Uncertain Destiny

A True Story

by
Dorothy Kovalchick Roark

Dorothy Kovalchick Roark

ISBN: 0-615-12681-2
Library of Congress Control Number: 2004098498

Copyright © 2004
Dorothy Kovalchick Roark

Printed 2004, 2005, 2008, 2009, 2012, 2013

Published by
Dorothy Kovalchick Roark
112 Maridale Drive
West Monroe, LA 71291
318-323-8756

Printed by

ᴍECHLING
BOOKBINDERY
PRINTING & BINDING
1124 Oneida Valley Road - Rte. 38
Chicora, PA 16025-3820
www.mechlingbooks.com

ACKNOWLEDGMENTS

I am grateful to my husband Earl for his patience and encouragement in writing this book. I am grateful to my brothers, Edward, Johnny and Nicholas, and Aunt Veronica, and Uncle Andy, for their help in furnishing facts, figures, and other pertinent information. And I am forever grateful to my father, for the 55 handwritten pages of information he left me, especially knowing how difficult writing was with his poor vision.

I wish to thank all my friends who encouraged me to write this book. I shall not attempt to list them all for fear of omitting a friend in error.

I thank Charles "Cork" McKee who was so helpful and generous with his time and patience in putting my type written pages on a disc, ready for printing.

I thank my friend Adam Harkins, who did all the beautiful sketches for this book.

And, above all I thank my friend Bob Fulton, who did all the proof reading with such perfection.

Names throughout this book may be changed to protect privacy.

Parts of this book are written in native dialect, spelling, with and without quotation marks.

Read it, enjoy it! Do not be concerned with grammar and the rubric of "Academicians"!

Here is a history of early America: people in coal mining, commerce, baseball (the only original American sport), and the United States Government.

Many U.S. History books were researched for dates and locations. No intentional direct quotations have been made.

Thank you,
Dorothy Kovalchick Roark
Author

INTRODUCTION

This is the story of the immigration of my father's parents to the United States in 1899 and the generation that followed.

I recount their challenges and how they met them, and how I met them as an immigrant's daughter. The question and surprises of life touched them all. Dad's questions of why in his life and the surprises that came his way will thrill and sadden you over and over again. What could have been different. Why did it all happen?

JOHN KOVALCHICK
BORN FEBRUARY 10, 1898 IN CZECHOSLOVAKIA FIRST
BORN CHILD OF NICHOLAS AND ANNA KOVALCHICK
IMMIGRANTS OF 1899
SHE HELD HIM CLOSE IN LOVE AND FEAR
THIS LITTLE ONE-YEAR-OLD,
HE DID NOT CHOOSE TO BE AN IMMIGRANT
THIS LITTLE ONE-YEAR-OLD,
THE STREETS OF GOLD WOULD NOT BE HIS
NOR HAPPINESS UNFOLD
FOR SO MANY DREAMS WERE UNFULFILLED
HIDDEN IN HIS HEART UNTOLD
FOR UNCERTAIN FATE WOULD TAKE COMMAND
HIS LIFE IS HEREWITH TOLD

CHAPTER I
A FATHER'S WISH

I am writing this book in fulfillment of my father's wish. My father, JOHN (BOUNCE) KOVALCHICK 1898 – 1988, died at age ninety in Binghamton, New York. His last and final residence for one and one-half years, was at one time A Sheraton Hotel, beautifully located along the banks of the Chenango River, in downtown Binghamton. This lovely hotel had been converted into a home for the elderly, and named Riverfront Center, and some years later it was renamed Renaissance Plaza.

My first visit in May 1987, is still as vivid as yesterday's memories. I can see him now, standing there waiting for us near the entrance of that huge carpeted lobby with its impressive cathedral ceiling. To his right was a massive stone fireplace, surrounded by deep soft chairs and sofas, with books and papers accessible for those wishing to lounge and read. He looked so tiny in that huge room. He had shrunken several inches in his latter years. I stood there hugging him, expressing my happiness in seeing him. We were almost the same height, and I teased him, saying that I was catching up to him.

He proudly escorted my husband Earl and me from place to place as though it was all his and his alone, and it made me feel happy to see, that he was content there. He kept stopping to introduce us to passing residents and employees. They were his new friends now. They happily greeted us, and were quick to express what a joy he was, and that he was a valuable moral booster to those residents lonely and depressed. Dad always had a charming wit about him. Having spent most of his life in public, in one capacity or another, he could make friends at the blink of an eye.

After touring the first floor, we approached the huge elevator, brimming over with residents coming and going from the six stories

1

that made up the former Sheraton Hotel. "Well, Dad," I said, "At last I am in a Sheraton Hotel!" Dad agreed, and turned to greet those who entered the elevator with us.

The elevator stopped at the fifth floor. We stepped out, and headed down the hall toward Dad's room, No. 512. We passed a lounge area where residents were watching TV, playing checkers or card games, or just sitting and talking. Dad said every floor had such a lounge. Also, we noticed drink and snack vending machines, telephone booths for those not able to afford private telephones in their rooms, and a large bulletin board which held current announcements of interest to all. I noted that many contests took place between the residents and asked Dad if he was in any of them. He had been, he said, but not anymore because they were not honest. They cheated all the time, he said. "Maybe," I thought, "Because he wasn't No. 1 all the time." Dad always had to be No. 1 when it came to playing any kind of competitive game. Anyway, I assured him he always was a good sport. Even in baseball, when the umpire called them wrong, he put up a fight and then jumped back in the game, and played that much harder. I hoped I had inspired him to once again participate in the contests being offered.

Dad opened his door with his private key. That impressed me. How nice for one his age to have the secure feeling of knowing that this one private room, and bath was all his and his alone. Upon entering, I was immediately impressed by the largest plate glass window I ever saw. The floor to ceiling window was as wide as his room which was over twelve feet and was enhanced by beautiful draperies that were drawn wide open. I couldn't believe it. "Dad, this is beautiful," I said, "You can see everything, the Chenango River, and all of down town Binghamton. It's gorgeous." "You should see it at night when the lights are lit up," he said. "Especially at Christmas. I sit watching the lights for hours. It is unbelievable." "And," I replied, "You have the best room in the hotel. I could live here myself and be happy." I could tell it made him feel good, hearing me say that. I stood there for a moment taking in that beautiful view, then turned to preview the rest of his room, which much to my surprise again, was quite large. It had a three quarter size bed with two pillows, a night stand and private telephone. There was a reading lamp and desk which held many papers and books, and on the corner I noticed his well-read Bible. The one that Earl had given him the first year we were married. "I read it every morning and every night, and even during the day," he said, and he thanked Earl for it as he did many times before. His large mirrored dresser held all of his personal clothing, and the clothes closet was very ample. I commented that his private bathroom was larger than mine at home for it must have been ten feet by ten feet. Neatly hanging on his walls were numerous baseball pictures that told one much about his past. I suspected that my brother Nicholas had hung them for him. He was a real anchor for Dad. He lived approximately 17 miles away, and constantly visited and looked after his needs. He was as dedicated a son as any father ever hoped to have. And lastly, I noticed a small refrigerator. It was just right for his milk and other perishables.

We sat down and Dad began to talk about the past winter months, and of his enjoyment in watching the snow falling softly in large flakes past his window.

He said he would open the small panel in the window and reach out to touch them as they felt so good, and that when he looked out from his large spacious window from the fifth floor it was like being in heaven as everything as far as he could see was covered with a beautiful blanket of snow.

I held back tears as he reminisced. He talked about the melting of the snow, and the melting of ice on the Chenango River, and watching the coming of spring. He showed us how he opened the little

3

latch of his window panel and fed the pigeons. "It's against the rules to feed the pigeons," he said, "but I always ask for extra bread at mealtime and feed them. They don't know I'm feeding them." I felt there was a good reason for this rule and told him so. He said he couldn't give up feeding them for they were his friends and pets. I dropped the subject when a nurse's aide entered the room with a few pills in a cup, which he took with water. This also meant it was time for lunch. He invited us to eat with him because guests were always welcome to do so. So, we lunched in the old original Sheraton dining room, and enjoyed the architectural grandeur of days gone by, which was still evident. There was a fine buffet selection. Those in wheelchairs were personally attended by young girls, who patiently took care of their needs. It made me feel confident, that if Dad were ever in that condition, they would do the same for him.

Following lunch, we returned to the lobby and lounge again. Activity was everywhere. Dad said residents had the opportunity to go shopping right there in the lobby one day each month, and this was shopping day. Tables were set up, and merchandise of every description was offered for sale at low prices. I thought it was very considerate and charitable of them to do that for the elderly. I browsed, checking prices from curiosity, and saw that the merchandise was priced very low.

We spent the remaining hours of the afternoon sightseeing. Dad acted as our tour guide. I was surprised how informed he was about the city, but that was just like him. He always had a good memory as well as a good sense of direction. That evening, we dined at his favorite restaurant. My brother Nicholas always took him there when he came to visit him.

The time to say good-by seemed to come too soon. I choked back tears thinking that it would distress him, and end our happy day sorrowfully. I didn't want to leave him. So, we lingered a little longer, and Dad began talking about a wish that he had for a long time. He said that he had wished that someone in the family would write a book about the family. Then he turned and said, "Honey, I wish you would write it. You're the one who should do it. I never had the education to do it, but I know you can do it." I gave him a hug and a pat on the shoulder, and replied, "I'll think about it Dad. Maybe I will. We'll see." This was not the first time he had talked of this wish that seemed to be so important to him. Many times throughout the years he had talked about it. So, I promised myself that I would give it serious thought.

As we embraced I felt his body shaking from choked-back tears, and I was doing the same. We both expressed our love for each other, and I assured him that I would return in the fall, and we would go sightseeing again, and enjoy the colored leaves. He smiled and said he'd be waiting.

When we drove off and out of sight, then and only then did the tears come rolling down my cheeks. I sobbed as though my heart would break. Earl reached and gently patted my thigh, as if to say "It's all right. You go right ahead and cry. I understand."

The first week of October, 1987, we returned as promised. There he was, waiting for us in that huge lobby again, and looking so tiny. Just as I remembered him from our visit in May. We embraced, expressing our love for each other. "I've been looking forward to our trip to the country, to see the leaves," he said. So we didn't linger long before heading for our sightseeing trip. The fall leaves were the most gorgeous panorama of colors that anyone could ever dream of. Dad said, "Honey, you came at the right time. The leaves are at their peak," and I agreed.

At noon, we once again dined at Dad's favorite restaurant. He knew the menu by memory and didn't hesitate to order the moment our waitress came to take our orders. I was flabbergasted when he said, "I want an order of three hotcakes, the kind I always get, two eggs over light, and on a separate plate, I want a double order of smoked bacon, a slice of ham, two sausages, a large glass of orange juice, real butter, extra syrup, and a cup of coffee, extra hot with cream, no sugar." We just looked stunned and I said "Dad, are you sure? You can't possibly eat all that." My brother Nicholas laughed, and said, "Oh yes he will. That is his standard order." And, much to my surprise, he did eat most all of it.

Dad appeared to be his same old self through the day, but I knew something was wrong. That certain familiar spark was gone. His walk was slower. He couldn't fool me – after all, I was his daughter. I suggested we return to his room to rest. Once there, I saw him take several swallows from a bottle of cough syrup. I recalled that he had done that same thing when I visited him in May, but had never heard him coughing. I picked up the bottle and read the label. "Dad," I said, "you can't drink this cough syrup. It has a high alcohol content and you are taking medication. It could be dangerous." "I only take it once in awhile," he said, "when I feel sad, and one of my friends have died." Then, he went on to tell us how he grieved for the loss of close friends he met only a few short months earlier, and now they were gone. He talked about how common it was to hear the sirens in the dead of the night, and then, in the morning learn that another of his new friends had died that night. "I hate to hear the sirens coming in the dead of the night. They always seem to die in the night." He said. He took a handkerchief from his pocket, and wiped the tears from his eyes. I, too, wanted to cry, to share his grief, as though it would ease the pain, but knew in my heart I mustn't cry. I put my arm around his shoulder. Then I thought about his wish about the book, and said, "Dad, I've been thinking about the book you want me to write. I'm going to try it, but I won't be able to until I retire from real estate. You know how real estate is a 24-hour-a-day job. In the meantime, I want you to help me by writing down important things that I will need to know." He agreed that he would, and spent sometime just reminiscing about the good old days. He always loved that, and it seemed to bring him back to his old self again, and we all felt happier to see him that way.

Once again, parting came too soon. We stood there in the cold breezy autumn air, colored leaves rustling about our feet. We held each other close and a little longer this time, shedding tears that couldn't be held back. I asked him to take care of himself, and I'd be back in May, and we would feed the pigeons together. He agreed, as he wiped his eye with his handkerchief. As we drove away, I said, "Earl, I feel that I will never see my father alive again." My heart was breaking. Tears came falling down my cheeks and once again, Earl gently patted my thigh, as if to say, "It's all right, go ahead and cry, I understand." Our return trip to Louisiana was a very sad one that October in 1987.

We had frequent contacts by phone and letters in the months that followed. He was so lonely and depressed. I lived so far away, and felt so helpless. His only solace was reminiscing about the past, so I patiently listened and listened, sometimes in the wee hours of the morning when he would call because he could not sleep.

On February 10, 1988, Dad was 90. "Happy Birthday, Dad." I shouted over the phone. "Congratulations, you made 90, how wonderful. Wish I was there, we would celebrate." He sounded so down, so sad and hopeless, when he said, "Honey, I don't know what it is, but as soon as I was 90, I don't feel the same, something happened. I don't know what it is, but I don't feel the same." "Dad," I said, "It's 8:00 in the morning. You've only been 90 for eight hours. How can you not feel the same?" I tried to cheer him up with positive and happy conversation, but nothing seemed to change his mood.

On April 6th, my brother Nicholas called giving me the sad news. Dad had passed away at 3 A.M. of a heart attack. Last October's visit flashed through my mind. Just as Dad had so sadly said, "I hate to hear the sirens coming in the dead of the night. They always seem to die in the night." "Oh Dad" I thought, "How right you were," and I cried.

No words in Webster's Dictionary are sufficient enough to express the heart-breaking experience of losing one's parents. My dear Mother had passed away May 7th 1974, and now Dad had gone on to join her. For those of us left behind, the sorrow is great, but the precious memories of them are with us all the days of our lives.

It is now 10 years since Dad, and 24 years since Mother passed away. And today, I have taken pen to paper, for it is my desire to fulfill my father's wish and tell the story. It is as I perceived it through my eyes as a child, a teenager, and an adult.

Dorothy

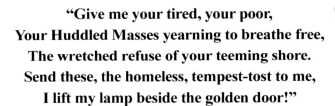

"Give me your tired, your poor,
Your Huddled Masses yearning to breathe free,
The wretched refuse of your teeming shore.
Send these, the homeless, tempest-tost to me,
I lift my lamp beside the golden door!"

CHAPTER II
THE BEGINNING 1899 - 1909

When I was growing up, it was a source of pride with me that both grandparents on mother's and father's side immigrated to America in 1899, when their homeland of Czechoslovakia was part of the Austria-Hungary Empire, and at the close of World War I, by the time the Armistice was arranged on November 3, 1918, the Czechoslovakian republic had declared its independence. Then in 1933, Czechoslovakia was divided into separate states. The northern part became the Czech Republic, and the southern part, where my grandparents were from, became Slovakia.

In 1899, my grandparents Nicholas (22) and Anna Pacan (23) Kavalycik wept as they said goodbye to their relatives and friends. They were leaving Slovinky, which was located near the Ukrainian border, as thousands of other immigrants did during this period of the great immigration to the promised land. They'd heard about this great place called AMERICA, where streets were paved in GOLD, and every man was FREE, and lived like a KING. Yes, they were coming to AMERICA, with a prayer on their lips, and hope and fear in their hearts. And, they were coming with their first-born son JOHN, who would one day be my father. Dad's passage was free because Grandma carried him in her arms.

First, there was the long tiresome journey overland by train. Then, the long, treacherous and dangerous crossing of the Atlantic Ocean, on the overcrowded ship. Most immigrants were poor and uneducated and could only afford to make the trip by ship as third-class passengers. They laboriously carried all their worldly possessions in bundles, sacks and torn bags and suitcases.

At last, their entry into New York harbor, as all incoming ships had to disembark at Ellis Island. The excitement and awe at the sight

11

of the Statue of Liberty was diminished when they saw the thousands of immigrants flooding into Ellis Island. Fear and apprehension gripped them, and Grandma had the overwhelming feeling of wanting to return to Slovinky. Grandpa put on a brave front, but he too felt the desire to return from whence they came. He pressed close to Grandma as she clung to their son John. He was so tiny for his age (1), but Grandma was barely five feet tall herself, and Grandpa was only five feet six inches. The lines of immigrants moved along slowly. They obeyed the signs, gestures and directions with the help of interpreters. They were tired and hungry, and so in need of a good bath. Immigrant never heard of colognes or deodorants, and body odor was everywhere. No one seemed to notice. They were used to it, but how they dreamed of a nice big tub of hot water with a big bar of soap. "Nicholas," Grandma whispered in Slovak, "John is needing a change of diaper, but where?" Grandpa replied, "Maybe we can change him here, I will shield you with my coat." So she proceeded to struggle with the changing, when suddenly the line abruptly moved, and someone from behind stumbled against her. "Oh," she cried as there at her feet lay the contents of Dad's diaper. She was helpless to retrieve it, as she was being pushed forward. "Move along," said the officer in Slovak. "Come on now, move along." And, as they moved along, Grandma cried softly as Grandpa squeezed her arm. At last, they stood before the immigration officer, who cried out, "Nicholas Kovalchick." Grandpa stepped forward, and quickly they were taken to be checked for certain diseases, and the condition of their general health. Having passed the health inspection successfully, they moved along. It all seemed an eternity when at last they were handed their entry papers. At that very moment, a ray of sunlight shown through a large overhead window. Grandma looked up toward the light and thanked God. They were legally admitted into this great country they had heard so much about. No longer would they be serfs under the rule of Czar Nicholas of Austria-Hungary.

Their sponsor, Mr. Matsick, a friend of the family, met them at the gate with a big smile and warm hug. Oh, what a wonderful feeling, and Grandpa and Grandma just hugged and hugged him back. Mr. Matsick looked down at their few precious belongings, then bent over and picked up one of the bundles. "Come," he said, "I have horse and buggy waiting." The buggy had no cover, just a plank across the front to sit on, with 18-inch planks along both sides. There was no plan to stay the night, nor food waiting for them. "Giddy up!" and they were on their way out of New York City, headed toward Pennsylvania.

Slowly, the horse plodded through the crowded, filthy slums of New York City. Grandma was raised on a dairy farm, and knew only country life, as hard and laborious as it was, and the sights she witnessed that day would remain with her forever. Her dreams of streets paved in GOLD were shattered. Now, Grandpa was a jolly sort, never having met a stranger – he was not going to let the experiences of this day frighten him anymore. He was in AMERICA, and he was going to make the best of it, and besides, it couldn't be worse than the poverty he'd endured in Czechoslovakia as a miner.

In fact, Mr. Matsick would be taking them to the small mining town of Horatia, located in west-central Pennsylvania, where a job awaited him. Yes, he again would be a miner, but this time he would be mining bituminous coal, instead of lignite. And, to hear Mr. Matsick tell it, it was going to be profitable. A man, he said, could work as long and as hard as he chose, making it sound like a man could make as much money as he wanted. Grandpa had a rude awakening to the truth, shortly after their arrival.

The town was new, as most mining towns were. Most had sprung up overnight, and were literally thrown together. This was THE

GREAT COAL MINING ERA IN AMERICA'S HISTORY, and they were part of it. The influx of immigrants was faster than coal companies could build houses for immigrants to rent. New arrivals were assigned numbers for houses. In the meantime, they lived with other families until their number came up. Not only was there a housing shortage, the towns were lacking in every accommodation necessary for decent living, by today's standards. Most water supplies were contaminated. All toilets were outside, called outhouses. Can you imagine, anyone today, going outside in zero weather to use the bathroom? I dreaded entering an outside toilet as a child for fear of falling into the hole of the seat.

Houses were narrow two story wooden structures, which were built in three sizes – either a small or large single, or a double which housed a family on each side. Everyone hated living in a double as both families from either side were tuned in to all the goings on next door. With absolutely no insulation in any of the house, one could also hear the goings on in houses a distance away. Now this brought about a lot of excitement at times. Without question, immigrants loved with a passion, and equally hated with a passion. They were loud and boisterous, in a way that swept you up. It was truly amazing how these people could live in such poverty and hardship, yet never seem to give up their love of life and God.

These houses had no electricity or running water until later years. However, houses built for bosses and their families, did have accommodations not allotted to immigrants.

Cooking was done on wood-and-coal-burning cast-iron stoves. These stoves also furnished heating for the entire house during long, cold winter months. A 12-inch hole was cut out of the upstairs floor, generally located in the center of the small hallway. This hole was covered with a metal grate and allowed heat from the stove below to reach the upstairs. At night, the fire in the stove was either banked or allowed to go out completely. By morning, one could find ice an inch thick on the inside window pane, and even snow on the floor below the window sill. Children admired the beautiful frost formations, and made a game of finding pictures in the formations.

As for summers, the houses were stifling hot. At times they felt they couldn't breath. With no air conditioning, and no fans, the cooking on the hot coal-burning stove added to the misery. The only means of cooling the house was to open all the windows and doors and pray for a good cross draft. Because cellars were cooler, many people chose to dig out their cellars a little deeper and turned them into kitchens, (that made excellent canning kitchens,) in the hot summer months. Also, clothes could be washed there, and hung to dry in the winter months. Everyone raised a garden and canned everything possible, and stored their canned goods in the cool cellar until needed in the long winter months.

Now Saturday was bathing day for most folks. Water was heated on the wood or coal-burning stove, then poured into a large galvanized tub (iron coated with zinc to protect against rust) that was placed near the stove. After everyone had bathed in the same water, it was poured out, and the tub put away until the next bathing day. Coal miners, however, bathed every day in their cellars or in small lean-to shanties, which they constructed in their back yards. This kept coal dust from being carried into the house. Years later, when water was installed in the houses, many miners invented showers, which enabled them to wash off the black coal dust from their bodies more efficiently. It was a sad sight indeed, watching coal miners coming out of the mines after a grueling 12-hour shift, completely covered with black coal dust from head to toe, and all you could see was the whites of their eyes. The sight always filled me with much compassion, especially seeing the older men, with bent backs, never to be straight again, from the years of mining coal, in tunnels only two or three feet high.

When my grandparents and Mr. Matsick arrived in Horatia, they, like all the other immigrants, had to live with another family until their number came up for a house to rent, which took several months. This was an embarrassing situation for Grandma, as she was very modest. You can imagine how difficult it was to have any privacy. Now all these inconveniences didn't bother Grandpa. He was being swept up in the excitement of his new life. Every day, after a hard day's work, the men would gather and tell stories about their lives in the "Old Country," referring to their birthplaces. Then too, there was gambling and drinking, which happened to be the men's favorite pastime. So men had an outlet, after a hard day's work, but women had little or no pleasures. Their lives were hard and grueling.

Women worked hard at creating as comfortable a home as possible out of these simple wooden structures. They were adept at needlework, carpet weaving, quilting, and sewing. Carpet weaving was profitable for those who could weave. They kept down the cost of having carpets woven by supplying their own scrap material. They would cut material and rags into one-inch strips, then sew the strips end on end, and then rolled the continuous strips into a ball, the size of a grapefruit. Flour sacks were printed in a variety of beautiful floral prints, and women were ingenious in creating beautiful curtains, and quilts, and children's clothing from these sacks.

One day Grandpa came home with two boarders. Many males immigrated without their families, and sent for them when they had earned enough money for their passage. During this interim, they boarded with other immigrants. Boarders meant additional income to a family, but added more burden to women already overworked and constantly pregnant. Such was the case with Grandma. Her second child, Joseph, was born in 1901. He was named after Grandpa's father.

Then came the proudest day of Grandpa's life. September 29, 1902. Grandpa became an American citizen. He proudly displayed the following document on his wall, for all to see, herewith copied from his original:

COMMONWEALTH OF PENNSYLVANIA

JEFFERSON COUNTY

BE IT REMEMBERED, That at a COURT OF COMMON PLEAS held at Brookville, in and for the County of Jefferson, in the Commonwealth of Pennsylvania, in the United States of America, on the 29th day of September, in the year of our lord One thousand nine hundred and TWO, NICHOLAS KAVALYCIK, a native of AUSTRIA HUNGARY, exhibited a petition to be admitted to become a citizen of the United States. And it appearing to the satisfaction of the Court that he had resided within the limits and under the Jurisdiction of the United States for five years immediately preceding his application, and that during that time he had behaved as a man of good moral character, attached to the principles of the Constitution of the United States, and well disposed to the good order and happiness of the same, and that he had in all things fully complied with the laws of the United States in such case made and provided; and having declared on his solemn Oath before the said Court that he would support the CONSTITUTION OF THE UNITED STATES, and that he did absolutely and entirely renounce and abjure forever all allegiance and fidelity to every foreign Prince, Potentate, State or Sovereignty whatever, and particularly to the EMPEROR OF AUSTRIA to whom he was heretofore a subject, Whereupon the Court admitted the said NICHOLAS KAVALYCIK to become a CITIZEN OF THE UNITED STATES, and ordered all

17

the proceedings aforesaid to be recorded by the Prothonotary of said Court, which was done accordingly.

IN TESTIMONY WHEREOF, I have hereunto set my hand and affixed the seal of the said Court, at Brookville, this 29th day of SEPTEMBER anno Domini 1902, and the Sovereignty and Independence of the UNITED STATES OF AMERICA the One hundred and TWENTY SIXTH.

CYRUS H. BLOOD Prothonotary.

ATTEST BLAKE R. GINN

PROTHONOTARY

Yes, Grandpa was a proud American, indeed, and it was well noted. There was a new bounce in his walk, and a smile of accomplishment on his face.

Some years later, the spelling Kavalycik would be changed to Kovalchick. It was common for immigrants names to take on new spellings for convenience sake. Many were changed as they embarked at Ellis Island. When they found them too difficult to pronounce, or much too long to write, immigration officers changed them.

In 1906 Grandma gave birth to her third son, and named him Nicholas after Grandpa. And, in 1908, her first daughter, Annie, was born.

In 1909 Grandpa heard of Sagamore, a new and prosperous coal-mining town, just 20 miles west. The reports he heard intrigued him, so he went to see this town that everyone was talking about. He saw Sagamore as an opportunity to better himself and made immediate plans for moving there. Moving trucks were scarce, and very expensive, so Grandpa hired a horse and wagon, large enough to hold only furniture and personal belongings, but not constructed for transporting the entire family. So, Grandpa, Dad, and Uncle Steve loaded the wagon, while Grandma got the children ready. Their goodbyes were hurriedly said to friends and neighbors, along with the shedding of tears. After almost 10 years, they were leaving Horatia. Grandma had four children now, and there was this gripping fear of once again going off into the unknown.

Grandpa would drive the wagonload of furniture and personal belongings. Grandma and the three youngest children would board the combined freight and passenger train for Sagamore, and meet them there. Dad and Uncle Steve, who had immigrated to America a year before Grandpa and Grandma, would stay behind, to lead Cherry, their Jersey cow, to Sagamore on foot. The train was primitive by today's standards. It was a very slow and boring trip, as it picked up coal and hauled food in box cars to the small coal towns along its route. Sometimes it took 8 to 10 hours to make the trip. Also, this single passenger coach was very dirty from the coal dust, so most people walked to Sagamore.

As for Dad, Uncle Steve, and the Jersey cow, Cherry, it was a trip Dad, as an 11-year-old boy, was never to forget. Uncle Steve led the cow on a rope, and Dad followed behind, carrying a four-foot tree switch, for the purpose of urging Cherry to follow Uncle Steve, in the event she refused to do so. It would take them all day to accomplish this long and weary trip on foot. The terrain of the Allegheny Mountains was rugged and difficult, with many twists and turns. Once they missed their road, and had to retrace five miles to get back on the right road. Uncle Steve became very ill, for he was elderly, and not very strong, so they stopped frequently to rest. The trip was far too taxing on him, so he climbed on Cherry's back, as he could no longer walk. Uncle Steve died a short time after the trip, and Dad always felt his death was caused by the hardship he endured that day.

Sagamore ~ The ball diamond on which Dorothy played 4th and 5th streets in the background and the town's water reservoir on the hill.

CHAPTER III
THE MIGRATION TO SAGAMORE
SUMMER OF 1909

In 1904, Sagamore was one of the hundreds of coal mining towns that were part of the great Appalachian bituminous coal fields, which extended from northwestern Pennsylvania to northern Alabama, and included parts of nine states. The town was founded by the B & S (Buffalo and Susquehanna) Coal and Coke Company, and was named after President Theodore Roosevelt's home in New York, "Sagamore Hill".

The land had originally been owned by seven families, who had cleared the land and were farming it, growing crops and raising cattle. It was uniquely located in the foothills of the Allegheny Mountain range, in west- central Pennsylvania. At first sight, it looked like a Shangri-La, with its narrow valley. And along this valley were the most beautiful hills, on which the town of Sagamore was constructed. Another unusual fact was that it was one mile west of the Armstrong County line, and one mile east of the Indiana County line.

Sagamore had the reputation as being the fastest-growing mining town in Pennsylvania, having eight mines in operation – four on each side of the valley and also having high coal, a miner's dream. Mining was done by the slope method, and their coal was classified as steam coal, used predominantly by factories and plants. It is unbelievable how improved today's mining methods are compared to those used during that period of coal-mining history. Slave labor conditions existed in the coal-mining industry as it did in every other industry in the United States during that period, when the industrial magnates took advantage of poor and uneducated immigrants.

However, despite all odds, these immigrants prevailed, as there was this unbeatable determination. They grieved over death, but did

21

not fear it. A short life span was common, due to lack of proper medical treatment as well as accidental deaths caused by the lack of safety measures provided in the mines.

Also, Sagamore had gained the reputation as being a rough, tough, and wild town. Dad's handwritten notes tell the story of the "Grand Opening" of the Hotel Sagamore in 1904. He writes, and I quote, "The hotel's 68-foot bar was four men deep, and the beer and liquor was flowing. Before long, the crowd was drunk and rowdy. Soon, the rowdiness got out of control and a brawl ensued, that turned into a wild west free-for-all. Before it could be brought under control, the basement floor of the hotel was in complete destruction, also part of the bar, and anything made of glass was broken. This marked the beginning of Hotel Sagamores' notoriety as the roughest hotel in western Pennsylvania. It became necessary to bring in the State Police every payday, to maintain law and order. Fortunately, only a few immigrants had guns. There was no arbitration, as differences erupted in seconds, due to short-fused tempers. As a result, disputes were settled with fists, knives, pick handles, clubs, or whatever was at hand. Many of these fights were due to the dislike of mixing with nationalities other than their own, which they were not accustomed to doing prior to coming to America. I don't like Pollocks, Yea, well I don't like Da-goes, and the fight was on. Seldom were these fights contained to the two in dispute. In fact, anyone harboring any kind of dislike for any nationality got into the act. However, when it came to baseball, then all the nationalities were best buddies, because all nationalities made up THEIR ball team, and THEIR ball team represented THEIR town.

So, for the five years prior to Grandpa's arrival, the town experienced its growing pains and never lacked for excitement. How could it, with the population comprised of Czechoslovakian, Polish, Hungarians, Italians, Russians, Irish, Swedes, Scotch, Welsh, Finlanders, French, Jews and English nationalities? All having to learn to live together for the first time since leaving their homelands.

When Dad, Uncle Steve, and their Jersey cow, Cherry, turned onto the narrow road leading into Sagamore, Dad saw the first of many sights that fascinated him that day. On the left side of the road was a huge dam, with massive projecting pipes, spewing water with great force. A narrow strip of land extended into the water, and along its bank was a lone fisherman, trying his luck, with a crude stick for a fishing pole. Dad had never seen anyone fishing before. The dam, in conjunction with a power plant and tipple, was constructed by the B & S (Buffalo and Susquehanna) Coal and Coke Company, for the purpose of generating power to run the tipple and furnish water and power for the mines and the town. In 1908, the power plant and tipple were lauded as being the largest in the world, and to Dad that day, they were. The tipple, an awesome black steel structure, stood majestically outlined against the sky.

The power plant ran the vast underground development of railway tracks and the ventilation shafts that provided air circulation for the mines. The number of shafts depended on how extensive the underground development was. At least two were provided in the event one was blocked by a cave-in, fire, or explosion, which was common during the early years when safety was not a priority and accidental deaths were common.

The coal was first steam blasted, and or dynamited, then hand shoveled into two-or-three-ton coal cars, with each miner tagging his car for identification. The loaded cars were pulled, by electric trains, to the tipple, where the weigh master weighed each car individually, removed the tag, and the miner was credited for the tonnage. Then, the coal was dumped onto a conveyor, and the bony, rock, shale, and debris were removed – we called it dirty coal. The cleaned coal was graded, and separated, and conveyors carried it to the top of the tipple, where it was dumped into waiting railroad cars. The loaded railroad cars were held in storage on the railroad tracks until a locomotive came to pull them to their intended destinations.

As for the dirty coal, it was stockpiled, on the hill behind the tipple. We called it "The Bony Dump". This bony dump burned continually, from natural combustion, we were told. The smoke from this continuous burning dump smelled like rotten eggs. When the wind blew in from the east, it blew this danged awful smell toward town. One didn't feel like eating when the wind blew in toward town.

Across the road from the dam was a mine slope that descended quickly into the black earth. A chill ran down Dad's back when he saw it. This mine slope fronted the gravel road that led to the town's five cemeteries, (Lutheran, Presbyterian, Greek Catholic, Greek Orthodox, and Roman Catholic).

As Dad walked that last mile to Sagamore, his heart skipped a beat. He thought he was dreaming, for there it was, the love of his life – "Baseball". A game was in progress. He promised himself he would be there with them soon. This love for baseball would be a driving force within him, for years to come.

Minutes later, he was gaping at the most beautiful sight he had ever seen, and momentarily, his thoughts left the ball field. This beautiful white building before him. A huge sign read " HOTEL SAGAMORE". It was the first structure built in Sagamore in 1903, for the purpose of housing construction workers, of every kind necessary, for the building of the new town. The owner W.I. Hay, had built it with financial assistance from the B & S Coal and Coke Company. It was a four story, 62-room white wooden structure, with the first floor partially below ground level, as was customary for that period. To Dad, it looked massive, and impressive with its mansard roof of bright green wooden shingles. There were lovely balconies, extending across the front of the second and third stories. Steep concrete steps led to the office and lounge on the second floor. The second-story balconies flanked each side of the entrance, and on the balconies were huge pots of beautiful evergreen ferns and several massive rocking chairs that looked inviting. Dad could not conceive that one day he would become its' owner, and also the salvation for many coal miners and their families in the bad days to come.

Dad was so fascinated by "HOTEL SAGAMORE" he completely missed the mule barn. It bordered the ball field that had him so mesmerized. He heard the clatter and clamor of mules hitched together. He turned and saw them coming, as in a parade. Instead, they were returning from a hard day's work in the mines. Soon, they would be in the hands of the mule barn caretaker. There, each would be watered, fed and bedded down in his own stall. Their workdays were long, and mornings came too quickly for them, just as they did for the miners. Mules would be used until the early 1930's when all the mines were completed and electric trains implemented. Dad felt sorry for the small mules, as they looked more like pets, and he hated their being worked so hard.

Grandpa had rented a house prior to their arrival, which was located on the hill behind the hotel. Dad couldn't be happier. It was near the ball field. Friends and relatives were expecting them, and had prepared a large kettle of soup, with fresh baked bread, and hand-churned butter. As always, the soup had very little meat, as folks, being frugal, used beef bones, which were boiled for hours to extract the flavor. The marrow was then sucked out of the bones for its protein.

After eating, everyone joined in unloading the wagon and arranging the furnishings. That's how it was in those days. Miners moved frequently, always looking for better working and living conditions, and more often than not, they found disappointment, as conditions were generally the same in all coal-mining towns. An important factor was the desire to work in mines having high coal seams. The misery of being bent over in three, four or five- foot coal, for 12 hours every day, was beyond human endurance.

CHAPTER IV
THE NEXT FOUR YEARS 1909 – 1913

The next day Grandpa reported for work as a coal-cutter, and Grandma went about adjusting to her new home, although she knew in her heart life would be no different.

Dad was in charge of the cow, and since there was no cow barn, he and Grandpa would build one right away. Cows were prized possessions for many families, taking precedent over home furnishings. From their cows came their milk, from which came their buttermilk, butter, and cheese. Also, cows having calves meant meat for the family, or additional income if they raised the calf and sold her milk. Every morning, after the milking, each family released their cow for grazing to young boys from the town. These boy cow punchers, as they were called, tended these cows for a fee of $1.00 a month per cow. Some boys tended as many as five or six cows. The cows were herded together and moved from one grazing field to another during the day. In the evening, the cows were driven back to their owners for the evening milking. Every month, Dad proudly gave his earnings to Grandma, realizing the family's desperate need. Dad enjoyed being a cow puncher, but the lure of the ball field was forever first on his mind and every minute he could get away, he was at the ball field.

Dad dreamed of becoming the teams bat boy. He chased fly balls in practice, caught behind the plate and also ran errands for the ball players as he was determined to become their bat boy. After all, he had promised himself that first day. Well, he realized that dream the following year. You'd have thought he had been elected president of the coal miners' union by the way he strutted after that happy day in his life – A BAT BOY for the SAGAMORE BASEBALL TEAM, WOW! And he was only twelve.

Ball players were really somebody in those days. Having the distinction of being a ballplayer on the town's team meant automatic respect from everyone in the community. It allowed them privileges other miners did not enjoy, such as being given the best jobs in the mines, or a day off before an important game, so the team could practice. Baseball rivalry between the towns was not for relaxation or fun, it was "WAR". Games were played with their hearts and souls, and the loyalty of the townspeople was unquestionable. They loved their ballplayers. The game commanded such admiration, and privileges, because baseball was KING, and every coal-mining town had their ballteam. A winning team brought a town recognition, and fame among the towns. However, they were envied, and other teams played hard to defeat them. And since coal miners were predominantly immigrants, it was immigrants challenging immigrants in their new country, in a newfound sport, and each wanted to be the best.

So Dad thoroughly enjoyed this newfound recognition he had acquired, by becoming the No. 1 team's BAT BOY. But he wanted more, so he organized his own team of young boys, and spent every spare minute he could for the next three years, developing his skills and mastering the art of baseball. Now he dreamed of becoming a player on the No. 1 team. Not just any player, but the best. Team players marveled at his ability, for he was so small. Full grown, he was only five feet six inches tall. They began calling him "BOUNCE", because his energy was boundless as he bounced around the ball field. The name stayed with him the rest of his life.

In 1910, Grandma had given birth to her fifth child, a girl, and named her Mary, and in 1913, her sixth child Helen was born.

In 1912, at the age of 14, Dad graduated from the eighth grade with high honors. His teacher encouraged him to seek further education. Sagamore had no high school until 1923, and further education was not possible.

He was still earning money as a cow puncher, but it was seasonal. He was able to make a little extra money by recovering and selling empty beer kegs for 25 cents each. Miners, on their days off, would purchase whisky for as little as 50c a quart, and eight or sixteen gallon kegs of beer for $1.00 or $1.75. Then they would settle under trees, on their favorite hillside, and drink and play poker all day. When the beer kegs were drunk empty, they rolled them down the hill, where Dad and other boys waited to retrieve them to sell. As many as six empty kegs came rolling down the hill in a day. The immigrants, thought that drinking and gambling was their inalienable right as miners.

Now, he thought about his future, and his choices. He concluded that miners' sons were destined to become coal miners. By the age of 14, boys were working side by side with their fathers, who trained them in the ways and means of becoming survivors in the coal-mining profession. Dad felt there was no future in being a coal miner, and besides, he didn't like the mines anyway. He would find another way to help his family.

He applied for work of any kind, with independently owned stores in town, and found work in a general store, which paid $9.00 monthly, including meals. Every payday, he proudly gave his mother the $9.00, along with the sack of groceries his boss Mr. Telly gave him every payday.

Mr. Telly was a short, robust, likeable fellow, very much dominated by his short, robust, nagging and prudish wife. Dad soon learned to stay clear of Missy, as he called her.

His job in the business world, delivering groceries house to house, meeting the public, and conducting business for the first time, gave him an astonishing realization as to how life was in a coal-mining town. No mining town had a more critical housing shortage than Sagamore. Three and four families were living in one house.

Sixty percent of the families took in as many as six boarders. These boarders paid $8.00 to $10.00 per month for room and board, which included laundry and ironing. He saw women on their knees, scrubbing wooden floors, two and three times every week, because there were no floor coverings. The only furniture in the houses were empty powder kegs to eat on, some benches, and a few wooden chairs. He saw people sleeping on floors for lack of space. He witnessed boarders using unkind and vulgar language, giving orders to the man of the house and his wife. This, he could not understand. It troubled him, because he loved his mother and father so much. "Why does the owner tolerate it?" He was too young to realize it was because they were in desperate need for money. Then, Dad wondered again, "How can miners afford to drink?" He thought of the beer kegs he retrieved and sold, but beer and liquor were cheap. So were groceries. Meats were as low as five cents per pound, and eggs ten cents a dozen. Dad said, "In those days, a dollar looked as big as a horse blanket."

In Dad's handwritten notes, he writes, "The work was hard, but I liked it. I did the delivery throughout the town, with a good strong wagon, and a mare named Maude, and took orders for groceries, meats, etc., and collected on payday. I curry brushed Maude every morning, and thought I was good to her, but sometimes, she would just stop and refuse to pull the load, and even get mean once in awhile, but I managed by always being on the alert. She kicked me once, when I was currying her, and I flew against the wall of the barn. I got some bruises, but was not severely hurt.

We had no refrigeration, only ice for the ice box and cooler. In the winter, ice was cut when it was 16 to 20 inches thick, and we packed it in saw dust, and stored it in a shanty. We had an opening for the ice to get into the cooler and ice box from the outside.

On one of my trips from the railroad station, after a heavy rain, I was hauling a good load of flour and sugar, etc., covered with a tarpaulin, just in case more rain should come. The road was rough, and very bad, and it ran along a valley with a creek running through it. I had to make a hill about a half mile from the store. The creek was high on account of the rain. I was doing O.K. and was 25 feet from the top of the hill when Maude stopped dead and refused to go on. I tried to coax her to go on, but instead she started to back down the hill, and I went with the wagon and load into the creek. Maude was shaken up also. So I jumped into the water, to save the sugar and flour etc. Most of the load was bulky, as they did not put everything in packages like today. I saved what I could, but the damage was bad enough. Mr. Telly was a real good man and he liked me, but his wife raised the roof. I did not say much, but I sure was mad at Maude".

When Dad went to work for the Tellys, they had been wanting to move to Detroit for sometime, and were seriously looking for a prospective buyer, for their general store and building. The thought occurred to Mr. Telly that Grandpa just could be the man. So he planned his strategy and approached Grandpa. First, he praised Dad, "Oh, Mr. Kovalchick", he said, "Your son is a natural businessman. He knows how to handle people, and he is a hard worker. He has a good mind that should not be wasted in a coal mine." Then he presented his plan. Why not buy his store and building, on a "Bond for Deed Agreement," which meant he would deed everything to him after it was paid in full. Until then, Dad could continue working for him, while learning the business. After some deliberation, Grandpa agreed, because he knew Dad loved his work and he wanted to give him the opportunity to better himself.

After the agreement was signed, Mr. Telly took Dad under his wing, teaching him every phase of the business. He had him observe all the business transactions when buying merchandise and paying sales agents, and introduced him to suppliers, paving the way for Dad to establish credit in the future. This knowledge and experience was the SPARK, that LIT the WICK, that GAVE the LIGHT, that SHOWED him the ROAD to one day becoming an independent businessman.

During this period, while training under Mr. Telly, Dad came to realize his dream of three years. He became a player on the town's No. 1 baseball team.

CHAPTER V
THE WAY OUT 1914 - 1919

Dad was almost 16 when Grandpa broke the sad news. He was taking him into the mines to work, because Grandma's seventh child, Michael had been born, and with nine in the family now, he desperately needed more financial help than Dad's wages furnished from working for Mr. Telly.

The first two months, they temporarily worked in another mine, because Grandpa's regular mine had been flooded due to an accident and was being drained. As he walked the three miles into the mine with his father, he kept thinking, "What am I doing here? Why am I in this smoke and dust? What future do I have here?" He hated every minute of it.

Within the next 10 months, Dad would experience two close encounters with death. First, a roof cave-in of several tons of coal missed him by inches. The second would have been fatal if it were not for his father's diligent training on safety.

Every day, he and his father sat in that damp, cold mine, eating their meager lunches from their two-tier tin lunch buckets, which held water or cold coffee, a sandwich or two made with home-baked bread, and something sweet, also home-baked. Only bosses were fortunate enough to enjoy that precious commodity they called store-bought bread. The rats gathered around them, looking for their daily handout. It was their lunchtime, too, and by the looks of them, many were better fed that the miners. The carbide lamps attached to their caps and the lights from the electric trains furnished the only light they would see for 12 hours every day. Grandpa and Dad sat there, feeding their rats and calling them by the names they had given them. In time, you recognized your rats, and they recognized you, too.

On July 23, 1914, when Dad was 16 ½ years old, World War I was declared. A great sadness and concern filled every immigrant, having relatives and friends still living in their homelands. Grandpa was especially filled with worry and concern, because the war began in the Austria-Hungary Empire, of which Czechoslovakia was part. A fighting spirit filled everyone in town. They felt the United States should immediately enter the war to help the Allies, but this would not happen for two years and eight and half months.

Grandpa knew Dad was unhappy mining coal, and had been conceiving a plan. Then one day, in that damp cold shaft, in the light of their carbide lamps, Grandpa revealed his plan. "Son," he said, "There is better way to make a living. I want to open up store in building I am buying. I borrow money from relatives, and friends. I got notice from Czechoslovakia. My father die, and $1,000 is coming from his estate. I don't speak good English. You have good business head, and good English. I want you run the store. You do best you can, Son. You not doing it for me, but for your brothers and sisters." Dad was filled with pride and love, to think his father had enough faith and confidence in him to turn over the responsibility of operating a store, and he wasn't yet 17. Tears filled his eyes as he said, "Dad, I will try." That day, he felt like a man, and a father too. "I must take care of my brothers and sisters," he thought.

Soon, the $1,000 arrived, and Grandpa set out to raise the balance needed to complete the purchase of the building. Many friends and relatives had immigrated to America as he had, and many were from his village of Slovinky. He approached those he felt could help him and successfully obtained the balance needed by offering enticing returns on their money.

Having raised the balance needed, Grandpa paid Mr. Telly and received a clear deed to the property and building, in his name. Mr. Telly was prepared to leave for Detroit immediately, but not before his loyal customers honored him with a humdinger of a farewell party. The year was 1915.

Grandma was happy to give up their small five-room rent house and move into the spacious living quarters adjoining the rear of the store, as well as living quarters above the store. "My goodness, could this be true?" she thought. Then, in her next breath, she said, "PAW! It doesn't have a COW BARN! I have to have COW BARN. I am not give up my COW!" So, the first order of the day, was the building of Grandma's COW BARN.

After the cow barn was built, Dad took stock of his competition and concluded the Keystone Company Store was his biggest competitor. Miners and their families charged all their purchases on credit, called a DUE BILL. Every payday, the coal company deducted the total of the DUE BILL from their paycheck, and the miner received the balance, if any, in cash. Every business in town and there were 17 – vied for whatever cash the miner had left.

Dad immediately devised a plan. He would be the store manager, handling all purchasing, bookkeeping and public relations. His brother Joe age 14 would work with Benny, the newly hired stock boy.

Mr. Telly's horse and wagon were not part of Grandpa's purchase agreement, and Dad wanted a good delivery horse and wagon desperately, explaining to Grandpa how vital they were to his business. So, Grandpa offered his beautiful mare, Nellie, a racehorse, having won many races at the county fairs. Dad said the horse was not the kind he needed, but Grandpa insisted the horse was just right. That is, until the day he and a friend took a trip out of town. When they didn't return, a search party was sent out which found them badly bruised and lying in a ditch, where the horse had thrown them, and the buggy was totally destroyed. Before long, Grandpa came home with a good delivery horse and a sturdy wagon, rigged with pull down curtains.

Now, Dad needed funds for purchasing merchandise, which Grandpa soon supplied, and would do time and time again as the need arose. Dad wondered, "How is he getting the money, and from where?" But he never questioned him, nor did Grandpa ask Dad how he was spending it.

Since wholesale distributors were located in cities 20 miles away, and since transportation was difficult, salesmen representing wholesale distributors called on independent retailers in coal towns, taking their orders to replenish meats, groceries, and other merchandise. Then, these orders were shipped by freight train and each merchant paid for his shipment when he picked it up at the train depot.

Dad wanted to know his wholesale distributors personally, and he wanted them to know him. So at six o'clock in the morning for three consecutive days, he could be seen riding out of town with his horse and wagon. And every morning, he would reach and pat the big roll of bills in his hip pocket. His ultimate goal was to pay cash for his first order and establish a credit account for future purchases. His first day, he traveled 20 miles west to Kittanning, the second day, 20 miles south to Indiana, Pa., and the third day, 20 miles east to Punxsutawney. His approach, which he well rehearsed, was well received, for he had wit and charm. It always worked for him. He asked for the owner, or man in charge, to whom he introduced himself, and his plan. Each distributor was surprised to see a young 17-year-old boy so knowledgeable and capable at conducting business. He pulled his grocery list from his pocket, and with it, his roll of bills. This was a deliberately planned move, but so impressed the man in charge that he had his men assist Dad in loading his wagon, and agreed to ship the excess by freight train right away. Also, his credit was henceforth established. Dad's goal was reached, and he was very happy indeed.

Soon, Dad, his brother Joe, and Benny picked up the balance of the merchandise at the train depot. Then, the three boys, ages 17, 14 and 15 worked into the wee hours until they heard Grandma's rooster crow. They were too excited to be tired, for payday was upon them, and that day would be their "GRAND OPENING" Day.

The eight foot sign had been installed above the front entrance, and spanned the width of the store. It looked very impressive in red, black and white, and read "KOVALCHICKS GENERAL STORE"

The "GRAND OPENING," however, was a disappointing, eye-opening experience, and Dad perceived for the first time what he was actually facing. He contemplated his facts:

(1)   Immigrants customarily patronized retailers of their own nationality

(2)   Sagamore was a mixture of many nationalities, each with their own customs and philosophies on life.

(3)   He wanted to do business with all the nationalities.

(4)   He would have to sell on credit, in order to meet competition.

(5)   Men controlled the money, and gave very little to the wife.

(6)   It was common that drinking and gambling took priority with miners.

But he was determined to overcome these obstacles, and meet them head on, and he would do it by being honest and fair with everyone.

The week following the disappointing "GRAND OPENING," a salesman walked into the store. He was promoting a "Sales Promotion" for the Arnold Coffee Company. The promotion offered a FREE CUP AND SAUCER of beautiful German China with every purchase of a two pound package of ARNOLD'S COFFEE. The cups were adorned with flowers and names, like Mom, Dad, Brother, Sister, etc. The salesman confirmed Dad's intuitive feeling, that the

KOVALCHICKS GENERAL STORE was the first retailer presented the offer. "I will make you a deal," he said to the salesman. "I will commit to purchasing every case in the company's promotion if you will give me the commitment that they will not sell to another retailer in the area, and to start, I will take 25 cases today." This meant an order of 600 two pound packages of coffee. The salesman was aghast. "You got a deal" he said. That year, Dad would purchase several hundred cases of the coffee, giving him a sales promoting edge over other competitors and bringing him much profit.

Twice a week, Dad loaded the wagon and traveled every street in town, ringing a big ole cow bell as he shouted, "Bananas, oranges, apples." He'd roll up the curtains, and hang out a whole stalk of bananas. They were considered an exceptional treat, and would bring folks out of their houses. Once out, he knew, he could sell them something, and with his wit and charm, he did. He offered a free banana to every family making a purchase, and with large purchases, he gave two bananas. To give better service, he installed an ice chest for meats and cheeses. He loved this part of the business. It took him outdoors, and being recognized as one of the town's baseball players helped his sales, as well as his popularity with the girls, who flirted with him. When he wanted to make an impression on a pretty girl, he offered her a banana.

Dad's popularity as a ball player was growing. He relied heavily on Joe and Benny to run the store when baseball games were being played in town and out of town. With Grandpa working hard days in the mines, they seldom saw him, and everything rested on the shoulders of the three boys.

After one year in business, the store was prospering and slowly making its way to becoming one of the top three in town. However, things would not become easier, as Dad had hoped. Instead, a new obstacle appeared on the horizon in the form of hucksters by the dozens began coming into town, offering fresh butchered pork and beef, and homemade head cheese and sausage, which miners loved. Miners were known to be great meat eaters, and every local farmer butchered cattle. Also, fresh fruits, such as apples, plums, pears, cherries, strawberries, and huckleberries were brought in by the local farmers. This presented a loss in business to meat and grocery retailers, as hucksters undersold the retailers. None were left untouched by the problem.

Now, much talk was circulating among the people. "The United States will have to enter the war," they said, and everyone was anxious to see it happen. The news came on April 6, 1917. The United States had officially declared war. And on May 6th 1917, Grandma gave birth to her eight child, Veronica. Patriotism swept the town like a hurricane. Continuous rallies and parades generated an atmosphere of excitement and everyone was buying U.S. War Bonds. Miners responded to the demand for coal by working seven days a week and overtime. One did not dare speak out against the war. In the beginning, those bold enough to do so were tarred and feathered, and one unfortunate objector did not survive the trauma.

Sagamore was now enjoying its biggest economic growth, and was reputed as the place to live when it came to coal towns, for it now had the following to offer its residents:

(1)   A company general store and pay office, and freight and passenger depot

(2)   Eight grades of elementary school, and five churches

(3)   Doctors, U.S. post office

(4)   Hotel, barber shops, and livery stable

(5)   Theatre, community park, social hall, town band, and baseball team

(6)   Independently owned retail stores

More streets were being developed and additional houses constructed to accommodate the increase in population. Dad's house deliveries became more difficult, as unpaved streets, deep-rutted and knee-deep in mud, were a constant problem. Also, young mischievious boys were stealing merchandise when he left his wagon to make house deliveries. One day, a man gave him a puppy. He quickly grew into a capable, intelligent watchdog, solving Dad's problem with the boys. The dog would hold the reins in his mouth, guard the wagon, and even learned to run one mile to the post office, get the mail from the postmaster, who knew him, and carry it home in his mouth. One day, a larger dog attempted to stop him, so Buff, as Dad called him, outran the larger dog, and as soon as Dad took the mail from his mouth, he headed down the road to fight the dog that tried to stop him.

Dad and the dog were inseparable and enjoyed many years together.

On December 18, 1917, Congress passed an amendment prohibiting the sale of alcoholic beverages. It was inevitable that Pennsylvania would vote in Prohibition. Dad hurriedly ordered 1,512 bottles of Jamaica Ginger from Pittsburgh, to be shipped by freight. It was one of his biggest sellers, having a 90% alcohol content, and when mixed with a soft drink, it tasted like whiskey. However, at the same time, the Government took control over Jamaica Ginger, making it illegal to purchase more than 24 bottles at any given time, to be used for medical purposes only. Too late, he had already received his invoice. The shipment was on its way. The next day, the freight station supervisor called Dad in a state of panic. "We have seven barrels of Jamaica Ginger sitting down here at our station. The law is in effect. You can't buy this much for your store. We're 40 miles away now, and you better be at the railroad station when the freight comes in, and get the damn stuff off the railroad premises before you get the railroad in trouble." Dad was waiting with the horse and wagon when the freight pulled in and received the fastest service he ever got. Dad, fearing for the worst, decided to store the Jamaica Ginger in a safe hiding place immediately. The kitchen had a false floor under it, "a perfect place," he thought, and before long he and Joe had all 1,512 bottles well hid. Two days later, the freight agent and the State Police arrived and searched the premises for the Jamaica Ginger, leaving no stone unturned in their effort to locate it. When their search inside the premises failed, they continued outside within a 100-yard radius before giving up the search and leaving. Dad would never forget the fear and worry of that day. However, they sold the Jamaica Ginger with great care, making a very good profit, as it was rapidly becoming more scarce, and the price was no object.

Dad had hired additional help during the baseball season, as he continued playing on the ball team. He dreamed of one day becoming a professional baseball player. It was his first love.

At last the long, cold winter and wet, muddy spring of 1918 was over, and that summer Dad made a wise decision. He realized the store offering the lowest prices would become the most successful. But with every retail grocer buying from the same wholesalers, it was difficult, unless the store sacrificed its profits. He thought, "Why not go directly to mills, factories, packing houses, and produce markets in Pittsburgh? Could this be the answer to obtaining better prices and passing them on to the public?" He would find out. So, he rode on horseback to Pittsburgh. He would never forget the trip, and spoke of it often, recalling that it took a week to recover as he was not accustomed to riding horseback. It was very late, and he was very tired when he arrived, so he found a secluded area where he and his horse, Dick, would sleep each night until his work was finished. The next day proved successful, as he bargained with a flour and seed mill for a car load of flour and feed to be shipped by railroad. This initial contact would pave the way for direct purchasing out of Pittsburgh, which would eventually make it possible for him to achieve his goal as the No. 2 grocery store in town. The Keystone Company store would always be No. 1.

The Armistice was signed on November 11, 1918, ending World War I, bringing an end to the demand for coal and leading to a postwar coal recession that would last for years. The B & S Coal & Coke Company's work days fell to one – two days weekly, not enough to feed and shelter large families with eight to twelve children. The War Bonds, so proudly purchased during World War I, were now being cashed in to supplement their meager wages. Those more financially established bought people's War Bonds for as little as one fourth their face value. People having any money in the bank drew it out, in order to live.

Dad began to lose money. In order to keep going, he made bank loans until they would no longer do so. With Grandpa working one or two days weekly, the store carried more and more of the burden. Grandpa learned to barter as a means of survival when growing up in Czechoslovakia. One day, he bartered for a FOX, in payment of a bill. Grandma was exasperated, ordering him to get rid of the FOX. But Grandpa took a liking to the FOX, and tied him to a post on the front porch of the store, and before the FOX was discovered and stopped, he had eaten two hams, hanging from the front rafters, along with other smoked meats, offered for sale. Then, there was the Christmas he came home pulling a piano on a sled, another exchange for merchandise.

In 1919 Congress ratified the 18th Amendment. Prohibiting the sale of alcoholic beverages, bringing to an end the long, hard struggle between those for and against the amendment.

Since the war was over, Grandpa was restless. He wanted to see what had happened to the "Old Country," as a result of the war. He worried about relatives and friends left behind. He felt sure he could make a trip to Slovinky and return before Grandma's ninth child would be born. So Grandpa left for Europe in the winter of 1919 – a decision that would change all their lives forever.

CHAPTER VI
DEALING WITH LIFE AND DEATH
1920 - 1922

Congress enacted the 18th Amendment on January 16, 1920, bringing in a period of 13 years of shame, crime and degradation, that today is recorded in history as "THE ROARING 20's."

Eight days later, on January 24, 1920, Grandma gave birth to twin boys, George and Andy. Grandpa was still in Czechoslovakia. Why Grandpa never returned as planned, I do not know. It was several weeks, before Grandpa learned of the birth of his sons, as mail was slow in those days.

The story is told, he celebrated the good news of twin sons, by drinking with his friends. It was a deadly cold winter night, when he was returning home, and fell in the deep snow, where he lay for some time, before he was found. From this, he developed Spanish influenza, and died March 20, 1920. He was 43 years old. When the news reached Grandma, she was told only, that Grandpa had died from Spanish influenza. Years later, Dad received more details from Czechoslovakia.

He learned, there was no gravestone on his father's grave, and vowed, he would one day go to Slovinky to erect one, and in 1960, forty years after his fathers death, he kept that promise. No son ever loved their father more, than my Dad loved his father.

All the towns people were saddened and grieved, at hearing the news of Grandpas' death. Only then, did they realize, how much love they had for this man, who at one time or another had befriended them, shared their good and bad times, and freely gave of himself so selflessly.

At the shock, of receiving the sad news, Dad wanted to be alone and cry, but he had to be strong, for his mother, and his brothers and sisters needed him. At age 22, through ill fate, he had become father to nine brothers and sisters, and the youngest were twins. He bravely held his hurt within, comforting his mother, and those brothers, and sisters old enough to understand, until friends and relatives came offering their support and love. Only then did he leave his mothers side.

He walked out behind the store, and thru Grandma's apple orchard, and slowly ascended the hill behind the orchard. There, he sat alone, away from watchful, curious or compassionate eyes, and for hours he wept and prayed, and wept again, unleashing all the hurt this loss had placed upon his heart. This heart-wrenching grief was the first of many he would experience in his lifetime.

He recalled the day of his father's departure. "It was as if Dad knew," he thought. He recalled the final private conversation with his father, in which he made his last request. "Son, should something happen and I do not return, promise me that you will take my place and raise the family. Always keep them together. Teach them to work together and help one another. Pay all my bills. I do not want to owe anyone. Go on with the business, and take good care of your mother. Always love and protect your mother. PROMISE ME?" My father replied in all sincerity, "Yes, Dad, I PROMISE. Don't worry, I'll take care of everything." And, with that, his father pressed him close to his chest, and said, "I LOVE YOU, SON," and kissed him on his right cheek, and then on the left cheek. Dad recalled seeing the tears in his eyes.

He recalled the trip to the train station. His father had forgotten to say good-bye to his horse, and he insisted Dad turn around and go back. He loved his horse, as Grandma loved her cow. He always talked to him, as though he was a human being, and the horse responded as though he understood. They had quite a relationship. After a hard day's work at the mines, he would peel a banana, and hold it for him to eat. He would stretch his neck, show his teeth as if he was smiling, and reach for the banana. When they came back, his father once again peeled a banana, fed it to his horse, and hugged hug good-bye. Dad remembered the stressful look on Grandma's face as she told them that their turning around and coming back was a bad sign. This was an old superstition she brought with her from the "Old Country."

As he wept for the loss of his father, he also wept for the loss of his dream of a baseball career in the major leagues. He had a great responsibility now, and he would keep his promise to his father.

That night, and for several nights to come, he lay awake, late into the night, as he analyzed his responsibility. If he was to keep his promise, he had to take charge. He concluded that each member of the family would have a responsibility. He would delegate in order to have a plan of stability. Joe, 19, and Nick, 14, would help him in the KOVALCHICKS GENERAL STORE, plus he would hire some extra help. Mike, 6, would help Grandma with her cow and her garden. The girls, Annie, 12, Mary, 10, and Helen, 7, would help Grandma with housework and caring of Veronica, 3, and the twins George and Andy.

Dad's hope for the help he desperately needed fell on his brothers, Joe, who was 19 and already falling into Grandpa's footsteps, as he had acquired a lust for drinking.

Within a few months of Congress' enactment of the 18th Amendment, people began making their own wine and liquor, which they called moonshine. Many grew their own grapes, and elderberries, blackberries, huckleberries, and crab apples to make their special brew. In fact, they made moonshine and wine out of just about everything. They soon learned their moonshine and wine was in demand, and began selling it to those in town who did not brew either wine or moonshine. They improved their skills, making more and better moonshine, for it was selling for as much as $20.00 a quart.

This brief period of prosperity would soon end, for the B & S Coal & Coke Company was still working miners only two or three days a week at $7.50 per day. With the scarcity of money, the demand for moonshine dropped drastically. Customers began offering Dad moonshine in lieu of money, in payment of their bills. He was opposed to taking moonshine as payment, but had no choice, for people had nothing else with which to pay their bills, and could not sell their moonshine.

One day he realized he had accumulated several hundred gallons of moonshine, and not knowing what to do with it, decided to go to a nearby city, where he knew it was being sold. Perhaps residents there would buy it. He loaded his old run-down truck, and was delivering it to illegal hidden places he knew of when a friend informed him the police were looking for him, as they were aware of his activities. Dad thanked his friend, and headed out of the city, with the police not far behind. He took every back road possible in an effort to elude them, as he still had moonshine on his truck. He thought of an out-of-the-way town, and fortunately was able to peddle the remainder of his load. This experience was to be the first and last time he would ever get involved in any kind of moonshining business.

Mobsters throughout the country were illegally trafficking alcoholic beverages to speak-easies which they controlled, bringing corruption and gang wars. Each gang fought for control, as it represented money and power. These mobsters sent their henchmen to the coal towns to purchase all the moonshine and wine they could find and to pay any price for it, as they learned that it was available in coal-mining towns. So once again the demand for moonshine brought a surge of prosperity to Sagamore, and other coal towns. However, this prosperity would come with a price.

Professional gamblers, realizing that moonshiners in coal towns had money from the sale of their moonshine, came into the towns under false pretenses of being ordinary folks, very naive in gambling.

Before immigrants realized they were being taken, it was too late. The gamblers vanished, and with them, the miners' money.

Then, thieves made their appearances, robbing people and burglarizing homes. Late one evening, Dad and Joe were working in the store when a stranger entered, wanting to buy a coal shovel. He said he had just gotten a job and was new in the coal mining business. After he left, Joe said to Dad, "He will never use that shovel mining coal. Look how well dressed he was. And did you notice his hands? They were clean, and if he ever worked anywhere, it must have been in a bank. He looked suspicious to me. And, did you notice how he was eyeing up our store?" That night, a gang of six robbers burglarized a number of homes, resulting in the death of one of the robbers. At the funeral home, Joe identified the dead man as the stranger who purchased the coal shovel.

Periodically, the U.S. Revenuers raided the town for illegal stills. Sagamore was only one of the many towns they raided. They may have caught the first one raided, but word flew from house to house with the speed of lighting, making sure they didn't catch anyone else. The runner would head out spreading the word, "THE REVENUERS ARE COMING. THE REVENUERS ARE COMING!" and things went flying in every direction as everyone in the family took part in camouflaging the still and brew before the revenuers appeared.

One story is told about one family that couldn't get a small keg of moonshine hidden in time. The Revenuers were knocking at the door, "OPEN UP IN THE NAME OF THE LAW!" The lady of the house, dressed in an ankle-length skirt, hurriedly moved the keg up to the table, and quickly sat astride the keg, covering it with her skirt. The husband answered the door and welcomed the Revenuers who searched the entire house while the lady sat smugly at the table, smiling and sipping a cup of coffee. "You fine-a-nut-ting?" she asked as they were leaving empty-handed.

Another woman, it is said, jumped into bed, putting a keg of brew on her belly, and covered herself and the brew with a blanket. When the Revenuers arrived, she proceeded to go into labor, howling in great pain. The Revenuers couldn't leave the house fast enough. You can't imagine how ingenious immigrants were about hiding their stills.

Grandma, desiring some financial independence during those desperate times, took to brewing small quantities of wine and moonshine, which she discreetly sold to close friends. One day, she got word the U.S. Revenuers were in town and cleverly hid her mash in her chicken coupe. After the Revenuers left town, she discovered the chickens had eaten her mash and every one of them were drunk. Soon the story got around, "Did you hear about the drunken chickens?"

In 1921, Dad saw his first major league ballgame at Forbes Field. Thereafter, during the season, he co-ordinated his business trips with the Pirates' home schedule. Before long, the ball players, their manager and the Pirates' radio announcer were his friends and calling him "BOUNCE."

Benny, who was very adept at handling every business aspect of the store, and Joe were left to manage the store when Dad was away, either for business or playing baseball. Joe looked forward to these trips as it gave him the opportunity to frequent the Sagamore Hotel for illegal drinking and gambling purposes without Dad knowing. Especially because Dad kept a constant vigilance on him when he was home.

It was in December, 1922, while Dad was in Pittsburgh, that Joe visited the hotel as usual to drink and gamble. He became quite drunk, and with a handshake he agreed to purchase the hotel from its owner, W.I. Hay. Immediately W.I. Hay called his Notary Public, and on December 18, 1922, Joe signed an agreement to purchase the SAGAMORE HOTEL, its furniture, fixtures, and 3.33 acres of land, and W.I. Hay agreed to sell for the sum of $9,000: five hundred dollars upon acceptance of the agreement, and $2,500 due on April 1, 1923 and $500 every six months at 5% interest. Final payment due April 1, 1929. He was 21 years old.

When Joe returned to the bar of the hotel, he invited everyone to celebrate the occasion. "The drinks are on the house, boys. I just bought SAGAMORE HOTEL," he said. A wild, drunken celebration continued non-stop for several days, culminating in people taking off with the hotel's furnishings and other accessories.

When Dad returned from Pittsburgh, he was met by a friend who gave a detailed account of all the goings on at the hotel. He immediately drove to the hotel, in time to stop a man leaving with a bed frame. Finally, he got control, putting a halt to the drunken party, and with the assistance of witnesses he began reclaiming the confiscated accessories and furnishings.

Now Dad was faced with an added burden, because Joe had no head for business. When it came to to manual labor, none could match him. His strength was unbelievable, and there was this inborn wisdom when it involved any type of construction. Through the years, many stories would be told of his almost genius ability for dismantling anything that had ever been built, from coal mines to factories. But when it came to paper work, or paying bills, he had no responsibility in that regard. So Dad knew it would be up to him to see that the terms of Joe's agreement would be met.

Three years had passed since World War I ended. The coal recession was still with them. Poverty prevailed with no hope in sight. People began migrating to more prosperous towns and cities, and states. Sagamore, indeed was stripped of its "GLORY DAYS."

Dad recalled surviving the coal strike of 1916, when he opened the store, but this was different. He felt he was in a deep hole with no bottom. Joe and Dad were certain the Hotel could not generate enough income to sustain itself, but Dad was determined to hold on to it.

51

Kovalchick's moving truck during the great 2 year strike 1925-1927

CHAPTER VII
DAD MARRIED - I AM BORN
1923 - 1925

Because of his father's early death, Dad's dream of a professional baseball career was lost. Now, with the purchase of the Sagamore Hotel, he was losing his brother Joe as co-manager of the Kovalchick's General Store.

February 10, 1923, was Dad's 25th birthday. As night fell, the snow glistened under the bright moonlight, and his heart was heavy. He wanted to be alone. So he donned his coat and overshoes, pulled a woolen cap over his head, and tied a scarf around his neck. Once again, he walked out behind the store, and through Grandma's apple orchard, ascended the hill and, once again he prayed, "LORD, SHOW ME THE WAY. I NEED YOUR HELP. I'VE LOST JOE AND I AM HEAVILY BURDENED. AM I TO GIVE UP BASEBALL, THE ONLY JOY IN MY LIFE? SHOW ME, DEAR GOD, WHAT I MUST DO." The tears began to fall, feeling icy cold upon his cheeks. He took a handkerchief from his pocket, and wiped away the tears. He knew his mother was unhappy and depressed since the death of his father. She took no interest in disciplining the children and after 23 years, still refused to speak English or accept anything American. He realized that the children were out of control, doing only as they pleased. "DEAR GOD, PLEASE HELP MY MOTHER. THE CHILDREN NEED HER," he prayed. Again, the tears fell. As he wiped his eyes, he thought, "If I got married, Mother would have someone to help raise the children. A wife could help her with the cooking and housework, and take care of the store when I am away." The idea filled his mind like a light in a dark room, and he accepted the thought as a message in answer to his prayer. A great burden lifted with the thought that marriage was the answer. The cold was now penetrating his coat and shoes, and he descended the hill, his mind filled with the thought of MADGE. He had been in love with the olive-skinned exotic beauty for some time. Yes, he would marry MADGE. "I'll call on her parents tomorrow, and ask for permission to court, and for her hand in marriage," he thought. Happiness filled him as he settled into bed. His newfound happiness would end the next day.

When he called on Madge's parents, and presented his proposal, they frankly refused him. "She is our only child," they explained. "It is only natural we would want the best for her. You already have your mother and nine children to care for." Dad was heartbroken. In his sad and deep disappointment, he knew her parents were right. They had prepared her for a better life than he could offer her.

He felt life had cheated him again. Still, he knew in his heart what he must do. He must find the right woman to meet his needs. In his mind, he began a process of elimination, for he knew many young and eligible girls.

He recalled the John Lucas family, who had moved to Yatesboro, a coal town ten miles away. They had several strong and healthy looking daughters. He recalled being impressed by the eldest daughter, MARY. "Yes, MARY would be perfect," he concluded, making plans to travel to Yatesboro, only to learn that Mary was betrothed to another. Immediately, Mr. Lucas suggested he court his second daughter, ANNA. She had suitors, but was not betrothed. Anna, 20, entered the room, surprising Dad, for she had grown into a tall and beautiful young lady. Four years had passed since the Lucases left Sagamore. He remembered her only as a skinny little girl. However, she had not forgotten him. She had been in love with him since she was 14. One day, when watching a baseball game, she asked her friend who this "Bounce" was that everyone was shouting about. Her friend pointed him out, and from that moment, she knew she loved him.

In 1899, Mother's parents, John (21) and Suzanne Janosov Lucas (20) immigrated to America from the Austria-Hungary Empire, just as the Kovalchicks' did. Their village was Michalovce, Slovakia, 60 miles east of the Kovalchicks' village of Slovinky, Slovakia. John Lucas, also a coal miner, moved frequently, as most coal miners did. The Lucases, more robust and taller than the Kovalchicks, were a very happy, loving and hard-working family, that enjoyed each other's company.

Dad was pleased when he saw mother and began to court her. It was a short and unromantic courtship, with Grandpa Lucas always sitting in the room, visiting with Dad, while Mother sat and listened. There were no parties or dances, no flowers or love notes, not even walks hand in hand in the night air. But, to Mother, it was a dream come true. He quickly proposed, and Mother accepted. She preferred a wristwatch in lieu of an engagement ring. Both agreed to marry with simple gold wedding bands. They journeyed to Pittsburgh, where they purchased their rings and wedding clothes. Mother's wedding dress was absolutely beautiful.

Dad broke all wedding traditions and customs of the day for it was he who gave the wedding instead of Mother's parents. They were married in the St. Mary's Byzantine Catholic Church in Sagamore, May 7, 1923. With 13 ushers, 13 bridesmaids, and two flower girls as attendants. Sagamore celebrated the town's GRANDEST WEDDING ever. Dad knew thousands of people and invited them all. In order to accommodate the massive crowd, the celebrating took place in the community dance hall and Hotel Sagamore also, at Dad's 10-room home above the General Store, and on the hillsides of both east and west sides of town. The celebrating became so rowdy and out of control, with all the eating, drinking, and lively dancing, that the police were brought in to maintain order. Before long, they too joined in the revelry and excitement. The wedding celebration continued for three day, with everyone having the time of their lives.

Wedding gifts came from everywhere, every kind of gift imaginable. Dad's importers, grocery suppliers, and meat packing houses shipped elegant pieces of cut glass and crystal, goblets, tableware, and tea and coffee servers, and trays of sterling silver. They filled two rooms in the Hotel Sagamore, and the house above the store was laden with them.

After the three day celebration, it was a week before life in Sagamore returned to normal. Then came the sad and shocking revelation that Mother's most beautiful wedding gifts were gone, and no one could shed light on their disappearance. One day, Mother explained their disappearance to me, saying, "In those days immigrants' lives were a constant struggle with poverty. Even the first American generation, which I was part of struggled in poverty. They had never seen such lavish and beautiful gifts, and in their minds, the wrong-doing of taking them was overruled by their deep desire to own something beautiful." She had no bitterness concerning their being taken, and I was amazed by her forgiving nature, one of Mother's extraordinary qualities.

After the wedding, Mother moved into the large 10-room house above the General Store with Dad's mother (my grandma) and eight brothers and sisters, ages 17, 15, 13, 10, 9, 6, and twins 3. Her starry-eyed expectations were only a dream. Grandma resented her immediately, feeling intimidated by her youth, and 5'7" slim beauty. She thought of Mother as an intruder in "HER DOMAIN." Mother realized the children were unsupervised, each going his way, doing his thing, knowing Grandma was on "THEIR" side. When Mother attempted to better their lives together with some organization or supervision, she would quickly affirm, "Leave my children alone. They are mine not yours." She was infuriated by Mother's delicious American cooking, accusing her of wasteful spending on food, calling it fancy cooking that they didn't need in "HER" family. Mother could not please her. Dad was non-supportive. Any private conversation with him concerning the situation was brushed aside with the assuring statement, "My Mother means well." end of conversation.

Three months later, Mother learned she was expecting a child. There was no joy expressed by Grandma, no advice given by her, and no compassion shown. Also Dad was gone from their bed most every night from 11 P.M. until 6 A.M. explaining to Mother that he owned a gambling hall nearby and was working there nights in an effort to earn additional income to pay off debts still pending since his father's death, and those incurred during the five-year coal recession, and the purchase of the hotel.

Mother began working longer and harder hours, hoping Dad would give her some time and attention if he didn't have so many debts to worry about. Nothing changed. Instead, she spent long, lonely nights, crying as she walked the floor and watched out the window towards the gambling hall, hoping for a glimpse of Dad coming home. She held her swollen stomach, and talked to her unborn first child, Edward John. "I love you little one, You are my only joy." He was born April 28, 1924, an exceptionally beautiful, but a weak and tiny child whom we called Ed or Eddie. Ironically, Mother's unhappy situation did not improve with Eddie's birth. On the contrary, her hours became longer and harder, for now there was another mouth to feed, and worry about, and Grandma offered no help. Still, Eddie was a comfort to her, as she hugged him close during the long nights of loneliness.

In the summer of 1924, Joe married Julia Hospodar, a lovely girl in whom Dad was pleased, feeling certain she would be an excellent assistant for Joe in managing the hotel, and would hopefully keep Joe's drinking under control.

Since his father's death in 1920, Dad alone was shouldering the stress and worry of the family's bad financial circumstances. In time, this would prove detrimental for him, because his brothers and sisters were never given to fully understand how deeply in debt the family was then, and would be for years to come. He was concerned that his brothers and sisters acquire an education, and that they or his mother not have to worry of the family's financial problems. Also he realized Joe got drunk every time he told him things were rough, and he got drunk every time he told him things were doing pretty good, so he kept everything to himself.

That summer, the renowned P.J. Sullivans baseball team offered Dad a contract with pay and all expenses, to play with their team the rest of the year. A once in a lifetime opportunity, he could not refuse. This would be the closest he would ever come to realizing his dream of a professional baseball career. The P.J. Sullivans, impressed with his baseball ability, offered him a contract for the following year. Fate would prevent his returning, and again Dad's baseball dream would be shattered.

Returning home from baseball that fall, he found Benny anxiously waiting, quaking in his boots. "BOUNCE." He said, "We're in deep trouble. Professional gamblers from Pittsburgh are using our town as a hideout, and they're taken over our gambling hall. They're on the run from the law, and are staying at the hotel. They're carrying guns and knives under their coats. What are we going to do?!" Dad, swift to size up the situation, fearing the worst, quickly devised a plan. "Hurry," he said. Benny went running at lightning speed, breathlessly rushing into the gambling hall looking scared. "THE REVENUERS ARE IN TOWN!" he shouted. "THEY'RE HEADED FOR THE HALL AND THE HOTEL! THEY ALREADY ARRESTED BOUNCE!" No gambler doubted the rumor, because no one looked more scared than Benny, except the gamblers, who were scrambling to evacuate Sagamore at breakneck speed, leaving everything behind. That day, fearing for his family, Dad closed the gambling hall.

It was now six years of struggling through a coal recession, and minors were working only two or three days a week for minimum wages. Their war bonds had long since been cashed and their savings spent in order to survive. Now they were more desperate than ever, little realizing the worst was yet to come in April, 1925.

The Sagamore mines would have a two-year major shut-down. The B & S Coal & Coke Company's refused the demands of the United Mine Workers of America's (UMWA) for safer mines to curtail the horrific death toll of miners due to unsafe mines. Also, they demanded an increase in wages. The coal company refused their demands, and closed the mines. Then, the coal company re-opened the mines five weeks later, paying $1.50 less per day. Immediately, the UMWA's Union Party leader John L. Lewis called a walk-out. Then the trouble began.

WHAT IS A COAL STRIKE LIKE? Unless you have lived it, you can't imagine it.

IT COMPARES TO WAR: The coal industrialist is your enemy. He does not care if you live or die. There is always someone else to take your place. Coal miners call them scabs. They come from distant places and appear out of nowhere, ready to take your job, even for less pay.

IT COMPARES TO A FAMINE: You never know when your next meal is coming, or where it is coming from. You make coffee from the same coffee grounds, over and over again, until the ground refuse to expel the slightest taste of coffee. So you drink the colored water. You are fortunate if you still have home canned goods left in your cellar, or some potatoes buried in the dirt or straw. Your cow is gone. You could not afford to feed her. You are forever hungry, and you can't stand to hear your children crying for something to eat. You have nothing to give them.

IT COMPARES TO BEING IN PRISON: Where can you go? Where can you hide? No means of transportation is available. No money to buy even a horse and wagon. You are trapped in a house not yours, and the walls feel as though they are closing in on you.

IT COMPARES TO BEING A SERF: You own nothing. The master owns everything and you are at his mercy. Unless you work for starvation wages, while he lives in luxury, you are replaced by one who will. Yes, you are a serf as you work the land, and you never rise above it.

IT PRODUCES FEAR AND HOPELESSNESS: Fear for yourself and your family's survival. Will we have enough to eat? What if we become ill? The children have no shoes for their feet or clothes for their bodies. Does anyone realize we are starving? Is anyone going to try to help? Is anyone?

Yes, these were the desperate thoughts and feelings the people of Sagamore faced those two dreadful years, in which the face of Sagamore was changed forever. I would be remiss if I did not relate conditions as they existed for those courageous, and brave miners and their families during this time, when all were sacrificed in an effort to better their lives, and the lives of those who would come after them.

The coal company ordered the miners out of their homes. If they did not vacate within he given time, the coal company brought in their own police and sheriff and evicted them bodily, furniture and all, into the streets, rain or shine, day or night. The Miner's Union immediately contracted with private property owners, of which Dad and Joe were one, Dad and Joe quickly built rows of two room wooden barracks for those evicted. The Union also rented room from the Sagamore Hotel, and housed one family per room, resulting in as many as eight people living in one room. These families remained until they could make arrangements for moving elsewhere. This rental income made it possible for Dad and Joe to meet the payments due on the hotel.

Black strike-breakers from out of state were brought in by the coal company to re-open the mines. The miners countered by organizing picket blocks, carrying pick handles, shovels, and clubs, resulting in fights between them and the strike-breakers. The strike-breakers, however were successful in re-opening the mines.

Dad purchased a large moving truck, agreeing to move people's furniture for any price he could get from them. Roads were rough, with very few black-topped and most made of dirt. In his own words, he wrote, "For a 2 ½ ton load of furniture and 150-160 miles, I received $50. Half the time, I did not eat all day, maybe, sometimes a cup of coffee and a doughnut. Trips were long and hard, and the profit was small."

One day, by chance, Dad met a man in Pittsburgh who sparked an idea. The man explained he was a scrap-iron dealer, selling scrap iron to the U.S. Steel Corporation. The idea excited Dad, who thought he could use his truck for hauling scrap iron as well as moving furniture. When he returned home, he began buying scrap iron from everywhere, stock-piling it behind the hotel, accumulating a truck load, then delivering it to Pittsburgh. The work, heavy and laborious, proved to be more profitable than the moving business.

On June 4, 1925, Nick, 18, graduated with Sagamore's first high school graduating class. Only four of Grandma and Grandpa's 10 children – Nick, Mary, Helen and Veronica – would ever graduate from high school. As Dad proudly listened to the addresses of the valedictorian and salutatorian during the commencement exercises, he felt a deep hunger for more education, a ceaseless desire through out his life. He was proud, feeling he, too had prepared Nick for facing the world. He began by training him in the general store, at the age of 11. Noticing his quick mind and natural ability for business, he was determined that if anyone in the family graduated from high school, it would be Nick. He had been waiting for this day, and now it was here. His plan was that Nick would manage the moving and scrap-iron business.

During this period of struggle for survival, I was born on December 31, 1925. A paralyzing snowstorm had hit western Pennsylvania, closing down everything. The doctor arrived in a horse and buggy, hours late, having been snowbound. The mid-wife had already delivered me. Dad was snowbound for two weeks in Pittsburgh. Friends of the family called to give him the news of my birth. "You've got another boy, Bounce," they said. Dad happily passed out cigars. "Have a cigar, boys, my wife just had another boy, my second ballplayer," he boasted with pride. When he arrived home, Mother had to remove my diaper to prove I was a girl. He just wouldn't believe it. Mother named me Dorothy Ann, in memory of a little girl she once sat and loved when she was 12.

CHAPTER VIII
THE TURNOVER OF A TOWN
1926 - 1929

One year passed since the strike began, with no hope in sight, except the dogged determination to survive. The miners refused to give in to a power greater than they or allow that power to control their lives like a yoke that could only be removed by a revolution in the form of a strike, such as the one they were enduring.

Slowly, the strike-breakers were driven off. A popular scare tactic was attaching dynamite to auto tires that were rolled downhill, through the streets, under darkness of night. A second wave, in larger force, was quickly brought in by the coal company, along with an increase in police support. The union miners continued their picketing and various tactics, frightening many off.

Merchants were going broke, claiming bankruptcy. Then mysteriously, their stores burned down, whereupon they collected their fire insurance and left town. One could only guess as to the cause of the fires.

The KOVALCHICKS GENERAL STORE was also in trouble. Dad's bank refused him further loans. The store was mortgaged to the limit, and his line of credit was exhausted. For years, loans had been renewed over and over again, only the interest having been paid. Wholesalers terminated his credit, for failure to pay them. He, in turn was forced to terminate credit to his customers, who were unable to pay him, resulting in a virtual business standstill.

During this time Dad's brothers and sisters were removing merchandise from the store, giving it to friends less fortunate than they. Also, it gave them a sense of importance and prestige among their friends and neighbors. Mother's efforts to dissuade their practice of removing stock was rebuffed. "This is our store. It's not yours" they said. Mother felt Dad should know, and was surprised to hear him say, "I would rather my own family take it, than a stranger." Mother said no more.

Again, Dad climbed the hill behind Grandma's apple orchard. Once again he prayed for guidance, meditating for hours. The next day, he called on the president of his bank, then his wholesalers in days to follow, explaining his circumstances, and that after 12 years, he was closing the KOVALCHICKS GENERAL STORE. However, he was determined not to claim bankruptcy, desiring to re-open the store when things got better. They came to acceptable agreements, giving him time to re-establish himself.

During these trying times, Grandma's cow furnished milk, butter and cheese for the family. Her chickens furnished eggs. One could always find a pot of chicken soup simmering on the stove, and her garden produced vegetables for all.

Since the strike began, the United Mine Worker's Union aided the striking miners, providing them with food, clothing, medicine, and rent. The cost was more than the Union could bear, resulting in the inevitable. The Union regretfully announced "IT WAS BROKE," bringing an end to the hotel's rental income.

The loss of the rental income was a blow to Dad and Joe. However, the moving business still prospered, as miners continued moving out of town.

Dad and the few remaining merchants called on their wholesalers, explaining the hopeless plight of the miners, and pleaded for help on their behalf. "We can't let them starve!" Dad pleaded, promising to pay them when the strike was over and things got better. The wholesalers, much to Dad's surprise, eased their burdened hearts by responding with truckloads of meat, groceries, and milk. The poor hungry miners patiently stood in line, with tears in their eyes, awaiting their share, which Dad and the merchants distributed according to the number in the family.

Another blow was quick to follow, when the coal company brought in a third wave of strike-breakers, followed by a posted public notice. The notice warned the striking miners, their families and private property owners that they would be arrested if caught trespassing on company property. Consequently, many people were arrested.

Union miners began meeting secretly in homes of private property owners, resulting in police guarding private properties in an effort to prevent their meeting. People feared leaving their homes, as police on horseback patrolled throughout the town. Dad recalls stepping out of the house one night and surprisingly walking into a policeman on horseback.

After two long, suffering years, only a few hundred striking miners remained of a population that at one time exceeded 3,000. The spring of 1927, heartbroken and weary, the miners faced the realization of having failed and returned to work for starvation wages. Wives and children stood crying in the streets, embracing each other, not in happiness, but with heavy hearts, to hard to describe. Women weeping for their children, and for the men they loved. Children crying, because now their bellies might be full again. And everyone crying because their battle was lost, with nothing gained. Their heartbreak was filled with fear for their future.

In May, Dad's second sister, Mary, graduated from high school as valedictorian.

Mother, pregnant, heartbroken and weary after four years of stress, living under the same roof with Grandma and her eight undisciplined children, went to live with her parents, who had fled the strike and were living in Warren, Ohio. Dad immediately followed, pleading for her return, promising they would move into a two-room apartment in the HOTEL SAGAMORE, with a private bath. Mother agreed, for she loved him so much. On July 17, 1927, she gave birth to her third child, John Andrew, nicknaming him Jackie, and then Johnny in later years.

When Mother and Dad moved into the hotel, he was deeply in debt and penniless. He borrowed money from everyone he could in order to re-establish the KOVALCHICKS GENERAL STORE. He cashed in his life insurance policy, and borrowed from a bakery, a hardware owner, and his insurance agent. The store occupied the first floor of the hotel, where the bar had been prior to Prohibition. It was smaller than the original, but the location on State Highway 210 was a prime location, more apt to generate business.

To update the new store, he conservatively purchased used store fixtures and equipment.

All efforts to revive the store would eventually be doomed to failure, as Dad could not conceive the depth of the miners' despair. His heart grieved as he watched them returning from work, staggering from weakness and sheer exhaustion. Their starvation wages were never sufficient to cover their Keystone Company Store DUE BILLS. Consequently, pay envelopes were empty, leaving them helpless to do business with him.

The store, however, was beneficial for furnishing meats and groceries for the hotel at wholesale prices.

With new immigrants moving into Sagamore, many sought room and board at the hotel until they were financially able to bring their families to America. Soon Mother and Julia were taking care of 35 boarders, every day preparing their lunch buckets before 5 A.M. as well as their breakfast and supper meals. Young girls were hired to help with the housework and laundry. Mother cooked constantly, baking as many as 26 apple pies daily. Apples were plentiful in the area, and Dad purchased bushels from local farmers, storing them in the cellar for the winter. In the fall everyone joined in cooking apples outdoors in huge vats, producing sufficient apple butter for the winter.

When miners rooming and boarding at the hotel returned from work, covered with coal dust from head to toe, they first entered the first floor by a side entrance leading to a 15 x 40-ft shower room that had two large shower heads, eight galvanized sinks, and several commodes. This shower room adjoined the furnace room, making it warm and comfortable for their showering. Miners stripped off their coal-black mining clothes, hanging them on personal racks, ready for the next working day. Only their long-john underwear was changed daily.

Mother and Julia's washdays were from dawn till dark. Clothes were washed by hand, and by an antiquated washing machine. The machine had to be filled and drained by a hand-held water hose, and the clothes rung out by a hand-turned wringer. Coal miners' clothes were boiled in large galvanized vats, using homemade lye soap. In the spring, summer and fall, clothes were hung outdoors on 150 feet of clotheslines. In winter, they were hung next to the furnace and shower room, on the first floor, and in the dining room on the second floor. On washdays everyone dined in the kitchen, including boarders.

Because of the income generated by the rooming and boarding business, at last there was a little light at the end of the tunnel, giving Dad a sigh of relief. Yes indeed, this little surge of prosperity was a welcome relief, and he began making payments on his bank loans, and small payments to his wholesalers.

On May 6, 1928 his eldest sister Annie married John Fedock, a fine gentleman. He felt John would be an excellent provider and good to his sister. She would be happy, and he was glad. There marriage would be a happy one, and would produce three beautiful daughters, Ethel Reda, Eileen and Joanne.

John was a man of great strength, having an undisputed and envied reputation for years as being one of the best coal loaders in

Sagamore. Every coal miner strived to become a top A-1 coal loader, for everyone admired these unbeatable men. A coal car could hold as much as three tons of coal, or as little as two tons. In the U.S., the long ton of 2,240 pounds is generally used in the coal industry. John could load as many as ten three ton coal cars in a day's work, or 22,400 pounds of coal, a phenomenal feat for a coal miner, being that coal cars were hand loaded using a coal shovel.

While the hotel continued to prosper in 1928, a sad event would break Dad's heart, from which he would never recover. This blow would come from his brother Nick, age 21, who had been managing the moving and scrap-iron business with Mike, almost 14. In 1928 (exact date unknown), Nick approached Dad as he was closing the store one night and disclosed that he was going on his own, and wanted his share of his father's "INHERITANCE," Dad was AS-TOUNDED! He thought, WHAT INHERITANCE? His Dad left NOTHING BUT DEBTS, some still unpaid.

For a time, he was speechless. He thought of how he had helped his mother raise Nick from the cradle. His father did not get much work, and he could always make a little money and give it to his mother, and he always helped her with the children. And, to make matters worse, his Dad was a heavy drinking man.

He recalled his burdens of past years. He thought about the family's hardship during the immigration years, then his struggle to open the KOVALCHICKS GENERAL STORE, and his determination to make it succeed for the benefit of his brothers and sisters. As his father had said, "You are not doing it for me, Son, but for your brothers and sisters." He recalled his struggle against his competitors during World War I. Then, came the six-year coal recession, and his father's death, and the devastating two-year coal strike that brought the family to the brink of total disaster.

He thought of the loss of the woman he had loved because he was burdened with too many responsibilities. He thought of the loss of a baseball career. He looked forward to the day his brothers and sisters would graduate from high school and help bring the family back to its feet. Nick was his hope at this trying time. He loved his brother Joe, but drinking prevented his giving Dad the desperately needed support he hoped for.

Realizing Nick was 21 and had the right to go on his own, he recalled March, 1920, when his father died. He was 22, and also had to make a decision. He refused to abandon his brothers and sisters, because they needed him. He now felt he was being abandoned by his brother Nick when he needed him so desperately. He did not feel he owed him anything.

Nick interrupted his thoughts, when he said, "It may be for the best, as you have been up and lost out. And, if I do or make good in the future, I will help you out." The hour was growing late. Again, Nick asked Dad for what he owed him. Dad thought, HOW IRONIC, I OWE MORE THAN I AM WORTH, BUT I WILL GIVE HIM A START.

They came to an agreement. He offered Nick the moving truck and $800 cash, which he could borrow right away. Nick would pay Dad $30 per month for room and board, an office, and the use of the hotel's property for the scrap-iron business. Nick reiterated, "If I do any good, I will help you," and left. Dad writes in his memoirs, "He went to his bedroom, as it was getting to be early morning. But I stayed in the store for hours, and I cried like a small boy. I wanted the family to stay together. He was my best of help. I needed him badly. I had a long rough road ahead of me, with mother and her still seven children. I was sick at heart, but did not show it to no one, as things were bad enough."

The next day, he would face another shocking revelation. Mike was dropping out of school, to join Nick. He pleaded with him to remain in school, with no success, as he was determined to join his brother Nick. Dad's heart was breaking. Now he was losing two brothers. He slowly climbed the stairs to his bedroom. He locked the door, fell to his knees and prayed, "God, will it ever end?" He was only 30 years old.

This start given by Dad would enable Nick to become financially independent, and in 1939 he and his wife and family would move to Indiana, Pennsylvania, 20 miles south of Sagamore. The promise to Dad, "If I do good, I will help you," would never be fulfilled, contributing to Dad's depression in later years.

Dad would liquidate many of the family's oldest debts in 1928, giving him a feeling of accomplishment, having resolved to repay every debt ever incurred in raising the family. He knew that thousands of dollars extended on credit to miners who had moved from town could never be collected, but he vowed to repay every wholesaler, every bank or individual who ever loaned him money or extended him credit. He valued his name, always living by the philosophy that "A MAN'S WORD WAS HIS BOND."

Recalling a time following his father's death eight years before, he wrote these words: "One of father's friends would come to the store often, I could see he was worried. Finally, one day I said, You seem to be sad and worried. Then he said to me, Your father, I loaned him some money, and I never asked you for the money, because I did not even get a note from him. I asked him how much money he gave to father. He told me, and it was a large sum. I said to him, I can't pay you in full, but I will give you a number of checks. The first one, you can cash at once, and the others as dated. He did not care about the interest on the loan, but I had added to the checks all the interest that was due. He did not know what to say, and I said to him, Henry, if you ever need help, don't forget, I will remember you, as I knew father was a real friend of his."

Years later, when Henry became too old to work in the mines, Dad kept his word, giving him and his wife room and board, plus a salary, in exchange for light handy work throughout the hotel. They lived in the hotel until they died, as they had no children.

The hotel's room and board business continued to prosper into 1929. Its success due to long, hard, and laborious hours expended by Mother and Julia. However, as boarding miners succeeded in bringing their families to America, they moved into rent houses owned by the coal company. Young, single boarding miners also moved as soon as they married.

In February 1929, at age 3, I successfully battled tonsillitis and scarlet fever, which left my legs crippling weak. Mother administered daily doses of cod liver oil, which I hated, and exercised my legs to strengthen them. The hotel's antiquated steam radiator system caused a continuous variation in temperature and drafts throughout the building, leading to frequent colds and other health problems. More so for children.

Dad's sister Helen graduated from high school that May. Following graduation, she commuted 40 miles daily to a college, completing a two-year business course in one and one half years.

One day in September, 1929, late into the night, the sky glowed light as day. Screams and yelling awoke the town. People came running to see what was happening. Dad, Mother, Joe, Julia, and Nick, who were living in the hotel with their five children, were also awakened, and rushed to investigate the cause of the excitement. They climbed the hill towards the old general store, where Grandma and six of her children still lived. Upon ascending the hill, their fears were confirmed. The store and house were in flames, billowing smoke reaching high into the sky and flames shooting higher than anyone had ever seen. The general store and Grandma's 10-room house above the store was a huge wooden structure. Nothing could be saved. The fire was out of control.

At a safe distance, Grandma, the twins George and Andy, Mike, Veronica, Helen and Mary, sat on the ground, in their nightclothes, crying and in shock. Mary screamed hysterically, unable to be brought under control. It was a chaotic night.

The massive hunk of rubble smoldered for days. One could feel the heat from it for a week. When it was safe to venture among the rubble, each cried as they reached down to retrieve the remains of a once treasured object, hardly recognizable. One picked up a clump of melted coins, ironically having been the secret cache belonging to one of them. The fact was, many secret caches burned in the fire, which accounted for some of the hysteria.

The cause of the fire could not be determined. Fortunately, everyone could escape through a door that exited the rear of the house. Nothing being saved, friends and neighbors gave clothes to the family, and Grandma and the children went to live in the hotel.

So, it was that the hotel became home for 17 members of Dad's family. Dad, Mother, Eddie, Johnny, and me. Joe, Julia, Martha and Betty. Grandma, George, Andy, Veronica, Helen, Mary, Mike and Nick.

In an effort to make living quarters for Dad's family as private and comfortable as possible, Mother and Julia moved coal miners, still rooming and boarding to the fourth floor. Much to Mother's relief, the few remaining boarders chose to prepare their own lunch buckets and cook for themselves. They also rented an extra room, which Mother converted into a kitchen.

The kitchens had meager furnishings with a small dining table and two chairs. A second table held a two-burner hot plate, having a curtain to shield storage underneath. A third table held a dishpan and towel rack, also with a curtain for shielding storage. A picture hung on the wall, and a sheer curtain covered a single window with its pull down shade. A small rag rug lay on the wooden floor.

Everyone on the fourth floor shared a common restroom, having two lavatories and two commodes, and everyone used the shower room on the first floor.

Mother and Julia continued doing their laundry and cleaning their rooms, changing bedding weekly.

Hotel beds were iron, having a single narrow padded mattress on a single sheet of iron mesh. This mesh gave little support, and one continually rolled toward the center. Periodically Mother and Julia would purge the mesh for bedbugs, which were brought in by the miners. The purgation method was performed by first diligently searching every crevice of the mattress for bedbugs, then removing them into a pan of boiling water. Certain of their removal, the mattress is set aside, and a pan placed beneath the mesh, at the head of the bed. Boiling water is poured over the mesh, flushing out the bedbugs into the pan below. This is repeated as the pan is moved across the head of the bed, and then continued across the foot end, assuring success.

As the family was adjusting to living on the third floor of the hotel, another crisis shocked the entire world.

On October 24, 1929, called "BLACK THURSDAY," the U.S. Stock Market took a sickening plunge and wiped out many private investors. The following Monday, the market fell again. Then, on October 29, called "BLACK TUESDAY," THE MARKET COLLAPSED, AND THE INEVITABLE GREAT DEPRESSION WAS UPON THE NATION.

THE GREAT DEPRESSION WAS INEVITABLE FOR MANY
REASONS:

1. The ROARING '20 were out of control, with widespread
   contempt for the law.
2. Political factions controlled the country, satisfying their
   personal desire and quest for power.
3. Many politicians, controlled by high-powered mobsters,
   falsely claimed they were working for the people.
4. Women, having received the constitutional right to vote,
   flaunted their new "equality" in the greatest fashion
   revolution of all time.
5. The United States, having remarkable economic growth since
   the turn of the century, had too much of the nation's wealth in
   the hands of a wealthy minority. The entire world would feel
   the effects of this greed.
6. By 1929, production capacity in the United States exceeded
   market demand.

The STOCK MARKET CRASH brought immediate panic to
Sagamore. The poor miners were asking, "What does it mean? What
is the STOCK MARKET? What does it have to do with us? The
poverty and suffering endured in the previous 10 years still haunted
them. Realizing that the crash would bring more terrible times filled
them with anguish. How much more could they endure? they thought.
Little knowing it would be 10 more long years.

Every day, newspapers and radio announcements were filled
with gloom and doom, depicting a desperate nation in depression.
People, having lost fortunes overnight, were jumping to their deaths.
Those unaccustomed to hardships were unable to cope with the shock
of having lost all their wealth. It was as though the end had come.

Mother, determined to make Christmas as cheerful as possible
that year, chopped down an eight-foot evergreen and dragged it across

the snow to the hotel. Joe installed the lovely tree on a stand, placing it in a corner of the large 30x40-foot kitchen, as the entire family dined there at two 12-foot tables. Sparkling lights and loads of icicles created a lovely vision. For many years to come, the annual Christmas tree would be placed in that same corner, always reaching at least eight feet high.

Sagamore Hotel 1939

CHAPTER IX
THE YEARS 1930 - 1935

Regretfully, Dad carried only $2,500 fire insurance on the store. It was all he could afford and he always struggled to pay the premiums. The bank applied the $2,500 toward the stores outstanding mortgage, holding Dad liable for the balance. Making matters worse, he and Joe were unable to pay the hotel's final payment, being eight month past due. The stress was overwhelming, causing him sleepless nights while he sought an answer, for so many were depending on him. Feeling that his world was crumbling, he prayed for a solution. It would come during on of his sleepless nights.

He called on the president of his bank and presented his plan with all the sincerity and determination he could muster as he silently prayed within. After a very amicable meeting, they came to an agreement, satisfactory to both. The bank loaned him the funds sufficient enough to secure a clear deed to the hotel.

On January 18, 1930, Joe received a clear deed to the HOTEL SAGAMORE. On January 20, 1930, he and Julia deeded half interest to Dad, and the bank received a first mortgage on the hotel, covering the cost of the hotel's final payment, as well as the unpaid mortgage balance on the store.

After seven struggling year, Dad and Joe at last had their deed. Dad recalled his migration to Sagamore in 1909, at the age of 11, when he and Uncle Steve, along with Cherry, their cow, walked that last mile down highway 210 to Sagamore. He recalled his awestruck fascination at the sight of the hotel, little dreaming that one day he would be one of its owners.

Dad, realizing the hotel's grave need for extensive repairs and remodeling as nothing had been maintained since it was constructed 26 years before – began to plan a remodeling and repair program. It would be a slow, but continuously never ending 10-year program, accomplished with much effort during the depression years. His first project was the conversion of the antiquated gas lamp lighting system in the hotel to electricity.

Since the great coal strike of the mid '20, many coal-mining towns in western Pennsylvania had begun to fade away as their mines closed. Of these coal towns, Meko and Tyler were two. Houses were torn down, and their secondhand lumber sold at give away prices. Dad and Joe purchased enough of the secondhand lumber to construct two huge barns behind the hotel, in which hay and straw were stored for winter resale at premium prices to the Pittsburgh Plate Glass Co. in Ford City, Pennsylvania. A third barn was constructed and used in Nick's scrap-iron business. A fourth building served as a slaughterhouse, having a corral for animals until they were butchered. A cow barn with a small corral was built behind the slaughterhouse, and Mother established a garden next to the cow barn. Joe, being a gifted carpenter in the family, was responsible for the construction of these buildings, with the help of a man called Figlar.

Every conceivable plan in making a living was implemented. Once again, Dad rang his ole cow bell as he peddled meats and produce throughout the town – this time in a truck, instead of the old horse and wagon of bygone days. However, sales were poor with money so scarce. Also, farmers patronized the nearby flour mill, where their wheat was ground into flour. They exchanged their flour for its grinding and groceries, as the mill also sold groceries. However, Dad was thankful for what business he had.

Every family, as well as Dad's implemented every means for survival. Gardens produced their vegetables. They hunted deer, quail, grouse, dove, rabbits, and squirrels. They raised chickens, cows, pigs, pigeons and goats for meat, eggs, milk, cheese and butter. Berries and fruit were canned and made into jellies. Hickory nuts and black walnuts were dried and stored. Bread was home baked. Everything possible was either canned or dried in preparation for the long cold winters. Clothes were mended over and over again, always passed down from older to younger children. Hair was cut by Mom or Dad. Absolutely nothing was wasted.

On August 2, 1930, Julia and Joe celebrated the birth of their third child, a boy, naming him Joe Jr. after his father.

Two months later, on October 8, Mother and Dad celebrated the birth of their fourth and last child, a boy named Nicholas Donald, whom we called Nickie or Nick.

Responsibilities weighed heavily on Dad's shoulders in 1930, resulting in his decision to retire from the Sagamore baseball team after 8 years of dedicated loyalty. This decision left him sick at heart. He was also disturbed in his unsuccessful effort in helping Joe with his heavy drinking problem. It was a constant worry to him, for he loved his brother greatly.

Joe was a good-hearted man whom everyone loved. He was a hard worker when he was not drinking, and unbelievably strong. The story is told that he once drove his bare fist through a solid marble sink without getting as much as a scratch on his hand. This feat was performed one winter, when Julia hid his shoes to prevent his leaving the hotel to obtain more liquor.

He dearly loved children, always spending time with us, taking us places, and sharing with us. I remember many times, when he was drinking, he would sit at the head of the table, having his and our families children seated around him. He would raise his arms into the air, like a choir director. "O K," he would say, 'Now let's all sing When It's Spring Time In The Rockies.' That was his favorite song. We sang it over and over again, until he broke down crying. Something about that song seemed to make him cry. Many times, I think about him, and begin humming.

"WHEN IT'S SPRINGTIME IN THE ROCKIES, I'LL BE COMING BACK TO YOU.

WHEN IT'S SPRINGTIME IN THE ROCKIES, IN THE ROCKIES FAR AWAY.

ONCE AGAIN I'LL SAY I LOVE YOU, AS THE BIRDS SING ALL THE DAY.

WHEN IT'S SPRINGTIME IN THE ROCKIES, IN THE ROCKIES FAR AWAY"

Another song he loved to sing, bringing us to laughter when we sang it, was "SHE'LL BE COMING AROUND THE MOUNTAIN," and it went like this:

SHE'LL BE COMING AROUND THE MOUNTAIN WHEN SHE COMES,

SHE'LL BE COMING AROUND THE MOUNTAIN WHEN SHE COMES,

OH, SHE'LL BE COMING AROUND THE MOUN-TAIN, SHE'LL BE COMING AROUND THE MOUNTAIN, SHE'LL BE COMING AROUND THE MOUNTAIN WHEN SHE COMES.

SHE'LL BE RIDING SIX WHITE HORSES WHEN SHE COMES,

SHE'LL BE RIDING SIX WHITE HORSES WHEN SHE COMES,

SHE'LL BE RIDING SIX WHITE HORSES, SHE'LL BE RIDING SIX WHITE HORSES, SHE BE RIDING SIX WHITE HORSES WHEN SHE COMES..

WE WILL KILL THE BIG RED ROOSTER WHEN SHE COMES,

WE WILL KILL THE BIG RED ROOSTER WHEN SHE COMES,

WE WILL KILL THE BIG RED ROOSTER, WE WILL KILL THE BIG RED ROOSTER, WE WILL KILL THE BIG RED ROOSTER WHEN SHE COMES.

WE WILL HAVE CHICKEN FOR DINNER WHEN SHE COMES,

WE WILL HAVE CHICKEN FOR DINNER WHEN SHE COMES,

OH, WE WILL HAVE CHICKEN FOR DINNER, WE WILL HAVE CHICKEN FOR DINNER, WE WILL HAVE CHICKEN FOR DINNER WHEN SHE COMES."

In February, 1931, Nick, supposedly on a business trip to Detroit, Michigan, surprised the family when he returned with his 16-year-old bride, Fannie, whom he married March 4 while on his trip.

At the time, he was engaged to another woman, who, unable to cope with the news of his marriage, suffered a nervous breakdown.

Mother and Julia rearranged living quarters for several members of the family, availing to Nick and Fannie four rooms and an office on the third floor. Their marriage would produce three girls, Rebecca, Sally, and Millie, and one son, Joe or Joie as he was called.

Helen, having completed her two-year business course in one and a half years moved to Kittanning, 20 miles away, where Dad obtained a job for her with a grocery owner friend of his.

The day after Labor Day, September 1931, Mother enrolled me in first grade at Sagamore Elementary. I do not recall being aware that one day I would be going to school. School was a complete surprise. There I was, in this large room with strange little boys and girls everywhere, wondering what on earth was I doing there.

I looked up, up, up at my teacher, Miss Hildy, who was six feet tall, thinking she was the tallest person I had ever seen. She looked down, down, down at me, smiling. "My, but you are a tiny little thing," she said. "I will have to put you in the front row, or I won't be able to see you." I weighed only 32 pounds. From that first day I liked Miss Hildy, as did all the hundreds of children she taught through the years.

At Christmas, the class drew names for the exchanging of gifts. Upon opening my gift, my heart leaped at the sight of my first ever, a beautiful strand of red beads from Donald Flickinger. At that moment, I fell in love with Donald, thinking he must feel the same or he would never have given me such beautiful beads. Soon, I realized, he didn't even know I existed, ending my first love.

I enjoyed learning in school. However, I missed the freedom enjoyed in our 62-room hotel and its 3.33 acres of land. I felt too restricted, too confined, craving the freedom of the outdoors. Still, this new life of regimentation and learning fascinated me, as I was hungry to learn.

For Valentines Day, Miss Hildy brought a beautiful decorated box to school, explaining how we were to exchange cards. Miss Hildy's card was the prettiest one I received, and when Mother died in 1974, we found it in the attic. Mother had kept it all those years.

It was difficult to walk the two mile round trip to school, as my legs were still weak from my bout with scarlet fever. Unable to walk the distance to our end-of-the-year school picnic, I sat on the ground crying as I hugged my legs. Miss Hildy stopped her friend, who was driving by, and asked him to drive me to the picnic. They picked me up, carried me to their car, drove me to the picnic, and then brought me back home. I could not believe anyone could be so nice to me.

My philosophy of life was now taking shape. I concluded that adults expected children to be seen and not heard. Consequently, I quietly listened and learned, gaining knowledge about life and things transpiring around me. Their not realizing that I was comprehending gave me a secret satisfaction.

In June, 1932, Franklin D. Roosevelt won the Democratic presidential nomination. Rumors were circulating that if Roosevelt were elected, the 18th Amendment would be repealed. Realizing the general store was not making enough to support the family, and being delinquent on his bank loans, Dad began planning towards obtaining a liquor license, should the amendment be repealed. The hotel would definitely qualify, if he could raise the money for the license. He began working diligently with the county commissioner, who headed Roosevelt's campaign headquarters in Armstrong County. Being a strong influence in the county, Dad had campaigned for Armstrong County political leaders for years and was much respected by county politicians, who vied for his support.

That summer, the circus inspired my first aspiration. The tightwire walker and beautifully costumed trapeze artists held me spellbound. The thrill of the crowd, the cheers, and screams filled me with the dream of becoming a grand circus performer. However, this aspiration ended the day I straddled the iron railing in front of the hotel while attempting to run along its one-inch width. Coming out of unconsciousness, I saw the doctor hovering over me, looking where I felt he had no business. Mother was crying, and several others were standing nearby, looking down at me in grave concern. As I laid on the bed, greatly embarrassed, my aspiration of being a circus performer vanished.

In September, I entered Miss Miller's second-grade classroom, thinking she was the most beautiful teacher in the world. It surprised me to see children coming to school in their bare feet, little knowing it was because they had no shoes to wear. However, I thought it was great, so I took to hiding my shoes in some bushes nearby, proceeding to school in my bare feet, then reclaiming my shoes after school. Mother wondered why my shoes never showed signs of normal wear and tear. This continued until the weather got too cold. However, many of the children continued coming in their bare feet even after the snow began to fall.

On my way to school one day, I happened upon a MOONSHINE STRAINER. They are shaped like an oversized funnel, and made of natural colored wool. I'd never seen one before, so innocently believing it to be some sort of cap, I picked it up, put it on my head, and walked into my schoolroom wearing my newfound possession. My teacher, knowing what it was, could barely refrain from laughing out loud while questioning me about my cap. I walked home from school, wearing my funnel-shaped moonshine strainer cap, and felt quite proud, until my mother saw me walk into the house. It was years before I understood why she snatched that strainer off my head, yelling "DON'T YOU EVER DO THAT AGAIN! NOT EVER!" Oh, the innocence of childhood, as I now reminisce.

Being that Mother worked full time in the general store with Benny, my care was predominantly in the hands of others. Therefore, unbeknownst to Mother, every Saturday I was given a bucket of lye water and a bucket of rinse water, with a scrub brush and rag. Lye acts as a bleaching agent on wood. I was told to scrub the 20 wooden kitchen chairs, and the front and back stairways of the hotel, each having over 20 steps. While working, I could hear children playing outside. The desire to be outside laughing and playing with them would bring tears rolling down my cheeks. One night Mother was teaching my brothers and me our prayers in Slovak, when she noticed me scratching my red hands and questioned me. She looked in disbelief as she rubbed them with a soothing salve. I never again had to scrub those steps and chairs with lye water, much to my joy and happiness.

I would have several brushes with death as a child. My first occurred the day I climbed the corral fence to see our cow, Bessy's newborn calf. Bessy, thinking I was coming to take her calf from her, charged, and I took for the fence as fast as my little legs would go, but Bessy overtook me, and as she lowered her horns to gouge me, they caught in the collar of my coat. Unable to free her horns, Bessy headed for the wooden fence, ramming me into the fence in an effort to free them. I screamed as she rammed me up against that fence again and again. Mother, working in the hotel kitchen, heard my screams and headed for the cow barn. With much effort, she freed me from Bessy's horns, but not before I was badly battered and bleeding.

Dad's brothers, George and Andy, were identical twins. No one could tell them apart. Dad thought, "What a great drawing card they would make, if they boxed against each other in a boxing ring. He contacted a trainer in Kittanning, who felt the same as Dad about the novelty of twins in a boxing ring, and at only 12 years old. Soon they were boxing with great success in Kittanning and Ford City. Before long, they were in demand for performances in Pittsburgh and other cities. Dad had their first names embroidered on the left leg of their boxing trunks. Audiences found it a unique thrill, trying to read their names while they boxed, for no one was able to identify them otherwise. A corner of the hotel's dining room, the size of a boxing ring, was used for their practices. I was seven when Dad laced a pair of gloves on me, and to his surprise, I was quite good in the ring. That is, until I was hit so hard I got a really black eye, ending my boxing career.

Grandma was bitterly against the twins boxing, accusing Dad of trying to kill her sons. Dad, therefore, withdrew them from boxing, and upon their completion of the eighth grade, they went to work with Nick and Mike in the scrap-iron business, against Dad's wishes, and again he grieved that nothing was turning out the way he had hoped. The family was abandoning him even before they were coming of age.

On November 8, 1932, a ray of hope filled the hearts of the American people when Franklin D. Roosevelt won the election, having pledged "A NEW DEAL FOR THE AMERICAN PEOPLE," if elected. Experts considered the election the most crucial since Lincoln's victory more than 70 years before. Roosevelt received 22,800,000 votes and his opponent, President Hoover, received 15,750,000 votes.

Once again Dad was in trouble with his bank. It had been closed. When the government men opened the bank, they began to foreclose on delinquent loans. Just as Dad feared, he received a deadline notice for loan payment. He could not afford to lose the hotel with so many mouths to feed. He planned a last desperate plea for an extension as time was running out. He tells his story in these words. "I knew I had to have something extra to say, as I had talked with them so often. So, I thought, I would walk to the bank, which was three miles. The weather was below zero, and wind was strong. It was just one of the worst days of the winter. I had a pint bottle of apricot brandy on me, and as I was thinking just what to say, I was sipping on the nectar to keep from freezing. So, I do not know how I looked as I opened the door into the bank. Before I could say a word, the head man at the bank took me by the hand and led me out of the bank to his car garage, asking me into the car, and drove me back home. My wife thanked him, and asked him in the kitchen, as it was dinner time. He stayed a good while, looking the place over, and I was feeding my eight brothers and sisters, four of my own, and four of my brothers', my mother, my brother and his wife, me and my wife and a janitor, who could not get work. We had to feed 23 in all. My wife asked him to have coffee, and I was told to go to bed. After realizing it all, the worry I put her through, I did not like the way I done. But, to my surprise, I noticed the head of the bank changed so much, and was so good to me. I could not believe it. All I can say is, I think when he saw that group of children etc, we were feeding, he did not have the heart to push me. I could see, he would accept most any kind of offer to settle with the bank. So, I offered by brother, who had left me just four years before when he reached 21, to take over the mortgage at the bank, as I could get to settle the whole account for one third But, to my surprise, he and his wife refused. I told him when I paid him back his money he would give me back the deed, but he refused. So, I cashed the last of the insurances. It was a joint policy with me and Joe. Then scrapping and borrowing from anyone I knew, I finally paid off the bank. The head of the bank became our family's best friend."

When Franklin D. Roosevelt took the oath of office March 4, 1933, the weather was cold and rainy. Before tens of thousands at the inauguration, and millions of radio listeners at home, he carefully repeated each phrase of the presidential oath, rather than the traditional "I do." After he was sworn in, he turned to the crowd, with an aura that radiated a feeling of confidence, and spoke these now-famous first words of his inaugural address: "FIRST OF ALL, LET ME ASSERT MY FIRM BELIEF THAT THE ONLY THING WE HAVE TO FEAR IS FEAR ITSELF – NAMELESS, UNREASONING, UNJUSTIFIED TERROR." For the next seven years it would be an uphill battle for the United States of America.

Because Grandma was discontented living in the hotel, Dad and Joe deeded a small lot out of the hotel's 3.33 acres on which to build her a house. Joe dug out for the foundation, but Grandma wanted to rebuild on the grounds of the old store and house, so Joe and Figlar went to work clearing the old store site and constructing a smaller house, with a small store attached, should Grandma or anyone in the family want to re-establish another store in the future. When the new house was completed in 1933, Grandma, Mary, Veronica, Mike and the twins moved in. However, the store was never re-established, and Grandma used it for storage.

Mother's health was beginning to fail. The years of long, hard hours, working with little sleep or rest, had taken their toll. She entered the Cleveland Clinic in Cleveland, Ohio, where a tumor was removed from her right side. Many bouts with health problems would prevail throughout her life. She never complained, always remaining her kind, good-natured self. She was a giver in life, never a taker. To know her was to love her, and all who knew her did indeed love her very much.

While Mother was in the Cleveland Clinic the summer of 1933, I experienced a never-forgotten highlight of my childhood – my first vacation, two weeks with Grandma and Grandpa Lucas in Warren, Ohio. Two weeks in a glorious world I didn't know existed. Banana splits, milkshakes, all the food I could eat, anytime, anywhere, bus rides, sliding boards and swings, swimming, singing, dancing, laughing and playing. I thought I'd died and gone to heaven. It was so overwhelming, I didn't want it to end. When Mother returned from the Clinic, extremely pale and thin, I knew my wonderful vacation was over and began to cry. "We have to go home," she said, "but you can come back next summer." Still, I cried as her brother drove us the 120 miles to Sagamore.

Medicine shows and small carnivals came to Sagamore every year. However, the Dayton Fair, which was 10 miles from Sagamore, was special, drawing thousands from miles around. One day, Uncle Joe took us to the Dayton Fair. Some six or seven happy children, ages seven to nine, climbed into the 1930 four-door Oakland, each having 50 cents or less to spend. At the fair's front gate, Uncle Joe sent us on our own to enjoy the fair, saying, "You all have a good time now. When, it's time to go home, I'll come get you." Several hours passed. Our money was spent, we were ready to go home, so we began looking for him. At last, we found him among the farm animals with some friends, and he was very drunk. A feeling of fear came over me, as there was no one but him to drive us home. When we got to the car, he told me to sit up front in the middle which I did. Not for one second did I take my eyes off that road, good thing, too, for at seven years old I was faced with a decision, that miraculously saved all our lives. Ironically no one was aware of the near tragedy, with all the talking and laughter going on. We were heading straight into the path of an oncoming car. It was obvious to me that Uncle Joe was oblivious to the critical crisis before us. In a split second of fear, I grabbed the wheel with both hands, turning it to the right with all my might. We missed the oncoming car by inches. Not for one second did I remove my hands from the wheel the rest of the 10 miles home, steering the car until we stopped in the driveway. Mother and Julia were shocked when Uncle Joe stumbled out of the car. Aunt Julia gave him a well-deserved tongue lashing. "You could have killed those children," she shouted. I believe God placed me in there that day to steer the car home. How can one question a power greater than us?

Dad was happy because his hard work at campaigning for President Roosevelt was paying off. Thanks to the county commissioner, who paved the way, his sisters, Mary and Helen obtained public jobs during a period in history when few women held such jobs. Mary would obtain the position as postmistress of the Sagamore Post Office, a position she would hold for 30 years until she retired. Helen would obtain a position with the Pennsylvania State Government in the state capital of Harrisburg. She held this job until she married Gene Place, a fine gentleman from Warwick, Rhode Island. They later lived in Warwick, where their marriage produced on son, Philip.

As a child, I thought Aunt Helen was slim and very beautiful. I do not have any memories of her, except that she came to visit occasionally for Easter or Christmas, always recalling fond memories of my mother. She especially remembered one occasion when a special function required a new dress, Mother being a gifted seamstress, designed and sewed for her the most beautiful dress.

At age 86 Aunt Helen said, "I never forgot that beautiful dress, I can still see it in my mind. I was so proud of that dress."

I always felt justified in my not liking Aunt Mary, especially after she almost boiled me alive during the time she lived at the hotel. She never liked children, but when I was five and six years old, she was in charge of our Saturday baths. I cringed at the sight of her coming with those pails of boiling water, pouring them in to the tub, missing me by inches. No amount of pleading or screaming, "IT'S HOT, TOO HOT," saved the three of us, bathing in the tub. We'd jump up, bouncing from one foot to the other shouting, "IT'S HOT, TOO HOT," but Aunt Mary would push us back down into that hot water saying, "IT'S NOT TOO HOT. NOW SHUT UP AND TAKE YOUR BATH." We couldn't bathe fast enough, trying desperately to keep our bodies above water, except for our feet and buttocks, which remained scarlet red and sore for hours, even days afterwards. I remember peeling skin from my feet many times following those baths.

Aunt Mary was extremely eccentric, and throughout her life she was plagued with manic depression. She always hoped to marry the town's doctor, who was originally from Canada and still maintained a residence there. No one knew much about him, except that upon his death the bulk of his estate was left to a local boy, who people said was his illegitimate son by his one-time housemaid. However, the doctor did will the usufruct of his Canadian residence to Aunt Mary. She lived there for a short time, then returned to Sagamore, where she lived alone and never married. She did have suitors other than the doctor, as she had an elegant presence, but they soon drifted by the wayside. Her home was gorgeously decorated and filled with rare and lovely antiques. Upon her death at age seventy five, her possessions and monies were willed to a religious domicile for nuns of the Catholic faith. One might say Aunt Mary was born at the wrong time, in the wrong place. To me, she was like Blanche in the movie "A Streetcar Named Desire." Sad indeed, for Dad never received a kind word or thank you from Aunt Mary, never acknowledged him for what sacrifices he made in raising her. Not even a thank you for helping her obtain the job that brought security in her life.

In school again, my third-grade teacher, Miss Marshall, was great. I sat in the front row again, next to a boy who was crippled by polio. Not having seen a polio victim before, it filled me with deep compassion. I wanted to know why God let such things happen and pressed my mother for an answer. Mother could always soothe our fears and anxieties with perfect answers. Thereafter, I admired the boy, who bravely faced his disability and acted like one of us. How wonderful, I thought.

Joe and Julia's fourth child, Robert, whom we called Bobby, was born in November 1933.

My three brothers and I looked forward to Mother's bedtime stories. Her scary stories were our favorite. After story time, it was prayer time, then bedtime, with all four of us sleeping in one bed, like sardines in a can, one this way, the other that way. Her scariest story came from Czechoslovakia. I thought you might enjoy it, as we did when Mother told it to us.

THE RETURN OF THE DEAD

IN CZECHOSLOVAKIA AT THE TURN OF THE CENTURY, IT WAS THE LAW OF THE LAND THAT EVERY 18-YEAR OLD BOY MUST SERVE TWO YEARS IN THE ARMY.

YOSEF AND ANYA WERE JUST MARRIED, AND IN A COUPLE WEEKS, HE WAS OFF TO THE ARMY FOR TWO YEARS. ONE DAY ANYA RECEIVED A LETTER FROM THE GOVERNMENT. YOSEF HAD BEEN KILLED IN AN ACCIDENT WHILE IN TRAINING. ANYA WAS GRIEF-STRICKEN. SHE DID NOT BELIEVE HE WAS DEAD. SHE COULD NOT BE-LIEVE IT. NO! NOT HER YOSEF.

SO ANYA WENT TO THE GYPSY FORTUNE TELLER, ASK-ING HER TO PLEASE BRING HIM BACK, SO SHE MAY SEE HIM AGAIN. "LEAVE HIM ALONE," SHE SAID, "THE DEAD ARE DEAD. LET HIM REST IN PEACE," "NO," ANYA PLEADED. "I MUST SEE HIM AND TALK TO HIM. I DO NOT BELIEVE HE IS DEAD."

SO, THE GYPSY INSTRUCTED ANYA TO GO AT MID-NIGHT TO THE CEMETERY, AND DIG UP SOME BONES OF THE DEAD, THEN PUT THEM IN A KETTLE OF WATER TO BOIL. SHE MUST DRAW A CHALK RING FIVE FEET IN DI-AMETER, AND SIT IN A CHAIR IN THE CENTER OF THE RING AND WAIT. THE GYPSY WARNED HER THAT SHE MUST NEVER CROSS THE CHALK RING. SHE SAID YOSEF WOULD COME, BUT SHE MUST NEVER-NEVER-CROSS THE CHALK RING. ANYA AGREED, AND THAT NIGHT SHE WENT TO THE CEMETERY AT MIDNIGHT. SHE DUG UP THE BONES, PUT THEM IN A KETTLE OF WATER TO BOIL, SAT IN HER CHAIR ENCIRCLED BY CHALK AND WAITED. THE WATER BEGAN TO BOIL. "PUTTS, PUTTS, PUTTS," IT SAID, WHICH MEANS "COME, COME, COME" IN CZECHOSLOVAKIAN. IT BEGAN

TO BOIL FASTER AND FASTER. PUTTS, PUTTS, PUTTS, COME, COME, COME, FASTER AND FASTER. AND THEN! YOSEF APPEARED. ANYA IN HER JOY AND SURPRISE, JUMPED OUT OF HER CHAIR, CROSSED THE CHALK RING AND THREW HER ARMS AROUND HIM SAYING, "YOSEF, OH YOSEF, I'M SO GLAD TO SEE YOU." HE WAS ANGRY. "WHY DID YOU BRING ME BACK FROM THE DEAD? WHY DO YOU BOTHER ME? I WAS AT PEACE," HE SAID. "I COULD NOT BELIEVE YOU WERE DEAD. I WANTED TO SEE FOR MY-SELF," SHE SAID. "AND SO YOU HAVE, AND NOW I WILL TAKE YOU BACK WITH ME." AS HE BEGAN SQUEEZING HIS FINGERS AROUND HER THROAT, SHE BROKE FREE AND RAN DOWN THE STREET, STOPPING AT EACH HOUSE AND POUNDING ON THE DOOR. "OPEN THE DOOR. LET ME IN," SHE SHOUTED. "OPEN THE DOOR. LET ME IN." YOSEF RAN AFTER HER AS SHE CONTINUED DOWN THE STREET, UNTIL SHE SAW THE CHURCH. THE DOOR WAS UNLOCKED. SHE RAN IN AND LOCKED THE DOOR.

IN THE CHURCH THERE WAS A DEAD MAN LYING IN A COFFIN. THERE HAD BEEN A DEATH IN THE TOWN THE DAY BEFORE, AND THE DEAD MAN LAY IN THE COFFIN READY FOR BURIAL THE NEXT MORNING. YOSEF STOOD OUTSIDE PEERING THROUGH THE CHURCH WINDOW. THEN, HE SAID, "DEAD MAN, GET UP AND TAKE THE LIV-ING," AND THE DEAD MAN MOVED HIS HAND. AGAIN HE SAID, "DEAD MAN, GET UP AND TAKE THE LIVING," AND HE SAT UP. EACH TIME HE SAID "DEAD MAN, GET UP AND TAKE THE LIVING," THE DEAD MAN MADE A MOVE TO-WARD ANYA, WHO WAS NOW COWERING IN THE CORNER OF THE CHURCH, TRYING TO HIDE. FINALLY, THE DEAD MAN CAME UPON HER AND WRAPPED HIS FINGERS

AROUND HER THROAT. "DEAD MAN, GET UP AND TAKE THE LIVING," AND HE BEGAN TO SQUEEZE THE LIFE FROM HER. AT THAT MOMENT, THE ROOSTER CROWED, AS IT WAS THE CRACK OF DAWN. YOSEF DISAPPEARED INTO THE SPIRIT WORLD, AND THE DEAD MAN LET LOOSE HIS GRIP AND MELTED INTO A POOL OF TAR.

THE TOWNSPEOPLE WERE AWAKENED BY ANYA'S CRIES, AND WERE NOW SEARCHING THE AREA TO SEE WHAT HAD HAPPENED. THEY FOUND HER IN THE CHURCH, COWERING IN THE CORNER. HER HAIR HAD TURNED SNOW WHITE AND HER MIND WAS COMPLETELY GONE. BESIDE HER THEY SAW THE POOL OF TAR, AND THEY WONDERED. (The end)

Today, this story is in my storytelling inventory, I hope you too have enjoyed it, as I did as a child.

Another of Mother's stories came from Grandma Lucas, who claimed the story was true, it having happened in her village of Michalovce, Slovakia. Being that it left a lasting impression on my imagination as a child, I want to tell you the story.

EVEN DEATH COULD NOT PART THEM

ANDREW AND ELIZABETH WERE FIVE YEARS OLD WHEN THEIR PARENTS BETROTHED THEM TO EACH OTHER. THAT'S THE WAY IT WAS IN THE 1800s IN SLOVAKIA.

ANDREW AND ELIZABETH KNEW THEY WOULD MARRY ONE DAY. AS CHILDREN AND TEENAGERS, THEY PLAYED AND WORKED IN THE FIELDS TOGETHER, ALWAYS ANTICIPATING THE DAY THEY WOULD MARRY. LOVE BETWEEN THEM WAS EVIDENT. THE WEDDING WAS TO BE ON ELIZABETH'S 16TH BIRTHDAY. SHE AND HER MOTHER SPENT MANY HOURS SEWING HER WEDDING DRESS, AND

ELIZABETH HAD FILLED A TRUNK WITH BEAUTIFUL HANDWORKED ITEMS FOR HER NEW HOME.

THE ENTIRE VILLAGE ANTICIPATED THE OCCASION. IT MEANT MUSIC, DANCING, EATING, DRINKING, JOY AND LAUGHTER. THE MORNING OF THE WEDDING, THE CHURCH WAS OVERFLOWED, AS ALL THE TOWNSPEOPLE WERE THERE. THE CANTOR BEGAN TO SING. HIS BARI-TONE VOICE RANG OUT THROUGHOUT THE CHURCH, AND THE PROCESSION BEGAN. FIRST THE BRIDESMAIDS AND THE GROOMSMEN, THEN ELIZABETH, LOOKING LIKE A FAIRY PRINCESS, WALKED DOWN THE AISLE IN HER BEAU-TIFUL WEDDING DRESS. SHE WAS RADIANT WITH HAPPI-NESS. THE PRIEST CONCLUDED THE CEREMONY SAYING, "ANDREW, YOU MAY KISS THE BRIDE." ANDREW REACHED AROUND ELIZABETH'S SHOULDER, AND AS HE PRESSED HIS LIPS TO HERS, SHE SLUMPED, FALLING TO THE FLOOR. THE CROWD GASPED IN HORROR WHEN THE DOCTOR PRO-NOUNCED HER DEAD. "NO!" SCREAMED ANDREW, "NO!"

THE GRIEVING FAMILIES AND ANDREW MADE A DE-CISION TO BURY ELIZABETH IN HER WEDDING DRESS THAT AFTERNOON, WHEREUPON THE MEN IMMEDIATELY PREPARED A SHALLOW GRAVE. AND SO IT WAS THAT THE TOWNSPEOPLE WOULD ATTEND BOTH THE WEDDING AND THE FUNERAL OF THE BRIDE IN ONE DAY.

AS NIGHT FELL, ANDREW WALKED TO ELIZABETH'S FRESH GRAVE, THROWING HIMSELF IN GRIEF ACROSS THE FRESH MOUND OF DIRT, SOBS RACKING HIS BODY. HE LAY THERE, SOBBING, "ELIZABETH, MY BEAUTIFUL ELIZA-BETH, WHY, OH GOD IN HEAVEN, WHY?" THEN, HE HEARD SCREAMS COMING FROM THE DEPTHS OF THE SHALLOW GRAVE. ELIZABETH WAS SCREAMING, "ANDREW, AN-

DREW!" HE JUMPED TO HIS FEET, AND BEGAN CLAWING THE DIRT AWAY WITH HIS BARE HANDS. THERE WAS NO TIME FOR SHOVELS. HE RAPIDLY CLAWED AND CLAWED, YELLING "ELIZABETH, I'M COMING, ELIZABETH, I'M COMING," UNTIL HE REACHED THE COFFIN. HE QUICKLY OPENED THE COFFIN, EXHAUSTED, BLEEDING, AND SHOCKED, AS IT WAS TOO LATE – ELIZABETH HAD DIED BY SUFFOCATION. THE SHOCK WAS MORE THAN ANDREW'S HEART COULD BEAR. HE FELL ACROSS ELIZABETH, AND WENT TO JOIN HER IN DEATH. THE NEXT DAY, THE TOWNSPEOPLE FOUND THEM TOGETHER LYING IN THE GRAVE, TOGETHER IN DEATH. (the end)

I felt the need to share this traumatic love story with you. It certainly depicts the uncertainty of life.

MARCH 4 - DECEMBER 31, 1933 THE NEW DEAL

Since President Franklin D. Roosevelt took office March 4, the most intensive executive-legislative co-operation in American History took place.

1. Two days after taking office, an emergency executive order temporarily closed the nation's banks in order to save the country's entire banking system by re-organizing.

2. Roosevelt pushed Congress to establish the Civilian Conservation Corps (CCC) on March 31.

3. Roosevelt had legislators abandon the gold standard.

4. On May 12, he pressed Congress to enact the Federal Emergency Relief Act, which set up a national relief system; the Agriculture Adjustment Act, which set a national farm policy; and The Emergency Farm Mortgage Act, which enabled farmers to refinance their farms.

5. Roosevelt and Congress enacted the Truth-in-Securities Act, the National Industrial Recovery Act – guaranteeing fair labor practices-and the Glass-Steagall Act, which guaranteed bank deposits.

6. On June 16, Roosevelt signed the National Recovery Act (NRA), forging an alliance between government and business. The law allowed representatives of each industry to set prices, quotas, wages and hours under NRA supervision. The Act included an endorsement of unionism and collective bargaining, and set up a National Labor Board to hear grievances. Section 7a was referred to as "Labor's Bill of Rights." After the June 16 signing of this Act into law, organizers began organizing throughout the nation (On May 27, 1935, the Supreme Court ruled this Act unconstitutional. However, the Wagner Act of July, 1935 replaced Section 7a of the National Recovery Act, helping labor)

AFTER NEARLY 14 YEARS, PROHIBITION IS REPEALED

In February, 1933, Congress had proposed the 21st Amendment for the repeal of the 18th Amendment. By December 5, 1933, Pennsylvania and 34 other states had ratified the 21st Amendment, ending Prohibition.

It was a long and costly wait for Dad. With miners working one or two days a week, the store wasn't doing any business. He was broke and unable to raise the $350 for a Pennsylvania State Beer License. The deadline was closing in on him. Despondent after six banks refused him a loan, citing his unpaid debts as far surpassing his worth, he tells of his last attempt to raise the money, when he went to "THE FARMERS BANK," one of the few banks that didn't close since the crash of '29. According to Dad's memoirs, "I went to the bank, and asked for the president, and they led me to his office. I am very nervous, as the time to apply is very short, and I tell him my story. But I got the same story, that I was over loaded in debts, more than the worth of the property several times. But I was desperate, and told him, if I got the beer license, I know I could do well, as I have the only hotel building for many miles around. He still could not be convinced. He sees I am very desperate. Finally, he said, if the bank gives me the loan, could I get some reliable property holder to co-sign the note? I quickly said "Yes." He asked me who it would be. I told him, and he said, As soon as you get back with the note, you can have the money. He was a tall, thin man, and looked like Honest Abraham Lincoln. I went for my little pickup, which was ready for the junk yard, hoping it would make the trip, as it was 14 miles one way. I drove faster than I did for some time, as the bank would close at 5 o'clock p.m. I did not want to take any chances until the next day, so he would not change his mind. I got there, and I told my story. He looked at me as if to say, Why you are so far in debt? You are in bad shape. You have so many to keep and feed. I did not say much, as I was at his mercy. He was in the bread and baking business. I know he must have thought of the days when he put as much as 600 loaves of bread in our store, in one week. He looked at me and said, "I will sign it." I thanked him more than once, and he said something like this: "God Bless You, your family and children." To this day, I think he was sorry for me, because of my Mother and family. Just as I started to go, I turned around to say something. I looked at him, and I must say, he had tears in his eyes, and was murmuring a prayer in my behalf. I myself wept softly inside my heart. I did not think that just a friend would be so worried for us all. I got the money, and applied for our first beer license."

Dad had a tremendous dislike for the beer and liquor business. His decision to acquire the license was a matter of survival. The Depression left no part of the nation untouched. Hopelessness, hunger, fear, and the struggle for survival was very real in every family.

Northern winters were always severe, as strong, cold winds, and deep snows blew in from Canada, across Lake Erie, Niagara

Falls, and Buffalo into Pennsylvania, frequently bringing zero temperatures from Thanksgiving through March. My feet and legs were often wet, icy cold and numb, as high snows filled my boots on my way to and from school. I appreciated our teachers, who permitted us to warm our legs and feet and dry our boots and socks by the steam radiators. Mother packed our lunch pail during the cold winter months, I enjoyed trading my sandwiches of store-bought bread with those having sandwiches of home made bread. I especially liked trading with Sally, who lived on a farm outside of town. Sometimes we would exchange our whole lunch pail. We each thought the other had the greater lunch.

In 1934, with the enactment of the National Recovery Act (NRA), in which Section 7a endorsed unionism and collective bargaining, union organizers united the common laborer in a courageous struggle against the industrialists, demanding from them better working conditions, better wages, and reasonable working hours. Never before had such courageous organizers been found in every industry throughout the country, and thousands of laborers, after suffering horrific slave-like conditions, were ready to give their lives in an effort to make life better for themselves, their families, and for those who would come after them.

John L. Lewis, born February 12, 1880, was one such dynamic man. He reorganized the United Mine Workers of America (UMWA) union, increasing the UMWA union membership from 100,000 to 400,000. Soon Sagamore miners realized an increase in hours worked and a small increase in minimum wages.

In condensing the history of the KOVALCHICKS GENERAL STORE, the original store opened in 1915, in that part of Sagamore, Pennsylvania, called Jewtown. The disastrous coal strike of 1925-27 caused it to close. When the strike ended in the spring of 1927, he re-established the KOVALCHICKS GENERAL STORE on the first floor in HOTEL SAGAMORE which was then operated by dad and his brother Joe. When dad received his first beer license in January, 1934, the KOVALCHICKS GENERAL STORE (1915-1933) was permanently closed and converted into a beer garden. The bar was cheaply constructed and sparsely furnished, offering beer only, at 10 cents a bottle. The few customers never realized Dad's complete stock was made up of no more than two or three cases of beer. Money being scarce, that was all he could afford to purchase from the beer distributor at one time.

He stubbornly hung on, not wanting to lose the hotel. From his small earnings, he strove to save towards his next year's license, knowing that liquor was being legalized and controlled by the state of Pennsylvania by way of Pennsylvania State Liquor Stores, and an additional liquor license was required.

He was disappointed and concerned that his 14-year-old twin brothers, George and Andy, had left school in favor of working full time with Nick and Mike in the scrap iron business. They had been working part-time since age 10, and at age 13 were driving trucks without a license. To dad, everything seemed to be out of control.

To help unburden himself, he returned to playing for the Sagamore baseball team. His years of experience were invaluable to them. At age 36, his reputation as a great baseball catcher was still remembered. People loved to watch the energetic and spunky catcher, who seemed to "BOUNCE" all over the place, playing baseball as a science, not a game, and whose determination to win was unsurpassed.

The last of his brothers and sisters to graduate that May was his youngest sister Veronica. After attending business college, than teaching high school for a year, she moved to Harrisburg, Pennsylvania, where she worked until 1945 as a private secretary and bookkeeper.

For years our local janitor was John Struhar, an elderly Hungarian immigrant who disliked children. He kept the furnace fires burning throughout the days and nights, always sleeping on a makeshift bed in the furnace room. We children instinctively kept our distance from him, especially after he presented mother and Julia with a handmade rubber tire cat-of-nine tails whip. Mother placed the whip on a china cabinet as a warning to us. She never used the whip, but she and Julia did put the paddle to us at times, never telling us what provoked the paddling. Struhar always stood watching with a big smile upon his face, wishing, I'm sure, that he was doing the paddling. I believe the Depression was so stressful on parents that their frustrations were taken out on their children.

I disenthroned Santa Claus that Christmas Eve as I sat waiting at the head of the stairs, determined to confront Santa over the fact that I had never received a Christmas toy in eight years. Surprisingly, the voices of mother and Julia came from below. The realization of who Santa Claus was quickly obliterated my fantasy world of Santa Claus. However, my quest for an explanation was satisfied. Thereafter, toys at Christmas were not important, knowing we had no money to buy them, especially with eight children to worry about, four in our family and four in Uncle Joe and Aunt Julia's.

Pets were an integral part of our childhood. There were dogs of various breeds, with German police being favored. I disliked cats after having experienced an attack by one when ascending our dark cellar stairs one day.

Mother's chickens were our pets, until they would disappear. We learned later that we had eaten them, then tears fell all over the place, especially when mother made soup from our favorite rooster, Tom. He acted almost human, and we kids loved old Tom. But, best of all, there was one dog that surpassed them all.

A DOG NAMED EDDIE

ONE DAY, BROUGHT HOME A LITTLE WHITE PUPPY. HE WASN'T PUREBRED OR ANYTHING LIKE THAT. HE WAS JUST A DOG, BUT THE CUTEST AND FRIENDLIEST DOG YOU EVER SAW, AND HE BECAME A MEMBER OF THE FAMILY IMMEDIATELY. MY THREE BROTHERS AND I NAMED HIM EDDIE. EVERYONE IN THE COMMUNITY LOVED EDDIE. HE WAS JUST ONE OF THOSE KIND OF DOGS,

OUR JOY CAME TO A SUDDEN END ONE DAY, WHEN WE CAME HOME FROM SCHOOL AND FOUND EDDIE LYING DEAD ON THE BACK PORCH. MOM SAID HE HAD BEEN KILLED BY A TRUCK. WE BURST INTO TEARS, CRYING AND CRYING OVER OUR LOSS.

THEN WE BEGAN DISCUSSING THE BURIAL OF EDDIE, AND DECIDED WE COULDN'T PUT EDDIE IN THE COLD, COLD GROUND. HE SHOULD HAVE A NICE BOX FOR A COFFIN, ONE THAT WAS SPECIAL, NOT AN ORDINARY BOX. SO WE SET OUT LOOKING FOR THIS SPECIAL BOX. AT LAST THE RIGHT SIZE BOX WAS FOUND. THEN IT WAS DECIDED THAT EDDIE COULDN'T BE PUT IN THIS BOX WITHOUT SOMETHING NICE AND SOFT TO LIE ON. SO WE TOOK ONE OF OUR BABY BLANKETS, PLACING IT UNDER HIM. NOW, TO FIND THE PERFECT BURIAL PLACE. WE REMEMBERED HOW EDDIE WOULD GO DOWN THE HILL AND DRINK WATER FROM THE NATURAL SPRING THERE. HOW NICE IT WOULD BE TO BURY EDDIE NEAR THE SPRING HE LOVED SO MUCH. A PERFECT SPOT WAS FOUND. WE TOOK OUR LITTLE PICKS AND SHOVELS AND STARTED DIGGING. WE DUG, THEN MEASURED, THEN DUG AGAIN, AND MEASURED AGAIN. IT HAD TO BE JUST RIGHT.

WE WANTED A REAL FUNERAL FOR EDDIE, SO ALL THE CHILDREN FROM THE COMMUNITY WERE INVITED AND WERE ASKED TO BRING FLOWERS AND SOME MONEY, SO EDDIE WOULD HAVE SOME MONEY TO SPEND IN HEAVEN. WE WERE SO SURE HE WAS IN HEAVEN. WE PLACED EDDIE IN A RED WAGON, SO WE COULD PULL HIM DOWN THE HILL IN A FUNERAL PROCESSION. I WAS CHOSEN TO ACT AS THE PRIEST. THE PROCESSION BEGAN, AND I BEGAN TO SING AND CHANT THE WORDS THAT I REMEMBERED FROM CHURCH: "HOSPODIE POMILLOW, AH-AH-AH-AH, EMYA OTZA SINAH SWATAHA DUHA AMEN AH-AH-AH-AH." THE CHILDREN FOLLOWED SINGLE FILE, HEADS BOWED, CARRYING THEIR FLOWERS. DOWN THE HILL WE SLOWLY MARCHED AND NOT A DRY EYE COULD BE SEEN. WE ARRIVED AT THE OPEN GRAVE, WHERE WE HAD PLACED TWO PIECES OF ROPE ACROSS THE OPENING. THE LITTLE COFFIN WAS PLACED ON THE ROPES AND SLOWLY WE LOWERED THE COFFIN INTO THE GROUND AS WE CRIED, AND I CONTINUED MY CHANTS AS THE PRIEST: "HOSPODIE POMILLOW, AH-AH-AH-AH." THEN, SINGLE FILE EACH ONE THREW A HANDFUL OF DIRT, A FEW FLOWERS, AND THEIR PENNIES AND NICKELS ON TOP OF EDDIES COFFIN. WE FILLED THE GRAVE WITH DIRT, MAKING A NICE ROUND MOUND AND COVERED THE MOUND WITH FLOWERS.

DAYS PASSED AND OUR HURT OVER OUR LOSS WAS BEGINNING TO FADE. WE BEGAN DISCUSSING THE MATTER OF EDDIE NEEDING THE MONEY IN HEAVEN THAT WE HAD THROWN IN HIS GRAVE. THE MORE WE DISCUSSED IT, THE MORE IT BECAME UNANIMOUS THAT EDDIE WOULDN'T NEED THE MONEY IN HEAVEN. WE WERE SURE HE WOULDN'T MIND IF WE TOOK IT BACK AND BOUGHT

SOME ICE CREAM AND CANDY AT THE ICE CREAM PAR-
LOR NEXT DOOR. SO WE AGAIN TOOK UP OUR SHOVELS
AND HEADED DOWN THE HILL. WE DUG UP THE GRAVE
AND RECLAIMED OUR COINS, FILLED THE GRAVE BACK
UP AND HEADED FOR THE ICE CREAM PARLOR. AS WE
ATE OUR ICE CREAM, WE ALL AGREED THAT EDDIE WOULD
BE REAL HAPPY TO HAVE GIVEN US HIS MONEY IF HE
WERE LIVING. EDDIE WAS EVENTUALLY REPLACED BY
ANOTHER DOG NAMED REX AND LIFE WENT ON.

Mother returned to Cleveland Clinic during the summer of 1934.
As she promised, I vacationed with Grandma Lucas in Warren, Ohio.
Again I experienced a way of life unknown to me in Sagamore.
Mother's parents and her seven brothers and sisters were an absolute
joy, full of fun and laughter and very kind to me.

The nation was in its fifth year of the Depression in 1934. Congress and President Roosevelt's enactment of the Federal Emergency
Relief Act in May, 1933, brought desperately needed food and clothing to the people of Sagamore. Government officials, with Dad's co-
operation, established a food and clothing distribution center in the
lobby of the hotel.

That August I watched, wishing there was something I could
do. I knew there was something terrible happening, but I couldn't
understand it, as I was only eight. Slowly, the line of men, women
and children moved, as they applied and received their allotment of
staple food items and clothing. Heavy khaki work clothes were issued to men, simple straight dresses to women and also to children.
They had no shape or style and looked like flour sacks, with holes
cut out for ones head and arms.

I remember the sugar, flour, cereal, powdered milk, rice, instant
potatoes, and soups being distributed in sacks, nothing being boxed.
Clothes were handed out, having no wrapping.

Labor Day meant school for children, as it always started the next day. It disturbed me, hearing that my fourth-grade teacher was a "MEAN" teacher. I visualized a "MEAN" teacher as a "WICKED WITCH," and decided I was not going to school. Besides, Mother had gotten one of the relief dresses for me to wear to school. "No," I thought, "I'll never wear that dress to school. It's for someone needy. We don't have outhouses, we have bathrooms. We're not needy." Oh, the innocence of childhood. Mother was not convinced.

"You will wear the dress, and you will go to school," she said I looked at five dresses intended to take me through nine months of school, and decided to wear the best dress on Mondays, the better one on Tuesdays, good on Wednesdays, fair on Thursdays, and terrible (the relief dress) on Fridays. Thereafter, the relief dress was blamed for every negative thing happening to me on Fridays. One happening was the Friday "Miss Meany" unjustly paddled me because I did not march out of class to her satisfaction.

Every day for nine months, government relief employees delivered milk to our class. Some days peanut butter, crackers, apples, toothpaste, toothbrushes, and other items were delivered for distribution. During the entire nine months I never was given one glass of milk, nor even one item. "MISS MEANY" said I was not entitled to anything because my father owned a hotel. The irony was the fact that I was the smallest student in the room. I cannot describe my joy, on that last day of school, knowing "MISS MEANY" was forever out of my life. Having survived "MISS MEANY," I felt I could survive anything.

Dad's brother Nick and his wife, Fannie, were blessed with their first child, Rebecca, born on October 18, 1934. I have no personal memories of them, as they acted indifferent toward me. Years later I learned the reason for it. When they were out of town, which was weekly, their refrigerator was being pilfered by an adult living in the hotel. Fannie questioned the culprit, who in an effort to divert suspicion blamed their pilfering on me. Why Me?, I thought. Then, I realized, how easy to place the blame on an innocent child.

The "ROARING '20S" had produced the Mafia, mobsters, gangsters, bootleggers, and outlaws. Now things were changing for them. The F.B.I. and all law enforcement agencies throughout the country were declaring WAR on the lawless, and were determined to rid society of these corrupt individuals. In 1934 they were successful in ridding society of the following lawless individuals, much to the joy of everyone.

1. May 23, 1934, the notorious Bonnie & Clyde were killed in Arcadia, LA.
2. July 22, John Dillinger – Public enemy No. 1 was killed.
3. October, Pretty Boy Floyd was killed.
4. November, bank robber Baby Face Nelson was killed.
5. January 16, 1935, Ma Barker was killed, ending the Ma Barker Gang.

In the cold wintry January of 1935, Dad and Joe received a disheartening blow when they failed in their constant struggle to keep the hotel's 30-year-old steam radiator heating system working. It was financially impossible for them to purchase a new heating system. Consequently, it became a difficult and impossible task to comfortably heat the hotel during the long, harsh Pennsylvania winters. For the following four years, the hotel was heated by individual gas heaters of various sizes, by pot-bellied coal-burning stoves located in the lobby and barroom, and by a commercial coal-burning kitchen stove. The struggle to keep warm was constant, as cold drafts were everywhere. Hallways, stairways, and unused rooms were icy cold. At night, ice crystals formed on the inside of windows. Blankets were piled high on beds, and heavy outdoor clothing worn indoors. Colds, influenza, pleurisy, whooping cough, and tonsillitis were ongoing. It was during those years I began dreaming of living in the South – a dream that would come true.

Dad's beer license renewal and his first liquor license for 1935 was coming due. He tells about this time in his life in his memoirs. He wrote, "Times were very bad. Mines only worked two and three days a week. Miners did not draw any pay as the company store took it all. The miners were always in debt to the company store. I was short $100 to send for my liquor license. I knew of a man that could help me, but he was drinking quite a bit, and I did not like to ask him. But it was time to apply and I took a chance to ask him. He loaned me the money. Then, when he sobered up, he was not sure I could be trusted. I signed a note for him, but he was told I was in debt so far, and it seemed to worry him. He came in to see me with two other friends of his. The two friends of his looked me over. They called me over to them and asked if I owed their friend so much money, etc. I said, "Yes, I got a loan from him just a month ago" and that I would pay him in the time I said I would, that they did not have to worry about it. They were from the big city from out of state. They looked to me like two tough men from the time I looked at them. To me they looked like just plain racketeers. I paid the man I made the loan from. Those days $100 was a lot of money to most of the miners. I must say that times were very bad. I could not buy a truck plate license. I drove my pickup truck by the back roads when I had to go sometime, such as to banks, etc. Finally, I received a telephone call from the police station telling me I must quit driving the truck without a license plate, as they had received complaints. I thanked him, and thought it was very kind of them. They knew me well, and they realized I was having it tough."

Dad, having received his beer and liquor licenses purchased a sign for the hotel which read "SAGAMORE HOTEL BEER AND LIQUOR." In his memoirs he writes, "I had a beer and liquor license, but I could only purchase a quart or two of whisky. When I sold it, I would get more. Finally, I could buy four or five at a time. Beer was the same. Sometimes, the beer distributor would get angry at me, thinking I was buying from someone else. I was ashamed to tell him I was doing my best. He remembered, and so did I, when the same hotel sold two railroad car loads of beer every week from 1904 to 1918."

Joe Reno was the town's barber. He was a World War I veteran, having been gassed in France and never having married. Following the war, he roomed and boarded in the hotel, and rented a space for his barber shop on the second floor adjoining the lobby. It was the social center for the town's miners. They spent hours discussing or debating past, present and future issues on everything. Joe Reno was well informed, as he constantly read, and his radio was never turned off. Dominoes and checkers were played there, as well as in the barroom on the first floor. Health problems resulting from the war plagued him, at times confining him to bed, whereupon mother caringly nursed him back to health. He brought mother bushels of mushrooms, hickory nuts, butternuts, and black walnuts every year after gathering them in the wooded areas outside of town. Mother either dried or canned the mushrooms, and the nuts were dried and shelled, lasting the year.

My brother Eddie learned to drive by age nine. Dad took him everywhere, thereby giving him the opportunity to travel to Kittanning, Ford City, Indiana, Punxsutawney, Pittsburgh, and many other cities where he learned a lot of things, experiencing and enjoying the world outside of Sagamore. For Johnny and me, it was chores, chores, chores every day. Brother Nickie was much too young to feel the impact of hardships like Johnny and I did. There was no resentment however, as the four of us were very close and knew Dad could not take all of us with him. When my seemingly endless chores were finished, my room became my haven. There, I designed clothes for my cut-out paper dolls, in a world of make-believe. Those moments of creativity consoled me and helped me accept things as they were. Because I hated standing on a chair, washing dishes for hours. I hated washing clothes by hand on a washboard for hours. I hated ironing clothes for hours. I hated peeling potatoes and vegetables and sweeping the kitchen. Hanging clothes on the line was O.K., as it took me outdoors. I liked setting the table, and I did not mind cleaning our three-room apartment. Johnny and I were recalling memories once when I asked him what he remembered most from his childhood. "Work, work, and more work," he replied. "I remember milking the goat every morning. In the cold winters, hauling buckets and buckets of coal for the hotel stoves, and for Mrs. Hodgson next door, then climbing the hill to Grandma's to carry in her buckets of coal, too. Working the garden, feeding the cow, cleaning the barroom." On and on he went, recalling those days of all work and no play. Johnny, it seemed, got the brunt of the hard work, but he never complained.

He and I often talk about our constant hunger as children. Our allotted portions were served at mealtimes, and there were no seconds, which meant we left the table hungry many times. At night, my brothers and I constantly talked about being hungry. We often fantasized about growing up and being rich then we would eat all the bananas, peanut butter and jelly, ice cream and candy we wanted. One night fantasizing was not enough, for Johnny and Nickie were crying because they were hungry. My love and compassion for my brothers gave me the courage and determination to slip down the hall and down the back stairs to the kitchen in an attempt to find something to eat.

Even though kitchen cabinets were locked after supper, I knew where the keys were kept and proceeded to get them. I took four slices of bread, stacking them after pouring a little sugar on each. Replacing the keys, I slowly ascended the stairs. Upon reaching the final step, I saw a pair of feet, and slowly my eyes followed the figure before me up, up, up, until I was looking at the face of Aunt Julia. "You little thief," she said. Her open hand came down across my face and I fell tumbling backward, down the stairs, and sugar bread flew in every direction. Miraculously unhurt, I meekly got up, reclimbed the stairs and slithered past her. "Don't you ever let me catch you stealing bread again," she said. Returning to bed empty-handed was the biggest hurt of all. After Nickie asked if I had brought him something to eat and I replied "no." I softly cried myself to sleep.

Next door to our hotel, the Hodgsons owned the town's only movie theatre and ice cream parlor, presenting movies for 10 cents and selling ice cream or candy for a penny or a nickel. We seldom frequented either, never having any money to do so. One day, however, I attended a Fred Astaire – Ginger Rogers movie, and was so inspired I wanted to become a dancer. Sagamore had no dance studios. Besides, Mother and Dad could not afford the cost of lessons. So, for hours I would dance until exhausted, creating my own choreography, and never realizing it was strengthening my legs for things to come.

In 1935, Dad was now buying four to five quarts of liquor and 10 to 12 cases of beer at a time. Still, not enough to generate sufficient income to support two families and maintain the hotel. During this time of uncertain destiny, Dad had no bank account. His most guarded possession was a small leather money pouch, which held all he had in the world – a few small bills and coins. He always carried the pouch in his pants pocket. To assure safety for his money pouch, Mother sewed extra material to the bottom of each pocket. As long as he could save a few coins in the pouch towards his next beer or liquor order, he never gave up. At night, he put the pouch behind his rocking chair pillow, where he sat for hours, meditating, praying and worrying about their future.

On May 6, 1935, the Work Progress Administration (WPA) was set up, designed to employ one-third of the nation's 11 million jobless. The Civilian Conservation Corps (CCC) planned to employ 500,000. Relief families with men 18 to 25 enrolled to receive free room and board at federal camps, and a salary of $30 monthly, $25 of it automatically going to their families. These men worked on public works construction, such as soil erosion, reforestation and national parks construction.

Then on May 19, Roosevelt established the desperately needed Rural Electrification Administration (REA), making low-cost loans to private companies to construct electrical generating and delivery systems to an estimated nine out of 10 farms that had no electricity.

On August 14, Roosevelt sign the Social Security Act providing pensions for those age 65 (beginning in 1942). It also gave assistance to dependent children, the blind and disabled, and established the Unemployment Compensation System.

That September was a very eventful month, both locally and nationally. First, there was the town's big Labor Day celebration with a parade, a ballgame, speeches, games, eating and drinking. Every event was special on Labor Day, but the baseball game drew the largest crowd and generated the most excitement. Watching Dad play was something. He was quick as lightning and seemed to be involved in every play. The crowd and the players were constantly shouting, BOUNCE, BOUNCE, BOUNCE. It made me feel very proud, that this BOUNCE everyone was yelling about was my father. People were never charged to see the ball games. It was the custom to pass the hat, with everyone giving according to his or her financial ability to give. Labor Day and Fourth of July games always generated the largest collections. These collections were used in defraying the cost of maintaining the team.

As always, school began day after Labor Day. I was ecstatic. My fifth-grade teacher, Miss Gorley, rekindled my love for school. She asked if I would like to help clean the classroom at the close of each school day. Even though I knew daily chores awaited at home, I quickly said "Yes." To my relief, Mother did not object, resulting in Miss Gorley becoming my fountain of wisdom and knowledge, as she took me under her wing, so to speak.

On September 10, news swept the country with headlines "HUEY LONG ASSASSINATED." Senator Huey P. Long of Louisiana was called the Kingfish. His enemies called him the first American dictator. His book, "EVERY MAN A KING," outlined a controversial plan for redistributing wealth in the United States. At the time of his death, it was ascertained that a Baton Rouge physician, Dr. Carl A. Weiss, was the assassin. Several biographical movies on Senator Long's life portray that assertion. Today there are many who firmly believe he was accidently shot by one of his bodyguards.

In October, not even President Roosevelt's "NEW DEAL" could make the wind stop blowing, as the biggest windstorm swept through Texas, Oklahoma and the Midwest. For several years, farmers endured droughts which developed into the now famous "DUST BOWL." The winds skimmed precious topsoil from prized farm land, forming tremendous clouds of dust that obscured the sun as far east as the Appalachian Mountains. On the Plains, the dust drifted up against fences like snow in winter and it was reported that cattle ate so much dirt, as they scratched for grass, that they died from mudballs in their stomachs. At least half of the Iowa farmers lost their land. Thousands just walked off their land, making their way to California via the Southwest to escape the "DUST BOWL."

On October 23, Dutch Schultz, and underworld bootleg whiskey operator, was shot down with three of his henchmen in Newark, New Jersey, ridding society of another gangster.

I was nine now, and had a deep desire in my heart to buy Mother a Christmas present. Having no money, my three brothers and I devised a plan. We cut a slit in the lid of a canning jar, creating a bank. Every day after school, we set out hunting soda pop bottles to sell. We could get a penny for two bottles. And, every day, I would hurry to the Christmas room of the old company store to gaze longingly at a cookie jar I had chosen for Mother. I hoped and prayed it would not get sold before we had enough money to buy it. The clerk told me it was 49 cents. Anxiously, I counted our pennies, getting more excited as we grew closed and closer to having the amount needed. I could hardly stand the anxiety, fearing the gift would be missing from the shelf before I could get to the old company store to buy it. Finally, we had the necessary 49 cents, and off I sped to buy the gift. It was still there. I was bursting with pride and joy as I watched the clerk place it in a box. My brothers agreed, it would be something my mother would really love. My mother kept that gift for the rest of her life. When she died in 1974, I saw it in her china cabinet. Tears ran down my cheeks as I recalled that Christmas of 1935. I packed it, bringing it with me to Louisiana, and placed it in my china cabinet.

It was two weeks before my 10th birthday when I encountered the ghost of the haunted house on 8th street. The old house had been vacant for years. No one ever moved into the old two-story house with the cellar door always standing ajar, looking black, cold and frightening, Parents forbid their children to cut through the yard on their way to school. They said the house was haunted. "I don't believe in haunted houses," said one. "Me either," said the other. As time passed, we never talked about the haunted house anymore, but we didn't cut through the yard anymore, either. No one talked about it except in whispers. So we kept our distance and passed only on the other side of the street.

As I said, it was two weeks before my 10th birthday. Our school was preparing a Christmas festival for the community. My teacher asked me to bring a bathrobe to school the next day, as I was to star in the play our class was producing for the festival. My heart sank - I had no such robe. No one did. It was Depression times. But that evening Mother assured me Grandmother had such a robe. "You can get it tomorrow," she said. "But I can't wait until tomorrow," I thought. "What if Grandmother doesn't have a robe? Maybe it won't fit me." I was determined to walk to Grandmother's and get that robe even though it was late, so I started up the hill. The darkness of night had set in. Our dim streetlights were hardly worth having. As I walked up the hill stumbling in the darkness, it occurred to me that it would be a tremendous shortcut cutting through the yard of the vacant house on 8th street. The stories I had heard came flooding through my mind and I wrestled with a decision, trying desperately to convince myself that they were only stories. I stopped as I neared the house, weighing the odds. "I am going to cut through," I decided. "It will be so much closer going this way, and I've got to hurry." So I pushed against the rusty gate. It would not open. I pushed again and again, then the rusty old hinges began to creak, moving just enough for me to squeeze past the gate, and I entered the yard. Slowly and carefully I walked as I approached the house. My heart began to pound! Something was wrong! What was this strange feeling? As I was standing in front of that open cellar door. THEN! I SAW IT, WHITE AS SNOW, JUST FLOATING, FLOATING AND COMING TOWARD ME. "IT'S COMING AT ME," I thought.

SUDDENLY, A VOICE WITHIN ME SEEMED TO IN-STRUCT ME. "MAKE THE SIGN OF THE CROSS," AND IN A FLASH, I RAISED MY HAND, AND BEGAN MAKING THE

SIGN OF THE CROSS OVER AND OVER AGAIN. IT CAME NEARER AND NEARER, AND OVER AND OVER AGAIN, MY HAND MADE THE SIGN OF THE CROSS. AS I MENTALLY CALLED ON GOD TO HELP ME. "JESUS, MARY, JOSEPH, HELP ME," I MENTALLY SAID OVER AND OVER AGAIN. I STOOD THERE AS THOUGH PETRIFIED. IT FLOATED NEAR AND NEARER. I COULD REACH OUT AND TOUCH IT, MOVING MY HEAD BACK AS IT WAS ABOUT TO HIT MY FACE. THEN IT STOPPED, JUST FLOATING THERE LOOKING AT ME. I REACHED UP, MAKING THE SIGN OF THE CROSS AS FAST AS I COULD, PRAYING JESUS, MARY, JOSEPH, HELP ME, OVER AND OVER AGAIN. AT LAST IT TURNED, FLOATING ACROSS MY FACE. I COULD FEEL THE TOUCH OF SOMETHING COLD AND BREEZY, AND IT WAS WHITE AS SNOW. I WATCHED AS IT FLOATED ACROSS THE YARD, AND THEN DISAPPEARED. MY HAND TREMBLED AS I CONTINUED MAKING THE SIGN OF THE CROSS.

THEN I RAN AS NEVER BEFORE, STUMBLING AND FALLING ALL THE WAY TO GRANDMOTHER'S HOUSE. SHE DID INDEED HAVE THE ROBE. SENSING SOMETHING WAS WRONG, SHE ASKED THAT I STAY THE NIGHT. REACHING FOR THE ROBE, THEN CLUTCHING IT CLOSE, I REFUSED, INSISTING I HAD TO GO HOME. AGAIN I BEGAN TO RUN. THIS TIME, IT WAS THE LONG WAY HOME, NEVER STOPPING, MAKING THE SIGN OF THE CROSS ALL THE WAY HOME. WHEN I WALKED IN THE HOUSE, THERE WAS MOTHER, NEVER REALIZING I HAD GONE. I TOLD HER WHAT HAD HAPPENED. SHE SCOLDED ME FOR EXPOSING MYSELF TO SUCH DANGER, AT LAST, THE STORY OF THE HAUNTED HOUSE IS REVEALED. "IT WAS THE SPIRIT OF MR. BABCHECK'S WIFE," SHE SAID. "HE WAS A CRUEL

MAN. THEY SAY HE KILLED HER. HER SPIRIT WILL NOT REST IN PEACE. HE LEFT TOWN IMMEDIATELY AFTER THEY FOUND HER. NO ONE KNOWS WHERE HE WENT. MAYBE SHE IS LOOKING FOR HIM. WE WILL NEVER KNOW," SHE SAID.

On December 22, the school's Christmas Festival was a success. Miss Gorley complimented me, saying I did real well, and that she was proud of me. That meant a lot, coming from Miss Gorley, and I felt a little closed to her after that. Two days later, December 24, was our last day of school until January 2, 1936. Children rushed out of the school building. They were excited. Christmas was the following day. I found the room deserted, except for STELLA. She was my friend, and she was waiting to walk home with me. She was a quiet, lonely, soft-spoken girl with thick, long, wavy hair, which was light in color, and she had the saddest eyes.

STELLA was 12, and I was six days away from my 10th birthday. But we were together in the fifth grade. She said she didn't start school until she was eight because her mother needed her at home. With 12 children and an immigrant boarder from Italy living in a small framed house, STELLA was put to work almost from the moment she came into the world. She had to pass our hotel on Main Street every day on her way to school. She was always alone. I wondered why. I felt so sorry for her. "I want to befriend this girl," I thought. "She is so sad," and so I became her one and only friend. Every day, when school was out, we walked home together. My other friends never joined us. They could not understand why I befriended her. She was not popular. She wasn't really pretty. And she wore that same old cotton print dress down to her ankles. No one else wore dresses that long. STELLA'S Mom and Dad were immigrants from Italy and she said her mother forbid her to wear her dress higher than her ankles. Then again, there were her high-top shoes.

Her mother and father demanded she wear them. But her one and only dress was clean. She said she washed it herself, every Saturday, and ironed it, ready for Monday morning. As soon as she got home, she changed so it wouldn't get dirty. Maybe that was why she sat in the schoolroom alone during recess. She never played outside like we all did.

I looked forward to walking home with her every day that she did attend school. There were days her parents kept her home to help wash clothes and tend to the children younger than her. Our friendship grew that September, October, November, and December of 1935. Winter was now upon us. We bundled up with high boots, big tossled caps and warm coats and gloves. I noticed STELLA'S coat was thin and ragged, and I felt so bad. I often thought how I would like to give her my coat, but STELLA was bigger than me, and besides, I only had the one coat myself. However, STELLA did have a big woolen scarf that she wrapped around her neck, and across her mouth, preventing her from breathing the cold, cold air.

It was a cold day, that December 24. The snow began to fall ever so softly as we were leaving the schoolyard. There was no wind, not even a breeze. The snow flakes were the largest I had ever seen. "Oh, how beautiful they are," I thought. We walked slower than usual that day, speaking very little. I felt STELLA'S sadness as we walked alone, children having long since rushed home, excited about the coming of Santa and the holiday week ahead. At the rate the snow was falling, it was going to be great for sled riding.

We arrived in front of the hotel and I turned toward STELLA. "Well, I'll see you January 2nd. Have a Merry Christmas, STELLA," I said.

"No," she said, "I won't see you ever again, and I want to say good-bye. I will not be back to school again."

"Why?" I asked in complete surprise.

117

"Because," she said, "I will be getting married tomorrow and I will be going off to live in another town with my new husband."

"Oh No!" I said, "STELLA, you can't be telling me the truth. Say it isn't true. Why? Why are you saying this?"

She explained that her parents had arranged it. She was to marry this immigrant boarder who was living with them. He was 39 years old. She was only 12. "There are too many mouths to feed. My Mother and Father said I would be safe. He would take care of me and I have to marry him."

The shock was overwhelming to me. "We're only kids!" I said, "STELLA, you can't do this. Come and live with me in our house. Mother will take you." "No, she said, "I cannot go against my parent's wishes." And with that, she threw her arms around me and I did the same as we began to cry and cry and cry, standing there along the lonely quiet highway with soft snowflakes coming down and covering us, as we clung to each other saying, "I will never forget you." Our hearts were breaking. We parted. I waved good-bye and watched her disappear in the snow, tears freezing upon my cheeks. I never saw her again.

My learning experiences were many, that year of 1935, remaining with me throughout my life.

CHAPTER X
THE YEARS OF 1936 - 1940

The beautiful snow-covered hills and valleys turned Sagamore into a "LOST HORIZON" in January 1936. Children, having thrown caution to the wind, laughed and screamed with delight as they flew at breakneck speed down icy slopes on everything conceivable. There were sleds of every description, a variety of makeshift slides, cardboard boxes and a prized homemade possession called a Yankee. The key to riding a Yankee was a lot of courage, with a superb sense of balance. One held their legs suspended in the air, as they rode down the icy slope on a single metal runner, their hands clinging to its 19-inch-high single seat, having no back or sides for support. Everyone admired these fearless riders.

Sagamore's frozen dam and Plum Creek created an ice skating paradise for young adults and older children, who loved playing hockey or just ice skating. And again, every conceivable kind of ice skates were invented. Huge bonfires burned thru-out the day and night, furnishing warmth to those wanting to remain outdoors.

Every day, people listened for the roaring sound of the snow plow coming down Hwy 210, running east and west thru town. To complete the highway clearing, a truck loaded with ashes or slack followed the snowplow, while two men using hand shovels, alternately spread the gravel-like materials over the cleared highway. This helped give automobile and truck tires a grip on the highway, preventing skidding and accidents. Without the snow plows, we were snow-bound. However, children welcomed being snow-bound, for it meant no school.

Since closing the general store in 1934, the slaughterhouse was used for slaughtering pigs and yearlings for the hotel's use. Also, farmers and townspeople used the services of the slaughterhouse in

119

exchange for the animals' hide. Dad cured the hides by salting them down for a period of time. When he accumulated a truck load, he sold them to a tannery in Pittsburgh. He did anything to help make a living during those trying times.

The holding corral adjoining the east side of the slaughterhouse was no longer necessary, so Mother had it plowed up and turned into a second garden. We children spent hours helping Mother hoe, fertilize, plant, water, weed and harvest abundant vegetables, most of which were canned for the winter months.

On the west side of the slaughterhouse were three barns Uncle Joe and his friend Figlar built from used lumber in 1930. Dad's brother Nick used one of the barns for storing valuable metals such as copper, zinc, nickel and brass that had been salvaged from numerous dismantling operations. Hay and straw were stored in the other two barns and sold during winter months when prices peaked. In winter Nick's employees used the straw barn as a place to rest and get out of the cold. It had a coal-burning stove, giving them an excellent place to eat there lunches and warm up before returning to work at loading and unloading scrap iron in the bitter cold.

February 10, 1936 was one such bitterly cold day, it was Dad's 38th birthday. One that he and the family would never forget. Already burdened with all he could carry, a shocking accident would indelibly mark that bitterly cold Friday afternoon of Dad' 38th birthday.

It innocently began with brother Nickie and Joe and Julia's son Joe Jr. playing in the straw barn. The men had returned to work after lunch, we children of school age were in school and everyone in the hotel was about their work, thereby leaving the two 5-year-olds unsupervised. They played among the bales of straw until, as children will be, they became fascinated with the fire. When Joe Jr., began stoking the fire with the poker, a hot coal fell upon some straw, bursting into flames, igniting other straw nearby. From there, flames spread with the speed of lighting. The frightened boys ran for the hotel as fast as their little legs could go, screaming and yelling FIRE! FIRE! HELP, FIRE! HELP, FIRE! Immediately people appeared from everywhere. It was apparent the fire was in command. No one was going to stop it, especially with no fire department available. All four buildings were going and there was no stopping it,

Get the truck out of the barn!" someone yelled. "Can't do it, it's going too fast!" "Get the cow out of the barn! It's going to take the cow barn!" another yelled as men ran for the cow barn, bringing out the cow, and the goat along with a few chickens and cats. People came running with their buckets and hoses. Someone yelled, "Get on the roof of the hotel! We've got to save the hotel! The sparks are flying on the roof! They'll set the roof on fire!"

Immediately dozens of men formed a bucket brigade, as another dozen climbed the fire escapes in a desperate effort to get to the hotel's flat-top roof, which was skirted by shingles as are mansard-style roofs. Quickly, they threw buckets and buckets of water upon the roof. The weather was below freezing, and before long, the water began to freeze. The men on the roof, having no protection from falling, were trapped upon a sheet of ice, unable to move. A rope was thrown to the men. "Tie the rope around your waist and throw it to another guy, form a chain and hurry!" But it was too late. The ice was dangerously slick, as one of the men began falling over the edge. As he came falling past the fire escape, someone grabbed his clothing, breaking his fall enough that other men on the fire escape below were able to hold on, bringing him to safety.

After school, the smoke-filled sky set all of us to running, to see what was happening. The entire school headed in the direction of the hotel. The street was lined with men, women and children. One woman wiping her eyes said, "Thank God, they saved the hotel," and another said, "Thank God, no one was killed." Nearby, I stood

121

crying, staring at the flames, the intense heat hot against my face. Crying, for I knew we were going through hard times, recalling Dad's constant worrying and Mother working so hard. I just knew this fire was BAD, BAD, BAD. I turned to watch the men on the fire escapes, spraying water on the shingles of the hotel's roof as darkness set in.

In the hotel kitchen, coffee continually brewed for the firefighters. Mother and Aunt Julia served pancakes with syrup, and bacon and eggs to everyone. That night, kneeling at my bedside, I prayed for God to please help my Dad and Mother, then quietly cried myself to sleep.

In assessing the fire losses, the three barns, slaughterhouse and cow barn were gone. Dad's truck, Nickie and Joe Jr's. tricycles, the hay and straw that would have been sold within weeks, the cured hides ready for delivery to Pittsburgh, and many other items of value were gone. And, most of all, it was said that the loss of Nick's copper, zinc, nickel and brass was valued at $25,000. Dad would collect $6,000 insurance on his loses, far short of the cost for replacing the losses sustained. However, the irony of the fire was the fact that once again insurance received from a fire had saved the hotel from bank repossession.

Because of the extreme cold, Uncle Joe immediately constructed another cow barn for the animals. And Dad concentrated on his last and only source of income, the beer and liquor business. First he would upgrade the antiquated bar and extend the east side of the hotel, allowing for a pool hall on the second floor and a dance hall on the first. He traveled to Pittsburgh, staying with a friend, long enough to purchase four used billiard tables, including their accessories. He then, contracted to have them re-covered and shipped to Sagamore along with several nickel and dime slot machines. A used back bar and tables and chairs were also purchased. Upon his return, he found Uncle Joe, who was tending the bar in his absence, drunk and celebrating with his customers, who were also drunk. The cash register was empty and the beer and liquor gone. It was not the first time this had happened when Dad was out of town. This time, Dad knew another person would have to tend bar with Joe at all times, given that Joe loved to open the bar as a free-for all on the house.

Soon Uncle Joe and Figlar were at work constructing a new 3x35 foot bar that had a bumper armrest along the front, preventing glasses and money from falling off its highly lacquered surface. A 35 foot spittle trough, replacing the old-fashioned spittoon of by-gone days, was built about four inches deep into the concrete floor, having continuous flowing water. A 35 foot brass foot rail ran along the spittle trough, and the concrete floor was covered with wood. The bar displayed gallon jars of dill pickles, pickled eggs and pigs feet for sale, and nut machines dispensed a fistful of nuts for a penny. There were new draft and bottled beer coolers installed and sinks for washing glasses, which were located under the bar, The new back bar was a real beauty with its high mirror and shelving for displaying liquors and wines. Along one wall were tables and chairs. Along the other was a nickelodeon and pinball machines. It was the classiest bar around.

Rumors spread about the classy new bar and pool hall at the HOTEL SAGAMORE. Rival ethnic gangs, who frequently battled it out, and men reputed to be pretty rough and tough characters, always looking for a fight, came to check out the rumor. Before long, things were really buzzing with excitement. Saturday nights and paydays were guarantees for a fight, unless Dad could stop it. Fortunately, Dad knew everyone, having lived 26 years in Sagamore and having played ball with many of these men. He was quite the diplomat, always playing the roll of arbitrator, counselor and friend. Nonetheless, HOTEL SAGAMORE was once again reputed as a rough, tough place to be.

In his memoirs, Dad recalls fights stopped and some he was unable to stop. I quote: "We had a constable and squire in town, but customers bought them all they could drink, and they were not much protection. Once I had trouble saving the constable from a beating. A gang was coming to beat him up. I called my friends to help. The gang came in to get him. I told them, 'O.K. men, we are ready when you are ready, but I just want you to know, this bar will be tore up and tore up good. It will be a fight to the finish, even if we tear the whole damn hotel up.' They saw I had good help and changed their minds. They left and said they would get him on the outside, but I kept him hid in a side room.

"In another incident, I had a bartender who had a temper. One night, two Italian gangs came in. There was a fight and a stiletto was drawn from a jacket and thrown at the bartender as he ran up the steps. The knife missed, or his back would have been ripped open. My wife hid him in one of the rooms while tempers flared downstairs. One of the Italians stuck a gun in my stomach when he thought I was being friends with the other gang. I convinced the hot-blooded young man I wasn't taking sides and he calmed down. Later, there was another uproar, when a gang leader blocked two doors, and wouldn't let anyone out. He lost his gun and was making sure it was found. The .45 German Luger was found on the rest room floor and I said 'Hell, this thing is like a cannon. It's so heavy, how can you shoot it?' The gang and the leader burst out laughing and everyone went back to their whiskey.

"Guns were pulled in the bar, though no killings took place. It took some talking to keep order while the boys drank. I had a customer so big, he looked like an animal. He stumbled into the bar drunk after he almost drove his truck load of dynamite kegs through a window. I had to 'shut him off,' as too much liquor was in him already. His huge fist came smashing down on the bar, and he shouted,

'No one ever refuses me a drink, and I'm going to kill you!' I said, 'You know there's so many Kovalchicks, that no one will miss me.' A few words were said and he took his loaded rig and left. The next morning, the trucker came back and thanked me for sending him home."

These stories, as told by Dad, gives one an insight as to how tough a bar in a coal-mining town was during the '30s.

The men, knowing Dad was against fighting in the bar, would challenge their opponent with, "STEP OUTSIDE" or "I'LL MEET YOU OUT FRONT" or "COME ON OUTSIDE AND I'LL BEAT THE HE—OUT OF YOU," and as they left the bar to settle their differences, every customer in the bar followed, for everyone enjoyed watching a good fight. Many times, the fight was not confined to the two opponents, as friends stepped in, taking sides. Others, having no squabble with either side, enthusiastically joined in, and it didn't matter whose side they were on. The next morning bloody shirts laid everywhere. Mother sent us to collect the bloody, torn shirts, which she laundered and made into clothes for all eight of us children.

Many men were reputed to be dangerous when drinking and beyond control when angered. One such man was Joe Bongiovanni. Everyone walked softly when Bongiovanni entered the bar. They said little and agreed a lot. He fought in World War I, fearing nothing and no one, and always carried a razor-sharp knife and sheath strapped around his waist. His loud, threatening voice frightened everyone. Even our dog Rex left the bar when he entered. One night, his anger exploded at one unfortunate customer. Bongiovanni drew his knife. The customer exited up the stairs and through the dining room, where I was trying to play the piano. Then, he crashed through the swinging doors into the kitchen and out the back door, just as Bongiovanni, filled with wrath and fury, charged through the dining room, knife raised to kill. "Where he go!?" he growled, holding that knife only inches from my face. Speechless, I pointed to the kitchen door. I breathed a sigh of relief when I heard him running out the back door. I have never forgotten that killer look in his eyes.

The pool hall on the second floor of the hotel's new east side addition was not to be outdone in popularity, as it too was experiencing glory days. The men took to the new game of skill called POOL with great enthusiasm. The challenge of the game stimulated their inborn competitive spirit to win, resulting in their arriving at the pool hall as early as 8 a.m. and staying as late as 2 o'clock the next morning. It was amazing, watching the talent of these men. It was common to see players breaking the billiard balls, then perfectly pocketing all 15 balls. Many fights erupted as betting on games, created poor losers. With only four billiard tables, the men played the nickel and dime slot machines while waiting. Also, checkers, dominoes, cards and chess games were played. Sandwiches were purchased and brought up from the bar, along with beer and chips. The town's barber, Joe Reno, moved his barber shop into the pool hall, managing it for Dad in exchange for his barber shop rental and room and board. There was always a line waiting for a shave and haircut. Joe Reno was one popular barber. The summer I was five, he cut several of us children bald-headed. I felt deceived. After all, I was a girl and I thought only boys got bald-headed haircuts.

The dance hall on the first floor wasn't to be outdone, either, and soon it could not accommodate the overflowing crowds. So Dad converted the huge dining room and main lobby on the second floor into multi-purpose rooms for dances, wedding receptions, baby and bridal showers, miscellaneous parties and dining. Uncle Nick's workers were constantly going to or coming from his office on the third floor, and the fourth floor efficiency apartments were filled.

All this excitement accounted for my lack of interest in school-work. However, I maintained a B+ and dreamed of becoming a history and physical education teacher, an unfulfilled dream, gone as many others did during my childhood.

That summer of 1936, a group of young boys built a swimming hole in the sulphur creek behind the bony pile* across the road from the hotel. They named it "SUNNY BEACH BARE AS-," because the boys swam naked and no girls were allowed. Five of us girls, ages 9 to 11, decided to go swimming there while the boys were at lunch. The girls undressed and jumped into the water. I volunteered to stand guard and act as lookout. Suddenly the boys seemed to appear out of nowhere, laughing and refusing to leave so the girls could dress. When the boys tried to confiscate the girl's clothes, I jumped into the water fully clothed, carrying their clothes with me. Having no choice, they dressed beneath the water. We walked the highway until our clothes dried. However, the sulphur water had stained our clothes yellow, and no amount of explaining convinced our mothers we had not been in the forbidden sulphur creek, resulting in our being punished. Never again did we visit "SUNNY BEACH BARE AS-." A sulphur creek is one that carries off the sulphur expended by the coal mines. (* dirty coal discarded by the coal company)

The popularity of "SUNNY BEACH" soon waned, in lieu of Sagamore's huge dam, which contained no sulphur. The most popular swimming hole however, was NORTH POINT, 14 miles north of Sagamore. Folks for miles around enjoyed swimming and picnicking in its lovely park. We children looked forward to several visits every summer. On one of those visits, several children taunted and dared me to jump from the third diving board. "I'm no coward," I thought. I climbed to the top, jumped in, sank to the bottom and sat there until realizing, if I did not get to the top for help, I would drown.

I began kicking my legs and thrashing my arms, slowly coming to the top. "HELP!" I yelled. "HELP, HELP!," and down I went. Coming up for the second time, again I yelled "HELP, HELP!" Going down for the third time, I saw people yelling and pointing toward me. As I lay on the ground, coming back to consciousness, an anxious crowd stood around me. Someone asked if I could swim. I answered "NO." "Then, why did you jump from the third diving board?" they asked. "Because, they dared me," I replied. To this day, I have not learned to swim.

Sagamore's five cemeteries located on a plateau one mile east of town, was the most peaceful and serene place in all the world. On Sunday afternoons, it was the custom that people visited the graves of their deceased loved ones, taking them flowers and objects of religion and through prayers experiencing a spiritual closeness to them. One day, I saw a marker that read DOROTHY KOVALCHICK – BORN AUGUST, 1926, DIED AUGUST, 1926. "I'm not dead yet! Why does it say I died?" I thought. Frightened to tears, I ran home to ask Mother. Much to my relief, she explained the marker was that of a cousin, also named DOROTHY KOVALCHICK.

Regardless of good times or bad, baseball still reigned supreme. Dad, now 38, was going stronger than ever. His love for the game seemed almost unnatural. Sagamore's children also acquired a love for the game at a very young age. They headed for the ball diamond as soon as they could pick up a bat or throw a ball. Even the girls, of which I was one, could be seen playing plain old sandlot ball with the boys, all summer long. We began games in the morning, stopped for lunch, then resumed the game, picking up where we had left off for lunch. Scores broke all baseball records, as you can imagine. This introduction to playing the game was actually the foundation for my inevitable baseball career. "Just like Dad," I thought.

August came quickly that summer, bringing an experience I was never to forget. The story is one I want to share with you.

IT HAPPENED AUGUST 23, 1936. SAGAMORE'S POPULATION AS I HAVE PREVIOUSLY STATED WAS MADE UP OF IMMIGRANTS FROM THE "OLD COUNTRY," AS WE CALLED IT. MANY DIFFERENT LANGUAGES COULD BE HEARD AS YOU TRAVELED THROUGH TOWN, AS PEOPLE WERE RELUCTANT TO GIVE UP THE LANGUAGE OF THEIR NATIVE COUNTRY, AS WELL AS THEIR OLD CUSTOMS AND TRADITIONS. INTERMARRIAGE BETWEEN THE NATIONALITIES WAS ALMOST UNHEARD OF, AS PARENTS DISCOURAGED IT.

AS OUR STORY BEGINS, THE HANCHICK AND THE BRUMSKI FAMILIES HAD NO LOVE FOR EACH OTHER. THE HANCHICKS WERE CZECHOSLOVAKIAN AND HAD A 20-YEAR-OLD SON NAMED JOHNNY. THE BRUMSKIS WERE POLISH AND HAD AN 18-YEAR-OLD DAUGHTER NAMED LENA. JOHNNY AND LENA FELL IN LOVE AND PLANNED TO GET MARRIED. MRS. HANCHICK WAS BITTERLY OPPOSED TO THE MARRIAGE AND TRIED DESPERATELY TO STOP THE WEDDING. BUT JOHNNY AND LENA WERE SO MUCH IN LOVE THAT ALL FAMILY OPPOSITION WAS IGNORED. MRS. HANCHICK, REALIZING THAT ALL HER EFFORTS HAD FAILED, BECAME ANGRY, FEELING REVENGE WAS HER ONLY SOLUTION, AND HAVING COME FROM THE "OLD COUNTRY," SHE CAST AN EVIL CURSE UPON THE MARRIAGE. "I CURSE THIS MARRIAGE," SHE SAID. "YOU WILL NEVER HAVE MY SON. YOU WILL NEVER BE HAPPY WITH MY SON. I CURSE IT, I TELL YOU, I CURSE IT." THE CURSE DID NOT SHAKE THE LOVE JOHNNY AND LENA HAD FOR EACH OTHER AND THE WEDDING DID TAKE PLACE AS PLANNED.

AFTER A COUPLE MONTHS PASSED, LENA AND JOHNNY RECEIVED GOOD NEWS, LENA WAS EXPECTING A BABY. MANY AN EVENING THEY COULD BE SEEN STROLLING DOWN LOVERS LANE, HAND IN HAND. THEN ONE DAY THERE CAME A FIERCE AND VIOLENT THUNDER AND LIGHTNING STORM. THE THUNDER ROARED, AND THE LIGHTNING CRACKED AND FLASHED ACROSS THE SKY. IT WAS THE MOST FIERCE AND VIOLENT STORM WE HAD EVER SEEN. MY BROTHERS AND I RUSHED TO HIDE UNDER THE BED AS WE WATCHED THE ADULTS RUSHING ABOUT, SOME CRYING, SOME PRAYING AND SOME LOOKING FOR A PLACE TO HIDE, SO FIERCE WAS THE STORM. BUT AT LAST, THE STORM SUBSIDED AND HAPPILY WE ENJOYED THE SILENCE. MY BROTHERS AND I RUSHED OUTSIDE TO PLAY IN THE FRESH AFTERMATH OF THE STORM. THEN SUDDENLY WE HEARD IT. A FLASH OF LIGHTNING CAME SWEEPING ACROSS THE SKY, FLASHING AND CRACKING AS IT MADE ITS PATH ACROSS THE HEAVENS. THEN IT HIT THE EARTH WITH SUCH FORCE THAT WE COULD FEEL THE EARTH TREMBLE BENEATH OUR FEET.

THEN I HEARD THE SHOUTS AND YELLING COMING FROM THE HILL, "JOHNNY HANCHICK IS KILLED, JOHNNY HANCHICK IS KILLED!!!" FOLLOWING THE STORM, JOHNNY AND LENA HAD GONE WALKING HAND IN HAND DOWN LOVERS LANE. THAT LAST BOLT OF LIGHTNING CAME SWEEPING ACROSS THE SKY, STRIKING JOHNNY IN THE TEMPLE, BURNING A HOLE IN HIS TEMPLE THE SIZE OF A DIME, KILLING HIM INSTANTLY. AT THAT VERY SECOND, LENA HAD LET GO OF JOHNNY'S HAND OR SHE TOO WOULD HAVE BEEN ELECTROCUTED. HOWEVER, THE

FORCE OF THE ELECTRICITY WAS SO GREAT AS IT PASSED THROUGH JOHNNY'S BODY THAT, AS IT LEFT HIS BODY, IT KNOCKED LENA TO THE GROUND UNCONSCIOUS.

THE TOWN WAS SHOCKED BY THE TRAGEDY AND EVERYONE WENT TO THE HOUSE TO PAY THEIR RESPECTS. I HAD NEVER SEEN A DEAD PERSON IN A COFFIN BEFORE, BUT FELT COMPELLED TO GO. SO, UP THE HILL I WENT, AND AS I ENTERED THE HOUSE, I COULD HEAR THE YELLS AND SCREAMS AND CRYING OF LENA AND THE OTHERS IN THE ADJOINING ROOM. AND AS I ENTERED THAT ROOM, I WAS SHOCKED!! LENA HAD CLIMBED INTO THE COFFIN AND WAS ON TOP OF JOHNNY, CRYING AND SCREAMING AS SHE TUGGED AND PULLED AT HIM SHOUTING, "JOHNNY, TAKE ME WITH YOU, I DON'T WANT TO LIVE WITHOUT YOU. I WANT TO DIE!" THEY WERE TRYING TO GET HER FREE AND OUT OF THE COFFIN, BUT SHE HELD ONTO JOHNNY AND WOULD NOT LET HIM GO. I TURNED AND RAN FROM THE HOUSE. AS I WALKED DOWN THE HILL, I THOUGHT ABOUT THE CURSE MRS. HANCHICK HAD PUT ON THE WEDDING. "YOU WILL NEVER HAVE MY SON!" SHE SAID. AND SO IT WAS, AND I WONDERED ABOUT THE CURSE.

The impact of this experience awakened in me an awareness of how short one's life could be, of destiny, and my own life. "I will live to be 30, and will face my destiny without fear," I concluded. Having arrived at this conclusion, I rushed to tell Mother. "I'm going to die when I am 30," I announced. "Don't you ever say that again! Don't ever talk like that, you hear me!" Mother replied in anger. I turned and ran for fear of being punished, never repeating it, but thinking it for years to come. I believe this experience, so firmly implanted in my subconscious mind contributed to my lack of fear that prevailed during my baseball career.

The little old peddler who came frequently to town was another example of how hard it was making a living in those Depression years. Watching him struggle, almost falling time and time again as he made his way up the hill with that heavy pack on his back, made me want to cry. Mother and Julia, having very little money themselves, always purchased something from him. That August, Mother purchased my first factory-made dress from him for $1.25.

Mother and Julia sewed all our clothes. When the billiard tables were re-covered, Dad requested the remnant material be shipped also. Mother and Julia made Martha, Betty and me identical green jackets from the billiard table remnants. For years people commented about those beautiful jackets, and how the three of us looked like triplets when we wore them.

Once again the patriotic parade kicked off the annual Labor Day celebration, followed by inspirational speeches from important union officials. There were games such as climbing the greasy pole, three-legged races and throwing the disk, to name a few, and a variety of foods for sale. The afternoon doubleheader baseball game, in which Dad always played, was the highlight of the day. Following the games, the men migrated to the bar and pool hall, continuing their celebration until the wee hours of the morning.

The next day, school began. I entered the sixth-grade classroom, delighted with my teacher, Miss Walker. She was a tall, thin blondeheaded beauty who I aspired to be like when I grew up.

Gambling was a passion with many immigrants and every coal town had their highly skilled gamblers. Sagamore's best was Russian Paul. No one could beat him. He had been an officer in the Russian Bolshevik Army, having defected during the Russian Revolution of 1917. Being opposed to communism, and fearing for his

life, he fled Russia without wife and child. Sadly, he never succeeded in getting them out of Russia. He lived alone on 10ᵗʰ Street,
not far from the hotel. His house and yard, with it's garden and
storage cellar that looked like a bomb shelter, was entirely fenced in
with wire and wood, and his gate was always padlocked. He was tall
and robust and had a solemn, stern look about him that frightened us
children. Many stories circulated amongst us. Some said they heard
he lured children into his storage cellar, where he killed them and ate
them. There was also the story that anytime a child entered his gate,
they were never seen again, so children never went near his house. I
pondered those stories time and time again, unable to imagine they
could be true, for I sensed a deep loneliness about him. I longed to
know the truth. He looked so harmless, working his garden or sitting
in his rocker on his porch. I wondered if he had any friends, I never
saw him talk with anyone.

The opportunity to solve the mystery came soon after school
started. While on an errand for Mother, I decided it would be closer
going by way of 10ᵗʰ Street, and as I walked past his house, I suddenly realized he was standing at the gate. I looked up and said,
"Hello." He replied, "Hello, little girl. You like candy? Come, I
give you candy," as he unlocked the gate, pulling it open. I was
filled with fear hoping it was not obvious to him. "I know you
Bounce's daughter," he continued. I wondered how he knew. "Your
father good man. I know him. He good man. I have little girl like
you in Russia," he said. Then, I saw his eyes were watery, as though
he was about to cry. "Why is she in Russia?" I asked, not knowing
exactly where Russia was. "She with her Mother. They no can come
this country. Come, I give you candy," he replied. I was afraid, yet
I wanted to know if all those stories about Russian Paul were true. In
my heart, I couldn't believe they were. The determination to know
the truth was beyond reasoning, regarding my potential danger. I

stepped past the open gate, and followed him, thinking, "I will scream and yell and bite and scratch and kick if he dares touch me."

We approached the back door, entering his dimly lit pungent-smelling kitchen. Rows and rows of sliced apples, peppers, assorted herbs and corn hung from the ceiling, drying for winter use, which accounted for the pungent smell. There was a small oilcloth-covered table, two chairs and a cabinet. Near the wood-burning cook stove was a single army cot, a small sink and wash basin. It was evident he lived in this single room. Drying mushrooms and nuts covered the floor of the adjoining room, otherwise vacant. A religious calendar hung on the wall by the table, giving me a feeling of security. He reached for a glass jar, removed the lid, then held the jar toward me. I reached in, removing a piece of hard candy. He encouraged me to take more than one piece. I reached in taking another, telling him two were plenty. He filled a paper sack with hickory nuts. "Here," he said, "You take. Come, I show you cellar." My heart jumped. I was never more frightened. A thought raced through my mind: "They said that's where he killed children, then ate them! But, he won't hurt me. He said he had a little girl in Russia. Maybe I remind him of his little girl. He wouldn't hurt his little girl, so he won't hurt me." I thanked him for the nuts and followed him to his bomb shelter-like cellar.

He unlocked the door, pulled a light string, lighting the stairwell and descended into his cold underground cellar. At the bottom of the stairs he pulled another string, lighting a large single room, encircled with rows of shelving, stocked with canned fruits, vegetables and jellies. Potatoes lay on the dirt floor, and apples on a bed of straw. Then, reaching in his pocket, he pulled out a knife. "Oh no! I've got to get out of here! He going to kill me! I thought. He reached down, picked up an apple, and proceeded to peel, core and half it. "You eat," he said, handing me half of the apple, then, biting into the other half. I thanked him, and bit into the apple. He pointed with pride at his home-canned goods, telling me he had canned them himself. I told him it was wonderful, acting excited about seeing so many canned things. He smiled. It made him feel good, hearing my words of praise. He turned and began to ascend the stairs. I followed, breathing a sigh of relief when we stepped out, then watched him lock the cellar door.

He asked me to come back to see him as we walked to the front gate. Assuring him I would, I walked away, then turned to wave goodbye, and shouted, "Thank you." He was wiping his eyes, "He's crying. I was right", I thought. "He is so lonely," and tears filled my eyes. Occasionally, I visited him, but as children will do, drifted away, as other interests came into my life. Through the years, Dad remained his one and only friend, getting him hospital care when he became ill. Then he arranged for his continued care in the County Home for the elderly. And when he passed away, Dad took care of his funeral. I have always regretted not having remained in touch with him.

Many great headlines would hit the nation's newspapers in 1936. Three main events triumphed, with the first on August 16th, which read "OWENS RACES TO VICTORY" The article read:

BERLIN, GERMANY, August 16

There were 5,000 athletes from 53 countries on hand for the Olympic Games, the world was in turmoil and everyone concerned was expecting the worst. Instead, the crowds, the revenue and the performances all set records, and Jesse Owens emerged as the world's fastest athlete. He won both 100- and 200-meter dashes and the running broad jump, and was a member of the 400-meter relay team. The United States took eight other gold medals among the 23 track events, with notable victories being scored by Archie Williams in the

400 meters and John Woodruff in the 800 meters. Women competed in swimming, track and field and gymnastics events.

There was some embarrassment for the host country when it turned out that 10 Negroes (an alien race, Hitler had called them) were on the American team. Hitler reportedly snubbed Owens, but he apparently didn't greet any athletes other than the Germans.

The second great headline announced the opening of the 726-foot high, 1,244-foot-long HOOVER DAM, which held more than 10 trillion gallons of water and was located on the Colorado River. It opened in October following three years of construction. It would also create the 250 square mile Lake Mead, the largest manmade lake in the United States.

The third great headline, from November 4, read, "FDR WINS IN LANDSLIDE," as President Franklin D. Roosevelt won a second term, he defeated Alfred M. Landon in the biggest victory in election history with 523 electoral votes and won every state except Maine and Vermont. He would begin his second term January 20, 1937.

Dad writes in his memoirs about the period in 1936. "I only knew the hard way, and everything we ever got was the hard way. I do not like to tell some of the life I had, and my experiences, but I must tell them as I remember them.

I was doing fairly well in the middle '30s, and at that time repairing the building, as I was unable to do it for a long time, and it was very much run down.

I had added a piece to the building, installed a pool room with four tables and a side room, where the men could gamble and shoot dice. I got a cut from it all and it helped. I did not care for the business or the pool room and gambling etc., but it seemed I could not keep the young people from it. They would make a mess when they gambled, and I had to clean things up, and I fed them as they would not go home for their meals. I was well paid, but I sure earned it, as I had to be on edge and tension was unnerving etc., as trouble came at any moment.

In fact, I never liked the hotel and the bar liquor and beer business, but I realized I could not be choosy. The life is hard on any man or family. If you can stand it for 15 to 20 years, you better get out, because if you keep at it, you either get to drinking too much, or if you do not, your nerves will get you.

I am saying this from the standpoint in the coal-mining towns. Most people see you as making money at it, but most of them, do not realize the life of it. Life is hard and rough. It was bad enough to run the business, but to do so without no real money is something that no one knows, only one who may have experienced it. As fast as I made the money, my creditors were there to get it. Even my relatives and best friends were tired of waiting for their money they loaned me, and I did not blame them, as I had lost out three times, and they began to think that I would never be able to recover."

December 31, 1936, was my 11th birthday. Birthdays came and went during Depression years. Mother and Dad had more to worry about that a child's birthday party. I always said, "If you never had one, you never missed it."

I enjoyed singing in our church choir. However, after February 1937, the joy of singing would never be mine again because of a bungled tonsillectomy. After being plagued for years with bad tonsils, Dr. Debutcher performed the tonsillectomy in his office. The gossip was that before operating the doctor consumed more of his narcotics than he dispensed. For six weeks, my survival was questionable, as I lay on a small cot next to Mother and Dad in their bedroom. During long days of suffering, unable to walk, talk or swallow due to the loss of blood and inability to take nourishment, Mother patiently nursed me, urging me to try to swallow. "You must try to eat," she pleaded.

One day, a new world opened, when Mother bought me a little radio, and for the first time I listened to The Lone Ranger, Fibber McGee and Molly, Amos and Andy and the Inner Sanctum Mystery! From that day forward, I was determined to get better.

One night as I lay in bed, unable to sleep, I overheard Dad saying to Mother, "Be sure and get the rent tomorrow, as I am needing it. It is embarrassing begging for it, and I am tired of doing it." Mother replied, "I am tired of begging for it too. She just smirks at me, and says she will pay it when she is good and ready, so what can I do? I am as embarrassed as you are." "Forget it, I will make other plans to get some money for bills I have to pay." I understood the conversation. The rent referred to was the $30 monthly rental that Dad's brother Nick agreed to pay for an office, three-room apartment and the use of the hotel's land for his scrap iron business. The "she" was Nick's wife Fannie, who managed their office. I could not believe what I was hearing, as everyone knew they had plenty of money, "Then why," I thought, "Do Mom and Dad have to beg for the rent?" And besides, I thought about all those muddy steps, I had been scrubbing for years. Muddy from Nick's workers plodding up and down those stairs to his office on the third floor. I felt so sorry for Mother and Dad. It broke my heart, lying there, feeling so helpless. After a two-month absence from school, my passing to the seventh grade was a happy surprise. Miss Walker said "You are an intelligent little girl. You will do all right. I wanted to reach up and hug her, but felt too shy to do so.

Sagamore had no hard-surfaced streets or sidewalks. Rubber overshoes were an absolute necessity during March and April, as mud was everywhere. When journeying on business to cities like Indiana, Kittanning and Punxsutawney, our muddy overshoes told then we were from a coal town. City folks had absolutely nothing to do with us. You'd have thought we were carrying a plague. "Why?"

I thought. "We all look like human beings, speak the same language, and live in the same country." It made no sense to me. However, class divisions existed in coal towns as well. Coal company employees and their families stayed within their circle and miners remained in theirs. Presbyterian and Lutherans shunned Catholics, and vice versa. Again, I thought "Why? We are all Christians, believing in the same God." I didn't spend time worrying about it, being that I had lots of living to do, having only 30 years in which to do it or so I thought.

That spring, when the ground got dry enough, Uncle Joe, Figlar and Dad began constructing a five-room house behind the hotel. Uncle Joe and Figlar performed the work. Dad supervised, always acting like he knew how the work should be performed, yet he had no carpentry ability. He couldn't drive a nail straight. Mother was the family carpenter. My greatest embarrassment came when we moved into the house, for it had no bathroom. Besides, the outhouse was located at the bottom of the hill. Everyone on top of the hill could see one's comings and goings to the outhouse, especially every morning, when carrying the chamber pot outdoors, "I'll die if anyone sees me," I thought. I'd cover it with a towel, thinking that camouflaged it. Every Saturday, my three brothers and I took turns bathing in the galvanized tub next to the pot belly stove in the living room. Soon after moving in, Mother made her annual visit to the Cleveland Clinic, leaving me in charge of the housework and cooking. One day, Dad asked me to cook chicken soup, as he loved soup. Never having made it before, I filled a kettle with water, dropped the chicken in and let it boil until it was tender. Dad never asked for chicken soup again.

Taking on the role as president, I, along with cousins Martha, Betty and EthelReda and our friend Helen, organized "THE T.F.S.G.D. CLUB" that summer, pledging never to divulge the meaning of our initials. Wanting to add mystery to our club, candlelight meetings were held in our cellar. Each assumed a nickname taken from the popular movie of the day, "THE DEAD END KIDS." Our purpose was to unite as a fearless gang against bad-boy gangs roaming the streets of town. Strangely, however, these bad-boy gangs became our friends. We learned they were not bad boys at all. Evenings, storytelling under the streetlight next door to the hotel became our favorite pastime, aside from playing baseball during the day. The evenings' finale was ghost stories, so scary that the group would escort each other home, until the last one had to brave it alone. Two boys (Ray and Dan) stood out above the others. They were more studious and well-mannered, in comparison to the average boy in a coal town, having dreams and aspirations to achieve, which they came to realize. Year later, having grown up together, Ray married cousin Betty and Dan married cousin EthelReda. Our club remained in existence for two years, then, faded away with growing up.

Without consulting me, Dad volunteered my tap dancing as part of September's Labor Day celebration. The stage for entertainment and important speakers brought in by the UMWA's union was a flatbed truck, patriotically decorated, having loud speakers and an ear-splitting band. My name rang out over the loudspeakers and the band began to play. My tap shoes clicked as I walked across the stage in pigtails with big blue bows, dressed in a blue crepe paper costume accented with silver stars. Looking out at the crowd, it appeared that everyone in town was there. Frightened, I froze, feeling unqualified to entertain them, never having had a dancing lesson. My feet and legs refused to move. Someone yelled, "That's Bounce's daughter." Suddenly, I spotted Dad in the crowd, dressed in his baseball uniform, watching me. "I can't embarrass Dad, I've got to do this for him," I thought, whereupon my feet and legs began to move, tapping out every tap step I had ever done. The crowd was kind in their response, much to my surprise. Afterward, walking through the crowd, I delighted in their compliments. Coping with stage fright that day was an invaluable experience, for my baseball career to come.

My seventh-grade teacher, Mr. Stroup, was stern-looking and strict. I would have liked him regardless of his personality if it weren't for what he did to my brother Eddie. Eddie repeated the third grade, bringing us together for our remaining years of school. He was a born mechanic and a people person. He carried miniature cars and trucks to school, like other children carried their books to school. During classes, he would place an opened book on its edge, pretending to be studying and instead played with his little cars and trucks. I always warned him when the teacher was coming, as I sat behind him. One day, it was impossible to warn him, as Mr. Stroup was standing beside me. He watched him briefly, then yanked him out of his seat, dragged him to the front of the room, and proceeded to paddle him. Not a sound came from Eddie, until Mr. Stroup began beating him on his legs. My temper flared and my blood surged, and out of my seat I flew, tearing into Mr. Stroup in an effort to stop him.

Within minutes, Mr. Stroup had us in the principal's office and we were being interrogated. "Mr. Smith," I answered, "Mr. Stroup was beating my brother on his legs, making him scream. It wouldn't be so bad if he only hit him on his behind, but not on his legs, and that's why I tried to stop him from beating my brother." Then, Mr. Smith asked what Eddie had done to warrant the paddling. "He was playing with his little car, making it wreck into the ink well, then pulling it out with a pulley. That's all."

Mr. Smith sat pondering this for awhile. Then he arose from his chair and escorted us to our room. He talked briefly in the hall with Mr. Stroup as we entered our classroom and took our seats, therewith ending the incident. However, at our next class meeting, Mr. Stroup enjoyed his revenge. Knowing bullies carried a lot of clout with students, he coached the class bully to push for my impeachment as class president. When he succeeded, I wanted to cry, and rushed for the privacy of the coatroom. Classmate friends gathered around, trying in their childlike ways to console me with hugs and loving words of praise. "They are just as hurt as me," I thought, their loyalty and kindness giving me courage and self-confidence again. Mr. Stroup never bothered Eddie again and we both passed to the eighth grade.

After years of misery struggling with gas heaters and coal stoves, Dad purchased a used locomotive boiler, concluding that if a coal-burning locomotive boiler could generate enough steam to pull thousands of tons of coal over a railroad track, then it ought to be able to heat the hotel. And heat it it did. A huge coal bin was built next to the furnace room, in which 20 ton of coal could be stored at all times. A chute into the furnace room made coal easily accessible. Our janitor, John Struhar, tended the boiler day and night, sleeping on a cot in the furnace room. That furnace room was the warmest place in town during the cold winter months. We children and our friends could attest to that. It was exciting, watching Struhar stoke and clean that old boiler, then fill it with shovels and shovels of coal.

The newspaper headlines in 1937 reported a nation in turmoil as these few headlines tell us much.

JANUARY 1ST – WASHINGTON, D.C. – FDR: "ONE-THIRD OF A NATION ILL-HOUSED, ILL-CLAD, ILL-NOURISHED"

FEBRUARY 1ST – CINCINNATI, OHIO – FLOOD HITS MIDWEST

FEBRUARY – CHICAGO – THE VALENTINE DAY MASSACRE

MARCH 2 – PITTSBURGH, PA. – UNION WINS AT U.S. STEEL

MARCH 12 – FLINT, MICHIGAN – G.M. GIVES IN TO STRIKERS

APRIL 12 – WASHINGTON, D.C. – HIGH COURT UPHOLDS LABOR RELATIONS ACT

MAY 6 – LAKEHURST, N.J. – HINDERBURG EXPLODES; FLAMES KILL 36

MAY 26 – RIVER ROUGE, MICHIGAN – VIOLENCE AT RIVER ROUGE

MAY 27 – SAN FRANCISCO – GOLDEN GATE BRIDGE SPANS FRISCO BAY

JUNE 22 – CHICAGO – JOE LOUIS TAKES HEAVYWEIGHT CROWN

JULY 18 – SOUTH PACIFIC – EARHART DISAPPEARS OVER SOUTH PACIFIC

DECEMBER 25 – WASHINGTON, D.C. – JAPAN APOLO-GIZES FOR SINKING U.S. GUNBOAT

Throughout the year photographers documented the Depression. Photographers Berenice Abbott, Walker Evans, Dorothea Lange, Russell Lee and Arthur Rothstein used their cameras as a social force, mobilizing the public to support New Deal programs. And Margaret Bourke-White recorded the plight of southern blacks, publishing her pictures in a book, "YOU HAVE SEEN THEIR FACES."

In January 1938, the United States entered the eighth year of the Depression. Sagamore miners were working but one or two days a week. The struggle for survival was faced by miners in different ways. Some found solace in leading Christian lives, finding strength and determination through God. Others found drinking and gam-bling as an escape from it all, living for each day, fearing they may not see tomorrow. It was the wives and children of those men, who bravely took on the challenge for survival.

In his memoirs, Dad confesses his dislike for the circumstances he was in, but he struggled on, praying for things to change. His escape from it all was the ball field. There he could forget all his troubles for a few hours by playing ball.

Mother and Julia constantly struggled to keep the hotel clean. Its reputation for cleanliness and hospitality were well known everywhere. They were proud of the compliments expressed and the questions frequently asked, such as, "How do you do it? I've never seen a place like this so clean."

As children in Sagamore, we never knew we were poor. It was a way of life with us. The joy of making it, being a survivor through hard times, will not be experienced by the baby boomers who were born during booming times. It didn't take much to make us happy. Receiving the smallest and most insignificant thing brought us indescribable joy, never to be experienced by children of plenty. Christmas meant something to eat, an apple or orange, nuts or candy instead of expensive toys as today.

It broke my heart, seeing children in poverty far greater than mine. Olga was one such person. She was being raised by an unkind aunt, as her mother died in childbirth. It was evident she had very little. Her clothes alone told me that, as they were nothing but rags. One day, she couldn't stop talking about her love for a dress I was wearing. After school, I asked and Mother allowed me to give her the dress, even though I only wore it the one time, and it was my second store-bought dress in 12 years. I never regretted it. The happiness I saw in Olga's face that day remains with me still. "It's the most beautiful dress I've ever had," she said, tears falling down her cheeks as we hugged.

Another incident that happened the summer I was 12 actually began three years earlier in 1935, when a group of young boys decided to go into the hills to seek a perfect spot for building a real log cabin. They wanted a camp of their own where they could hunt and fish and pick wild fruits and nuts. After finding a perfect location, they began felling the most perfect trees to turn into logs for the cabin. The boys kept the location a secret, meeting on top of the hill every day, then spending the day building their secret cabin. It became an image of their independence, pride and joy. Then one day, when the cabin was completed except for installing the windows and door, an accident happened. The leader of the boys, 19 year-old Billie Guda, was killed. The boys were filled with such grief they abandoned the log cabin, leaving everything just as it was. The boys made a vow never to return to the cabin again.

Three years passed and new young trees had sprung up around the cabin. It was lost to civilization as the shrubs and underbrush took over, obliterating the path. My four friends and I walked up the hill that summer to pick berries and wild crabapples. Before long, we had wandered off and were going deeper and deeper into the woods. We realized we were lost when we came upon the cabin. There it was, just as the boys had left it three years before. There were windows, but no glass, and a doorway, but no door. Light seeped in through these openings, just scarcely enough to see. "Let's go in and play," said one of the girls. The others agreed, we entered the cabin and began to play a game we called "Upset the fruit basket."

Immediately I heard a strange noise as I joined in playing the game. Again I heard it, and then a voice within me said "Get out of this cabin!" Then, again, "Get out of this cabin!" A deep fear came over me, as I ran for the doorway shouting, "Get out! Get out! Get out of the cabin!" Frightened by my shouting and actions, everyone came running out behind me. "What's the matter?" they asked. I replied that I did not know, except that a voice said to get out of the cabin. Everyone was filled with fear. What could I have heard?

Our thoughts turned to our quest for getting out of there. As we walked, occasionally a light peeked through the dense woods. Darkness was soon to set in. "It's late afternoon," I thought. That's the direction we need to go." At last, we began to leave the denseness of the woods, coming upon a little-used path. We chanced to take it, as it was headed toward the sun. Indeed, it was a good decision, for soon we began to hear echos of dogs barking. Then from the top of the hill, we could see the town below.

A couple months later, fall set in and hunting season opened. Hunters were everywhere. Our hotel was one of the few eating places available to hunters. One day a group of hunters were eating when I heard one of them say, "We came across that old log cabin up in the hills that the boys built years ago and we had to burn it down." My heart jumped. "Burn it down! Why burn it down?" I thought. Another hunter asked, "Why did you burn it down?" "It was nothing but a den of rattlesnakes," he replied. Again my heart jumped. Secretly, I knew the voice I'd heard was my guardian angel warning me to get out of that cabin. "Yes, it was my guardian angel," I thought. To this day I do believe that.

June 25, 1938, the American work force rejoiced when President Roosevelt signed into law the Fair Labor Standards Act. It set minimum wages at 25 cents an hour, eventually raising it to 40 cents. It mandated 44-hour work weeks, to be reduced to 40 hours over a period of time, and provided for time and a half for overtime, except in certain types of seasonal employment. Also, it prohibited hiring those under 16 years of age.

When Labor Day was a week away, word circulated that the Union's big Labor Day celebration was having its first "Most Beautiful Decorated Bicycle" contest. I was real proud of the Schwinn bike Dad had bought me and decided to enter the contest. For hours I worked, weaving one-inch red, white and blue crepe paper strips in and out of the spokes of each wheel until the entire bicycle was covered in red, white and blue, thereby creating a very patriotic-looking bicycle of which I was proud. I was even more proud when it was judged the winner. Happily, I walked across the stage. Simultaneously, a man rushed to the judge, whispered to him as I waited.

Then, speaking quietly to me, beyond hearing range of the crowd, the judge said, "We have to disqualify your bicycle from the contest. Your father is not a coal miner, and the contest is for coal miners' children only." Then, turning to the microphone, he announced, "There's been a mistake. Our first-place winner is Betty Shanger." Not a tear filled my eyes, for in my heart, I knew I had won. Also, discrimination was not new to me, being that I was neither a coal miner's daughter, nor a company boss's daughter.

The next day I entered the eighth grade, satisfied that Mr. Saxman was going to be a great teacher. At our annual weigh-in time, I proudly weighed in at 88 pounds. However, I was still the smallest in my class. We began hearing rumors we would be consolidating with several high schools from surrounding towns in Cowanshannock Township the following year. No one was happy about the news. We felt we were being invaded, just as they no doubt were feeling resentful about having to ride a bus to Sagamore.

In the fall, Dad opened a gambling room adjoining the pool hall. During the summer gamblers gambled outdoors. As cold weather was setting in, they asked Dad to furnish them a gambling room. His compensation came from what we called "pinching the pot," in which Dad received a small tip from each completed hand played. Brother Johnny at 12 years old handled the gambling room like a pro, bringing in more money than any hired hand Dad had working for him. Dad also partitioned the pool hall, making Joe Reno's barber shop private for the first time since opening the pool hall. Brother Eddie, now 16, responsibly managed it with some help. And as for handling the slot machines, he maintained them like a pro. Between Eddie and Johnny, they kept things going on weekends and after school.

They also had the laborious job of filling our 20-ton coal bin. Periodically, Johnny entered the coal bin, without breathing protection, to perform the grueling task of pushing the coal down for easier access to it from the furnace-room chute. Then there was the maintaining of the hotel's continuously eroding road and parking lot, which required tons of slack and boney. They smashed the slack and boney into smaller pieces with sledgehammers, then covered it with shell or dirt. Dad encouraged me to help them break up the slack and boney, saying it would make me stronger, and indeed it did.

Trouble brewed in many countries throughout the world in 1939. The United States had taken on the role of a neutral country, choosing the course of isolationism. Rumors of war were constant since Hitler rose to power in Germany in 1933. But now, the rumors were becoming real as Hitler's armed forces took over the countries of Austria, Czechoslovakia and Poland. People began to feel a deep unrest over the situation in Europe, despite their own struggle with the Depression. The question was being asked, "Is it possible for the United States to remain neutral?" Many were in doubt. Those immigrants from Austria, Czechoslovakia and Poland grieved for their relatives still living in their native lands. Everyone watched and waited, praying that WORLD WAR II would not happen.

With the rumors of war came the demand for iron and steel. The demand for scrap iron skyrocketed, which meant Uncle Nick's scrap iron business flourished. A huge number of men left mining in favor of working for Nick in the scrap iron business. Dad's brother Joe, who never liked the hotel business and felt he was of little help to Dad in the beer and liquor business, asked Dad to buy out his interest in the hotel. He wanted to work at demolition. Dad loved his brother as no man had ever loved his brother, but he knew Joe was right. He would not hold him back if he chose another route in his search for happiness. They came to an agreement, and Dad purchased Joe and Julia's half-interest in the hotel on January 10, 1939 for $1,500. The following day, he mortgaged the hotel for $4,000, giving him the much-needed funds for continuing the hotel repairs. As soon as weather permitted, we moved back into the hotel, and Uncle Joe, Aunt Julia and cousins Martha, Betty, Joe Jr. and Bobby moved into the house behind the hotel. Uncle Joe went to work for his brother Nick. Soon, he was regarded as a demolitian expert. Dad was happy that Joe at last had found his inborn natural ability.

After 11 years of conducting his business from the hotel and its 3.33-acre property, Dad's brother Nick announced he was relocating in Indiana, Pennsylvania, 20 miles south of Sagamore, where a house as well as acreage for his scrap iron business had been purchased. The plan was that eventually all the scrap iron stored on the hotel property would be removed. At last, after 11 years Dad could get the property cleaned up so it would not look like a junkyard anymore. Also, he would never again have to beg for his monthly rent of $30. Mother was glad, as her workload would be lightened. But no one was happier than me. I rejoiced as I thought, "No more muddy stairs to scrub." Besides, in my 13 years, Nick had never spoken one word to me and his wife Fannie spoke few, only through necessity.

In the spring of 1939, Dad organized his own baseball team. Since his dream of becoming a professional baseball player was shattered with the death of his father in 1920, he dreamed of one day owning his own team for the purpose of giving boys an opportunity to develop their baseball skills through special training and playing first-rate competition. To those showing the most potential, he would avail every opportunity he could to them in the hope that one day one of his prodigies would make the major leagues and ultimately the Baseball Hall of Fame in Cooperstown, New York. Little did he realize at the time that several would indeed make it to the major or minor leagues:

Mike Goliat - Philadelphia Phillies
Bud Souchock - Three American League Clubs

Alex Kvasnak - Washington Senators 1942

Bill Hunter - Baltimore Orioles

Gene Pompelia - Cotton States League

John A. (Johnny) Kovalchick - Coastal Plain and Pony leagues

Dorothy Kovalchick - All-American Girls Professional Baseball League

A baseball career was a way out of a coal town and players were eager to play for him, knowing he had the experience and contacts with scouts. Through years of attending Pittsburgh Pirate games, he had become acquainted with major league scouts, managers and players. Also, Dad developed such a close friendship with Rosey Rowswell, the renowned Pirates broadcaster, that on several occasions in the '40s, Rosey came to Sagamore to watch Dad's team play.

To see me play, that is, after I became a regular on Dad's team. But in 1939, my job was scorekeeper for his team. It was a job I enjoyed, but there was this constant desire to be in the game, especially as the first baseman. "I can do it. I know I can," was always on my mind.

The worse "bully" to ever hit Sagamore – 13 year old Tim Dewicked came to town that summer of 1939. His parents moved to our little coal town from Battle Creek, Michigan, in an effort to keep him out of a correctional institution. Upon arriving, they rented an apartment at our hotel. Ten months later they moved into a company house on Fourth Street. I immediately sensed an evil spirit in him as I watched him attempting to kick out the hotel's stairway bannisters. I knew one day we would clash, a premonition that one day would come true. Within weeks of his arrival, life changed in Sagamore. For no apparent reason he brutally beat every boy who crossed his path. Property was damaged at his whim. Death threats were made and shots fired. No one felt safe. Soon everyone stayed out of his way, including our friends, who no longer came to the hotel because of him. He beat upon brother Eddie continually. My three brothers and I constantly hid, but he would hunt us down.

That September the Cowanshannock Township High School consolidation was initiated, and I was a freshman. School buses carrying ninth to 12th grade students from the towns of NuMine, Yatesboro, Margaret and Rose Valley came rolling into Sagamore, and Sagamore High School became Cowanshannock Twp. High School. No student appeared happy with the merger. After eight years of enjoying the smaller classes of boys and girls from our own hometown, it was difficult for everyone. Learning came easy for me, for which I was thankful, because there was never time for studying and homework with all the work waiting at home.

When Dad's brother Joe purchased the hotel in 1922, a piano was part of the hotel furnishings, although it was terribly out of tune and many of its beautiful ivory keys were stripped of their ivory. Mrs. Dewicked had been a piano teacher before moving to Sagamore, so Mother hired her to give me lessons. After a couple of months of lessons, much to my relief, she refused to teach me. "You are only wasting your money, Mrs. Kovalchick," she explained. "Your daughter has absolutely no talent for the piano." That was a fact I had already come to realize.

On my 14th birthday, December 31, 1939, Dad kissed me on the cheek for the first time. "Happy Birthday, Honey," he said, always calling me Honey. Affection was never openly displayed in our family. There was this feeling of knowing with certainty that I loved my parents and brothers and they loved me. That being the first time Dad kissed me gave me a feeling of assurance that he cared, and I was glad.

Hollywood enjoyed booming times during the Depression. People turned to the fantasy world of movies to escape from their desolate lives and the all-to-familiar sight of the soup kitchens. In 1939, 388 movies were produced, but none could match the attraction and acclaim of "Gone With the Wind," which premiered December 15 in Atlanta, Georgia. I was impressed beyond anything I had ever imagined when I saw the movie and I dreamed of one day living in the South. As a result, I placed names of all the southern states in a box, then drew out one of the states. Twelve years later, I was living in Louisiana, the state I drew from the box.

In January 1940, temperatures fell below freezing, as snowstorms blew in from the Northwest. Following a heavy snowfall, my cousins and friend Helen and I were making a snowman on the hotel's front lawn when "bully" Tim Dewicked appeared. He began throwing snowballs soaked in water, which became a ball of ice. We called them watersoakers. We huddled behind our snowman. However, one of the watersoakers smashed into Helen's leg, knocking her to the ground, and she screamed in pain. My temper flared and my blood boiled when "bully" Tim walked away laughing. In seconds, I charged, leaping upon his back, bringing him down face first in the snow. Still clinging to his back, I pushed his face into the snow over and over again. After finally releasing him, I clenched my fists and shouted, "If you ever throw another watersoaker at a girl, you will get the same and more!"

Slowly, he got to his feet, wiped the snow from his grinning face, and said, "I'm going to marry you for that."

"Over my dead body!" I replied, still in the heat of anger. Little did I realize that six years later both our comments would be put to the test.

The freezing weather continued into February, when a paralyzing ice storm hit the region. Ice storms were not new to us, but this particular one was an emotional experience for me. It seemed the whole world had come to a standstill. No one dared venture out of their homes. As everything was covered with a sheet of ice. Cabin fever was felt by everyone. "I've got to get out of here," I thought, and devised a plan. I stomped the heels of my shoes into the sides of two empty evaporated milk cans, then hammered each end tightly against my shoes. This enabled me to walk on the ice. "Freedom at last," I thought as I walked across the ice. What a feeling of power over the elements. The entire town was a beautiful panorama of ice formations. At every turn of my head, their amazing beauty fascinated me. Hours of walking found me outside of town as cold was beginning to overtake me. Off in the distance, I saw a shack. "That's where Peg Leg Pete lives. I can get warm there," I thought and headed for the shack.

Peg Leg Pete is what everyone called him, because he had a wooden peg leg attached to a stump above his knee. The story was that he had lost his leg in the first World War. At one time he had been married and had a daughter. One day he returned home and found them gone. He never heard of either of them again. He tried, but never found them. So he lived alone in this shack down in the valley outside of town.

God gave Peg Leg Pete a talent that he shared freely with the world around him. He could play the fiddle. I was just a little girl the first time I heard him play that fiddle. He held me spellbound. No one, absolutely no one, could play the fiddle like Peg Leg Pete.

I approached the cabin and knocked on the door. No answer. Again and again I knocked, but there was still no answer. I reached down and turned the door handle. The door was unlocked, so I pushed it slightly ajar as I yelled out, "Is anybody home? HO-O-O is anybody home?" His one-room shack was dark and appeared cold and abandoned. Then I saw him! My eyes were not prepared for the sight. He was lying on the bed, an emaciated, starving, unclean man. He reached out his hand as though to speak, but no words came. He had been snowbound and icebound for days, perhaps weeks, with no food or fire to keep him warm. The place was freezing cold. "I must get him help," I thought, slowly backing toward the door. "I'll be back, Peg Leg Pete. I'll be back!" I shouted as I turned and ran in my makeshift ice shoes. No longer was I freezing cold. I ran nonstop until I entered the hotel. I immediately related everything to Mother. "Hurry, get the sled!" she said as she quickly gathered empty boxes, filling them with food, matches, newspapers, soap and toothpaste. We tied the filled boxes to the sled and again I was off across the ice in my makeshift ice shoes, pulling the loaded sled.

Arriving back at Peg Leg Pete's, I quickly unloaded the boxes on the table, then turned to build a fire in his stove. When the fire had a good start, I turned to unpack the boxes. There was Peg Leg Pete. He had crawled out of bed and was pulling at the boxes, frantically grabbing for the food I had brought. Having found a slab of raw bacon, he began chewing on it like an animal. It frightened me, and I stepped back, unable to handle the situation. Again, I backed toward the door. "I'll be back, Peg Leg Pete. I'll be back!" I shouted once again, as I sped across the ice once more.

Returning to the hotel, Mother called the Pennsylvania State Highway Department, pleading for a snowplow. We are still clearing the major highways," the man replied, "but we will try to get one into Sagamore right away." Then we heard the roar of the snowplow off in the distance, coming down highway 210. "Hurry! Stop the snowplow!" Mother shouted. I raced for the highway, waving my arms, shouting, "Stop! Stop!" "He's got to see me," I thought as I frantically jumped up and down. Slowly the snowplow came to a stop. I raced toward the driver's window. "We need your help real bad!" I shouted. "There's a man bad sick. We have to get him to a hospital right away. We need our driveway cleared so Dad can get his truck out, and he can follow us. I'll show you where he lives!"

Immediately the driver cleared the driveway, freeing Dad's truck as I jumped into the cab of the snowplow, giving the driver directions.

The driver and Dad entered the shack, wrapped Peg Leg Pete in a blanket and carried him to the truck, where I held him as Dad sped off for the hospital. Months and months of care brought new life back to Peg Leg Pete. The following Christmas, there he was, playing his fiddle once again. I smiled, took a bow and did a little dance for him. Peg Leg Pete and I had a special bond now, which was shared by Mother, Dad and a kindly snowplow driver.

One day, Dad partitioned the main lobby for an office. "How do you like it?" he asked.

"It sure is nice," I replied.

"I'm glad you like it, because it's yours. From now on, you are the hotel's official bookkeeper. I'm turning everything over to you, deposits, everything, and filing the income tax, too," he said.

"Dad, I'm only 14. I can't do all that," I pleaded with all sincerity.

"Then learn," he said, walking out of the office with no further comment on the matter. So I struggled along, learning as I went, using plain old common sense in keeping records of everything earned and spent and filing Dad's income tax return that year. The following year, I nervously faced an Internal Revenue agent who had come to audit the return. I was terribly frightened, thinking he had come to take me to jail. At last, he closed my books and said, "You're doing a mighty fine job, young lady. I've been auditing all the businesses in the valley and you have the best records I have found yet." I couldn't believe what I'd heard, nor can I explain the feeling that swept through me.

In the spring of 1940, Dad's team was anxious to begin spring training because they anticipated a successful season. Dad encouraged every boy interested in baseball to try out, furnishing gloves for those unable to buy them. The best of the lot joined as rookies, practicing daily. Dad reinforced the team with older, seasoned ballplayers from Sagamore and surrounding towns. He believed older ball players were inspirational role models for rookies and helped bring out their best possible talent. Brother Eddie frequently dragged and cleaned the diamond with our pickup truck, pulling a huge log or flat piece of iron. Dad was strict about playing on a smooth, clean diamond to ensure safety and enable infielders to perform their best. The desire to be on the team was growing stronger with every game. After all, I had been playing sandlot baseball for years.

At this time in my life, I became fascinated with stories of the Wild West. I visualized myself as a great crack shot horsewoman totting a .22 rifle or .32 revolver. Dad had came through when I hinted for a bicycle. "Why not again?" I thought. Before long, Dad and brother Eddie returned from a trip with a bald-faced brown and white quarter horse, whom we named Baldy. The whole horse episode turned out to be a complete fiasco. The moment I looked at Baldy, I realized how absolutely ignorant I was about horses, having never been near one in my life.

My brothers had a very knowledgeable friend, Dale Rairie, who agreed to teach me to handle and care for him. This arrangement would have gone well, except that Baldy happened to be an old horse, wise with experience. So old in fact, that he was headed for the glue factory when Dad bought him. He thought an old, gentle horse was a good start for me, but not when the horse is smarter than you are. Old Baldy sure knew he was in the hands of a greenhorn and he wasn't about to do anything except what he pleased. He would freeze stiff-legged at the edge of a bridge, whether large or small, refusing to cross until I personally walked across the bridge to show him it was safe. Then, he walked across the bridge as I held the reins. Finally I mastered riding him. All that summer of 1940, I'd get decked out in boots, western shirt with jodhpurs to match, and made a 12 mile round trip to Rural Valley to take care of Dad's banking.

One hot day in August, overcome by heat exhaustion, Baldy broke into a run toward a stream flowing through a deep gully. Unable to stop or slow him down, I just hung on till we went head first into that deep gully to reach the water. Over his head I flew. There I sat in the muddy water, while Baldy gulped and gulped it up. Exasperated, I shouted, "When we get home, Baldy, either you are going or I am going. Sagamore isn't big enough for the both of us." True to my word, I told Dad that Baldy had to go, as he was too independent. Dad returned him to his original owner, Mr. Caskle, who sold him to the glue factory. So ended my desire to become a great horsewoman. My experience with baseball and my new .22 rifle would prove to be more successful.

News spread through town that summer. Tim Dewicked had robbed the Sagamore Post Office, and was sent to a prison for boys under 21. That explained why we had not seen him for some time.

In September 1940, I entered the 10th grade. A rifle club was being organized in which rules and regulations as outlined by the National Rifle Association (NRA) would be followed. Having a .22 rifle, and anxious to develop my skill, I decided to join. Much to my surprise, I was the only girl member. I felt sure that was the only reason they elected me secretary – treasurer, Rifle practice soon took precedence over business subjects such as bookkeeping, shorthand, typing, salesmanship and civics. Participating in shooting contests from various distances in prone, kneeling and standing positions had captured my interest. "Just like baseball," I thought. Shooting my .22 rifle was as natural as breathing. It gave me great pride when I was awarded the marksman and expert medals by the NRA for prone, kneeling and standing positions at 100 and 150 feet. I wondered if they weren't preparing the boys for things to come: the entry of the United States into World War II.

Dad's baseball team was enjoying a very successful year and morale was high. Two games were left to finish the season, but still the team was practicing. Dad asked me to shag flys in the outfield. "Just for the exercise," he said. "I'll be doggone, that's my ballplayer," he thought as he watched me covering the field, shagging fly balls, then throwing the ball to the infielders. "Honey, come on in and hit a few balls," he yelled out. Again, he was impressed. "How would you like to play in the game this Sunday?" he asked. I was over-joyed. What a thrill to be in the game at last. That Sunday, I played two innings in right field, then Dad pulled me out. "Leave the girl in," the crowd shouted. "Go ahead, play another inning," Dad said. He was surprised by the response from the crowd shouting, "Put the girl back in, put the girl back in," after I left the game. Returning home, Dad said I would play a couple innings every game the next season, just for a drawing card. "OK, but I want to play first base," I replied. He was opposed because of the danger, in addition to the fact I was only 5'2" tall. I was determined and refused to play if I couldn't play first base. I pointed out that the boys could practice throwing to me on first. Also, I could jump real high. He agreed to think about it, as the next season was six months away. "We have a lot of training to do," he said, and I agreed.

Everyone constantly talked about the war in Europe, fearing for the worst, with Germany and Italy aggressively pursuing the invasion of other countries. Everyone felt it was inevitable that the United States would enter the war, but when?

By December 1940, Germany had taken possession of the following countries:

Austria - - - - - March 1938	Czechoslovakia – March 1939
Poland – September 1, 1939	Denmark - - - - - April 9, 1940

Holland - - - May 15, 1940	Belgium - - - - - May 28, 1940
Norway - - - - - - June 1940	France - - - - - - - - - June 1940

By December 1940, Italy had taken possession of the following countries:

Ethiopia - - - - - - - - - 1935	Albania - - - - - - Spring 1939
Libya - - - September 1940	Egypt - - - - - -September 1940

During the fall and winter of 1940, Hungry, Romania and Bulgaria were pressed into agreements which made them economic satellites of the Axis powers.

With the fall of France, Britain and its Dominions stood alone against Axis forces (Germany and Italy). Germany began raids on British ports and shipping in July, then began a sustained effort to knock out Britain's air defense. Britain battled raiding forces of 500 to 600 planes day after day. For a month London took terrible punishment from the air. But Britain struck back, for they had around 1,000 fighter pilots and some 640 planes. Though greatly inferior to Germany in numbers, they were high in quality and morale and were aided by radar screens that warned of approaching bombers. We stayed close by our radios, hungry for the latest news, dreading to hear the worst and fearing what we might read in the newspapers. Everyone prayed for Britain.

The United States now had a population of 131.6 million. It was being reported that a third of all America still favored neutrality and hundreds of isolationist groups sprung up. One viewed President Roosevelt as a "warmonger" and his military aid to Britain as "interventionist." Roosevelt had sent Congress a military supply measure to provide over $1.3 billion to build up the armed forces and he endorsed an agreement with the British to sell them large amounts of American surplus or outdated military equipment. However, President Roosevelt received a sweeping victory in his bid for re-election, thereby becoming the first man in history elected to a third term in the White House.

While Roosevelt insisted America had no intention of entering the European war, it was apparent he would not let the country get caught unprepared for battle. When he stated the need for a powerful two-ocean navy, Congress passed a bill appropriating $4 billion for naval vessels for both the Atlantic and Pacific. Funding was also set aside for the construction of 50,000 fighter planes. Then the first peace-time military draft commenced on October 29, 1940. By that date 16 million Americans between the ages of 21 and 36 were registered for the draft.

Children looked forward to snow for Christmas, I can't recall a Christmas without it. During the holiday season, the community en-joyed two main highlights: The Christmas activities presented by the elementary and high schools and those taking place at the churches. For those of the Catholic faith, Midnight Mass was the most spiritu-ally moving event. The pageantry and beautiful choir music touched our hearts, filling us with joy and happiness. There's something un-forgettable about walking to church at midnight in a little coal-mining town, especially when big cool snowflakes are drifting down to earth ever so softly with the air so still and the whole world seems to be quietly at peace. But that Christmas Eve of 1940 was overcast with the dark shadow of war and praying for peace was upon the hearts and minds of children as well as their parents, for no one wanted to see our young boys going off to war. Little did we realize that the following Christmas was going to be one of the saddest in our lives.

The week following Christmas was my 15th birthday. There was no birthday party as usual. In my heart, that was all right.

**Mother and Dad's Wedding Photo
May 23, 1923**

**Dorothy's 8th Grade
School Photo**

**Dorothy, age 7 and Nicholas, age 3
Taken July 1933**

Graduation May 1943

Left to right: Dorothy, cousin Martha, and cousin Betty

Cousin Betty

Cousin Martha

Left to right start at bottom: Johnny, Dorothy, Nick, Eddie, and Dad

Dorothy and her bicycle on Labor Day

Rear view of Hotel Sagamore from 8th Street

Hotel Sagamore

**Family photo left to right: Dad, Johnny, Mother,
Eddie, and Dorothy, Nicholas Kneeling
July 1945 Adrian, Pennsylvania**

Kovalchicks baseball team July 1945 Adrian

Dorothy's Father helping her select a bat

Dorothy out at home plate

Dorothy at play

Johnny   **Dorothy**   **Dad**

Brother Eddie

Brother Nicholas

Dorothy and Tim Wiles, Public Service Librarian
National Baseball Hall of Fame
Cooperstown, New York

National Baseball Hall of Fame
Cooperstown, New York

Dorothy sketched
by Adam Harkins

Dorothy in uniform All American
Girls Professional Baseball League
Fort Wayne Daisies 1945

Kovalchicks all male baseball team
Dorothy at first base 1939-1947

CHAPTER XI
THE YEARS OF 1941 - 1942

Our Pennsylvania winters came early and lingered long. Sagamore's dam and streams froze over during the coldest months of January and February, thrilling the young boys and girls who loved to ice skate.

Ever since the Norwegian ice skater Sonja Henie dominated the European, Olympic and world championships from 1927 to 1936, teenage girls dreamed of owning Sonja Henie skates and skating like the famous Norwegian star.

One day, Dad surprised me with a pair of white Sonja Henie skates. What a thrill it was. I never felt more inspired as I glided across the ice in those skates.

January 30, 1941, will always be remembered as one of the saddest days of my youth. That day, a shocking tragedy struck the Kovalchick family. Dad's brother Joe was accidently killed when demolishing the Johnstown Brewery in Johnstown, Pennsylvania. He was 40 years old.

"I'm going to die with my boots on. Take good care of the kids", he said, as he kissed his wife Julia good-bye that morning. In exasperation, she replied, "Don't talk like that! It's bad luck!" Ironically, by the end of the day, his words were truly spoken. His boots had caused him to fall as the building was collapsing. The fatal iron girder fell upon him, before he could regain his footing. Uncle Joe had died with his boots on, just as he had predicted.

In my bedroom across the hall from mother and dad's room, I heard the footsteps of dad's brothers, Nick and Mike, coming down the hall. They had come to tell dad, who was in bed with the flu, the terrible news of Joe's accidental death.

Dad, then Joe, were the eldest of Grandma's 10 children. Having endured many hardships together, the bond between them could not be denied.

Nick and Mike stopped at dad's door, knocked, then entered. By the sounds coming from the room, I knew something bad had happened.

At last, the door opened, and their footsteps disappeared down the hall.

Then, Dad's heart-breaking sobs reached my ears. In my fifteen years, I had never heard such sobbing. It tore into my heart. Between his heart wrenching sobs, he cried, "JOE, OH JOE – I LOVE YOU – OH GOD – OH GOD – WHY – WHY GOD?" It was truly the sobs of a man with a broken-heart. Emotionally shaken, I fell to my knees crying. Then, I began to pray, "GOD, PLEASE HELP MY DAD. PLEASE GOD, HE NEEDS YOU. HELP HIM TO STOP CRYING. I DON'T KNOW WHAT TO DO." I wanted to run and comfort him, but felt it would be an invasion of his private moment of grief, knowing he was unaware that I was sharing that very private moment.

Soon, I heard Mother enter their bedroom. She had come to comfort him. Again, I prayed. This time for the both of them.

Dad insisted upon leaving his sick-bed to attend the funeral. He dressed in his long overcoat, woolen gloves, galosh's and wrapped a scarf over his cap and around his neck. Mother and Eddie held him by each arm, as he was to weak to walk alone.

At the funeral, my fifteen years of memories of Uncle Joe filled my mind. I thought about the time he had taken us kids to the Dayton Fair, left us on our own, and how I steered the car home because he was drunk. I thought about how he loved us all, and how, when he drank a little too much, he'd have us sit around the dinning-room table singing songs, with him at the head of the table acting as choir director. The songs we sang so long ago, raced through my mind, "WHEN IT'S SPRINGTIME IN THE ROCKIES, I'LL BE COMING BACK TO YOU, and SHE'LL BE COMING AROUND THE MOUNTAIN WHEN HE COMES." Glancing about the church, I saw people crying. Only then did I let the tears fall with the realization of how much, I too loved Uncle Joe. Most everyone in Sagamore came to mourn the death of this man who they all came to love.

Following the funeral, a veil of sadness hovered over us. February 10, Dad was 43, and on February 17, Mother was 38. No one seemed to care. I longed for the snow to melt, and the mud to come, then baseball would be around the corner. Surely, that would bring Dad out of his depression. If only we could hear laughter again. Even the customers in the bar seemed sad or did I imagine it?

Soon, Dad's brothers Nick and Mike began building a house in Indiana, on the Kovalchick Salvage Company's property, for Joe's wife Julia, and his family of four children (Martha, 16; Betty, 15; Joe Jr., 10; and Bobby, 8). They would be moving in May, at the end of the school year. I felt a deep loss, as we had grown up together. Together, we gave our dog Eddie the wonderful funeral, cried over our rooster Tom when we ate him and went swimming in forbidden "Sunny Beach Bare As-." There was our T.F.S.G.D. Club, our baseball games, sled riding, ice skating, roller skating up the highway, and for years Mother and Julia dressed Martha, Betty and me like triplets. We found the long-lost log cabin together. The memories went on and on. I could not believe it was all over. They were going out of my life, just like that.

Everything was happening so fast. I felt alone. "I wish baseball would hurry and get here," I thought. "Baseball will be my life now, and after graduation, I will go to college in Indiana, and be a history and physical education teacher." With these goals in mind, I began preparing for spring training. Johnny, Nickie and I constantly

173

contested as to who could accomplish 100 non-stop push-ups. We all did, with Johnny being first. We measured our biceps often, competing for the largest. Johnny favored Mother's family, who were big-boned and tall. "He's got it," I thought. "If anyone makes it in baseball, it will be Johnny. Nickie has the brains. He'll be a scientist or professor. He's a genius."

Eddie didn't participate much during our training. He was 16, and the family driver. He drove our pickup to and from school daily. Being the only kid in school with a vehicle made him the most popular kid around. One could see him driving to and from school, with a dozen or more kids just hanging on. Having no law enforcement made life more daring. Eddie's buddies had top priority, so I didn't get rides to school, even on cold or rainy days. Neither did Johnny or Nickie. As always, teen-age boys will be teen-age boys, as they reach out for the friendship of one another.

Anxious to begin spring training, we constantly tested the ball diamond, wishing it would hurry and dry. Until then, we practiced on our hotel property. Dad bought me an outfielder's mitt, instructing me on how to keep it well oiled with neat's-foot oil and stored with a baseball in its pocket to mold the pocket. "Your glove will be your most important possession in baseball. It should be a part of you," he said. Finally, Eddie could drag the diamond, then serious spring training began.

Everyone in town was talking about United States entering the war. Global war seemed imminent. We anxiously read the Indiana and Kittanning newspapers and listened intently to our radios. They were our only sources for obtaining news of the outside world. Older and wiser people talked against our entering the war, fearing it because they understood the grave consequences of it. They constantly prayed for God's miraculous intervention and that peace would soon come to the world. But God gave man a free will, and man alone chose war or peace.

However, the young boys were anxious to go to war. They were optimistic that our going to war would ultimately bring peace to the world. Many were talking about enlisting. Since it seemed inevitable, they wanted to be ready to fight right from the start.

As for myself, I too felt it was inevitable and wondered if they allowed women to fight. "They'll need expert riflewomen as well as expert riflemen," I thought, "and I'm a crack shot."

In March, President Roosevelt signed the Lend-Lease Bill, allowing Roosevelt to lend or lease war materials to the government of any country whose defense the president deemed vital for the defense of the United States. Then in April America's automobile industry announced it would slash production of civilian vehicles by 20 percent to redirect resources toward the war effort.

Tension was rising by May with the sinking of the American freighter "Robin Moore" by a German U-Boat.

Dad, still recovering from his illness and the loss of his brother managed the team from the sidelines for several months, then resumed his role as a playing manager.

During practice and pregame warm-ups, brother Johnny, 13, already showing great promise, began catching and pitching. By age 15, he would be a regular on the team. Although we had older, experienced players, Dad always used a few young potentials, allowing them to get experience. We played teams that outclassed us in size and years of experience. Therefore, fearing for my safety, Dad wouldn't let me play but three or four innings in right field, saying, "Honey, if one of those guys should hit you with a wild pitch or line drive, they could cripple or kill you." Undaunted, I pleaded, determined to play first base. "Dad, give me a chance," I said. "Have your best players throw hard and hit grounders to me and have them fast pitch, then you can judge for yourself whether or not I can play first." Still skeptical, he said "OK, Honey," handing me a first baseman's mitt. Then calling in the boys, he explained that he wanted to see how I could handle first base, "It would be a great drawing card for the team," he said. "Besides, you fellas could develop your throwing skill to first, as your target would be smaller." "Let's give it a try," said Joe Stanavich Sr. Joe and Dad were the eldest players on the team, both in their forties. Other players readily agreed and immediately my training began, resulting in an impressive showing of ability to play first base. Following practice one day, I was thrilled when Dad said, "OK, Honey, I'm going to put you on first in our next game." Removing my mitt, Dad looked shocked. "HONEY! WHAT'S WRONG WITH YOUR HAND? IT'S BLACK AND BLUE UP TO YOUR WRIST!" he said. "Oh, I'm breaking it in so I can play first," I replied. My secret was out. I did not know how to handle a mitt. Immediately Dad taught me the proper way to handle a first baseman's mitt. The following day, we were shopping in Pittsburgh's finest sporting goods store, only to learn that protective chest or head gear was not available for women, nor were women's baseball spikes. However we purchased a new mitt and cap. By 1943, men's spikes in size 2 were available, and they did fit me.

My first base debut was a flawless three innings, played against Plumville. Following the game, Clyde Moore, a local hardware owner, approached us saying, "You got a Winner there, Bounce." Dad agreed as I smiled at Clyde, who winked and smiled back. Thereafter, I played four or five innings on first, and the remaining innings in right field. People were surprised to see a girl playing baseball. Children came as close to the bench as they dared, trying to get a closer look, like I was some strange object. "Hello, do you play baseball?" I'd ask. Their little faces would light up and they'd come a little closer. Little girls would say, "I want to be like you when I grow up." "You will. You just practice real hard," I'd reply. Little boys were quick to admit they didn't know girls played ball. I laughed when one little boy asked, "Are you a real girl?" "I sure am," I replied. "Golly," he answered. Children made it all worthwhile. As time passed, Dad seemed more like his old self again, for which I was happy.

The team practiced from 4 p.m. to 9 p.m. every Monday through Friday, an absolute must for anyone playing on Dad's team. Weekends, our team played as many as three games, winning most of them.

In 1941 Germany and Italy's conquests continued in their quest for supreme power. They occupied Yugoslavia and Greece in April and Crete in May.

Then, on June 4, Germany invaded their Russian ally by surprise, ending numerous cat-and-mouse games between these two countries, which were filled with tremendous hatred for each other. Not until years later would the world learn of the horrific details of the war between them. Volumes have been written. Every word of their four year war is beyond description, leaving one mystified as to how such inhuman acts could have been executed by supposedly civilized people.

I thought about Russian Paul, who had escaped from Russia during the Bolshevik Revolution in 1917. He would never learn the fate of his wife and daughter, who were still in Russia. I was filled with sadness and compassion for this family, whose lives were heartbreakingly sad, having been torn apart by war.

Labor Day came too quickly that September, Sagamore celebrated with its usual parade, speeches, entertainment and a baseball game.

The next day, I entered the 11th Grade. "Two more years to go. Will I ever get out of school?" I thought. My counselor made no inquiry as to my aspirations for the future, as she said, "You will be taking business subjects, bookkeeping, typing, shorthand, salesmanship, civics and history (which was compulsory), and that was that. The subjects required little studying, which I liked, and I did well in them, especially history. It carried me to worlds beyond Sagamore, which I loved, especially ancient history.

I resumed my position as secretary-treasurer in the rifle club, and again was awarded Marksman and Expert medals by the National Rifle Association (NRA). With all the talk of war, owning a gun gave me a sense of security and pride.

Our fears mounted as relationships between United States and Germany deteriorated. On October 17 Convoy CS-48 was attacked by a German Wolf pack, and several ships were sunk. President Roosevelt announced, "We have wished to avoid shooting, but the shooting has started. And, history has recorded who fired the first shot." On October 31, the destroyer "Reuben James" was torpedoed, killing 115 men. In November, Congress amended the Neutrality Act, permitting American merchantmen to arm, and granted them free passage to the war zone.

The complacency of the United States was shaken on December 7, 1941, by disastrous news from Pearl Harbor, Hawaii. The Japanese had launched a surprise attack on Pearl Harbor. At 7:58 on that peaceful Sunday morning, these words were blared out by Admiral Patrick N.L. Bellinger. "AIR RAID! PEARL HARBOR!! THIS IS NO DRILL!!!" One radar operator got some blips indicating a massive movement of planes. He looked more closely, thought the radar was wrong or that the blips were B-17 bombers being shifted from Wake Island to Pearl Harbor and did nothing.

The first wave of Japanese aircraft, consisting of 49 high-level bombers, 51 bombers, and 51 fighters deployed for Wheeler Field, Hickam Field and Battleship row where 26 destroyers, 5 cruisers and 8 battleships were moored. Most of the officers and men of the battleship Arizona were aboard when the first bombs and torpedoes began to rip it apart. Of its crew of 1,400, 1,103 men were killed. The Oklahoma was destroyed by three huge torpedoes in its hull. The West Virginia took six or seven torpedoes, but it was saved from the Oklahoma's fate by an exceptionally alert and well-trained crew. The California was also hit and rapidly settled into the mud.

Long lines of ammunition handlers were organized to feed the guns, which began to fire back at the Japanese Zeros. On the New Orleans, Chaplain Howell Foreby, a "sky pilot," was among the ammunition passers. When a Japanese plane was hit he called out, "Praise the Lord and pass the ammunition."

Within two hours, the Navy lost 2,000 men killed and 710 wounded, while the Army and Marines lost 327 killed and 433 wounded. Also killed were 70 civilians, mostly airfield workers and a few Honolulu residents.

By 9:45 a.m. the Japanese aircraft had returned to their carriers, but 29 did not make it back, which is a remarkable lose figure considering how completely the American had been surprised.

Radio stations and newspapers throughout the country blared out this terrible news, causing an anger such as the country had never seen, The Japanese attack was a military success, but it had stirred up a hatred demanding revenge.

President Roosevelt, declared Sunday, December 7, 1941, "a date which will live in infamy." On Monday he asked Congress to declare war on Japan. Congress hastened to comply and war was declared six and one-half minutes later.

Germany and Italy, in keeping with the terms of their Tripartite Pact, declared war on the United States.

The reality of war had come upon Americans with a bewildering suddenness, and the mood of the country was anger. The loss of 2,397 Americans in the assault on Pearl Harbor had aroused a nation that had shown no taste for war. Immediately signs were seen every-where: "We here highly resolve that these dead shall not have died in vain . . . REMEMBER DECEMBER 7TH" In Washington D.C. one overzealous patriot chopped down four Japanese cherry trees before he was arrested. Crowds pressed against the White House fence, five deep, hour after hour. The great white light that burned over the White House driveway was put out. And the "AMERICA FIRST" committee hastily called on all Americans to back the war effort.

The Japanese, following up on their surprise attack on Pearl Harbor, continued to astonish the world with successful assaults all across the western Pacific. In the early hours of December 8, Japanese naval and air forces struck almost simultaneously at Kota Bharu in British Malays, Singora in Thailand, Guam, Hong Kong, Wake Island and the Philippines.

The blows from sea and air were immediately followed by land invasions, which were virtually unopposed. Many of the briefly trained Filipino "divisions" simply melted into the jungle when faced with the tough and disciplined veteran Japanese military units.

The British and American forces fought back. In Kunming, China, Colonel Claire Chennault's American volunteer group, the Flying Tigers, shot down six Japanese raiders with no loses, and a combined force of Flying Tigers and the Royal Air Force in Rangoon, Burma, shot down several Japanese planes.

After successful Japanese landings at Luzon, Mindanao and Lingayen Gulf, American forces in the Philippines retreated to the Bataan peninsula and to Corregidor, a tiny island at the entrance to Manila Bay.

The speed with which the United States mobilized for war testified to both the efficiency and resolve of the American people. Recruiting stations across the land were flooded with men young and old, eager to sign up. Americans had made a commitment and were united in a common cause.

In Sagamore, our hotel was the hub of excitement. The town's young men filled the bar, fired up about enlisting. The patriotism was unbelievable. After all the past years of hunger and suffering through the Depression, their love for the United States was deep in their very being, and I admired their determination to put their plans on hold to become soldiers and go to war to fight for our country. By the war's end, Sagamore will have had more men enlisted per population than most towns it size in the state.

With sadness in my heart, I watched the boys saying good-bye to their buddies. They would be leaving for boot camp the next morning. The bar was generally their last stop. There were no tears amongst them, only an excitement hard to explain. But I knew all the tears were being shed by their parents and younger brothers and sisters. I thought about my brother Eddie. He was 17, and could be one of them one day. Now that the inevitable war was here, it was all happening too fast. I felt numb. "Many of the boys are not going to be home for Christmas." I thought, "and, it is going to be a very sad Christmas for everyone."

When Christmas came, I was surprised to see that many of the boys did come home on leave, each dressed in the uniform of their chosen branch of the armed forces. They wore their uniforms with much pride, and rightly so. Those boys not yet in uniform looked and listened with envy to the tales of boot camp training. For the duration of the war, our bar was the social gathering place for soldiers going to or coming from war.

With all the excitement about the war, my 16th birthday on December 31 wasn't acknowledged by anyone, like it was some long-lost secret and I was the only one privy to it.

On January 1, 1942, the United States joined 25 nations in signing the Declaration of United Nations, binding them to uphold the Atlantic Charter, to work toward the defeat of the Axis and make no separate peace with enemy countries. The charter was a declaration of common principles for war being fought. Among these principles were "the right of all peoples to choose the form of government under which they will live" and the outlawing of "territorial changes that do not accord with the freely expressed wishes of the peoples concerned." Also included were free international trade, full economic collaboration between all nations, freedom of the seas and "final destruction of Nazi tyranny" and a peace that will provide "freedom from fear and want." Finally, the charter expressed the belief that "all the nations of the world, for realistic as well as spiritual reasons, must come to the abandonment of the use of force."

The next three months brought the most disheartening news for the Allies. We listened intently to our radios and hastily read our newspapers. Our stomachs tied in knots from the tension of waiting to hear better news.

On February 23, people were shocked to hear that a Japanese submarine had shelled a Richfield Oil Company refinery in Santa Barbara, California, causing $500 damage to a pump-house roof.

Then on February 28, the country was saddened to hear that five Allied vessels were lost while the Japanese suffered one destroyer damaged in the Battle of the Java Sea in the South Pacific.

The greatest defeat for the American military to date came on April 9. Major General Edward P. King Jr., commander of the Luzon force under General Douglas MacArthur, had surrendered his army of 76,000 exhausted men to the Japanese. General MacArthur had left Bataan for Australia in March with a solemn vow that is recorded in history: "I shall return." Following the surrender of Bataan, Philippines, the inhuman "death march" began. The road to the P.O.W.

camps became lined with American corpses that had been bayoneted, shot or beheaded by the Japanese. Some 3,000 to 10,000 men died this way while others succumbed to exhaustion, dysentery or malnutrition. Thousands of horror stories have been revealed about this period of the war.

Everyone in town was talking about Bataan and the "death march." They were horrified that such cruelty had been done to our service people.

Throughout the world, the American servicemen's official newspaper, the STARS AND STRIPES, began calling the American soldier "G.I. JOE," a term for the ordinary soldier who bore the brunt of the fighting with no officer's clusters or bars, just a pair of dog tags and a snapshot of his girl or the family.

For convenience's sake, Mother had moved our family living room from the third floor to an area in the dining room on the second floor. This made it possible for others as well as our immediate family to listen to the news on our Philco radio.

Every day, the town's barber, Joe Reno, and I listened to the evening news. He knew what war was like, having fought and been gassed in World War I. His wisdom and knowledge about war amazed me. I acquired a great respect for him, and an in-depth awareness of the history that was being made at that time in my life.

With the arrival of April, and spring training on my mind, I began to worry about the upcoming baseball season. Many of my teammates had enlisted or were drafted. I recalled that a number of men and boys who were not on our team came out to play during practice. "Surely we could get a good team together using some of them," I thought. Dad was good at recognizing talent and bringing out the best in a ballplayer. The fact that we were at war did not deter my determination to constantly train in gymnastics and weight lifting that fall and winter. Dad's advice that, "A good ballplayer keeps in shape all year around" was seriously taken.

It was hard to believe that we were at war. For 12 years of the Depression (1929 – 1941), the Sagamore mines worked a meager one or two days a week, paying miners scarcely enough on which to survive. The constant struggle and feeling of hopelessness for their future was forever present. Those fortunate enough to find employment elsewhere in the country had gone. Those remaining had no place for escape. Dad and our family was among them. Dad's struggle to hold on to the hotel and his fears for the future were just as filled with hopelessness as those of the poor miners.

It is ironic and sad to say that the war brought prosperity back to Sagamore during its duration. The demand for coal was imperative to the war effort. Sagamore's three coal mines were soon operating six days a week with three eight-hour shifts around the clock. With so many young men gone into the armed forces, the demand for coal miners skyrocketed. New families began moving into town. Regardless of age, the coal miner was needed and welcomed.

Vehicles were not driven to work. The few in town were used for special purposes only. Therefore, miners walked to their mine entrance, where they boarded coal cars. These coal cars were then pulled by electric motorcars into the mines to where the miners were working. At the end of their shift, they again boarded the coal cars and the electric motorcar returned them to the mine entrance.

Miners going to or returning from work continually passed in front of the hotel. Many stopped at our bar, relaxing over a beer while visiting with friends and discussing the latest news about the war. My heart went out to them. Some were so stooped over from having been bent in that direction for hours on end for years. I visualized how terribly miserable it had to be working in those damp clothes covered with thick, black coal dust. I thought about the cold, black dampness of the mines with its damp-smelling air filled with coal dust that filled their lungs every day. I thought about the rats Dad spoke about. Then there was the constant danger of being killed or crippled for life. A coal miner's life was filled with so much uncertainly. "I could never marry a coal miner," I thought. "It is not a life, It is slavery of the worst kind."

No one was happy the way the war was going. On May 6, the country was filled with gloom and uneasiness over the loss of Corregidor. After months of bombardment from, sea, land and air and fierce hand-to-hand jungle fighting, Corregidor – "the Gibralter of the East" – fell to the Japanese. General Wainwright surrendered his 2,600-man force of soldiers, sailors and marines after 27 days of brutal fighting.

Then two days later a battle that had been strung out over several days in the Coral Sea ended. The Americans lost the carrier Lexington and the Japanese lost the light carrier Shoho.

Now Americans were feeling the effects of the war closer to home by the rationing of commodities and essentials. Everyone was proud to purchase war bonds, but rationing seemed to come all too soon that May when many of America's 131,669,275 citizens lined up at schools to receive their War Ration Book No. 1, limiting each to a pound of sugar every two weeks. Also, motorists received ration books limiting each to 25 to 30 gallons of gasoline per month. Many other items would follow in the months to come, thereby creating a black market. Most people accepted and learned to live within their rationed allowances, but those not willing to do so paid high prices to the black marketers, who could always be found if a person so desired.

By the time we played our first ballgame of the 1942 season, Dad had successfully re-organized a good ball team that was going into its fourth year of existence. The team was strictly a barnstorming team, reputed to be a team hard to beat, and regularly scouted by major league scouts. We drew large crowds who expected to see a hard-fought game with plenty of thrills and excitement. One thing was certain, we never disappointed them.

Joe Stanavich Sr. was Dad's excellent and faithful player. He would play on the team throughout the war. His two sons, Harry and Joe Jr. played until they went into service. Our lineup changed constantly as boys left for service. Younger boys, who were now grown up, stepped in and played until they were drafted. Dad frequently solicited players from surrounding towns, continually searching for talent, because a winning team was very important in his scheme of things.

Brother Johnny caught and pitched. Dad shared catching duties with him, as well as playing second base. I played four or five innings on first base and the remaining innings in right field. Brother Nicholas, age 11, handled the bat boy duties.

Brother Eddie, who was left-handed, was put to work as a pitcher. His pitching performances were something to see. As soon as the batter stepped into the batter's box, I would begin taunting him. "THROW IT IN THERE, ED, HE'LL NEVER SEE IT" and "COME ON, LET'S GO, THREE PITCHES AND HE'S OUT," I'd yell out. Other players joined in the taunting. That poor batter was so filled with anxiety and nervousness before the first pitch was made, he couldn't hit anything. Never in my life had I seen anyone deliver a ball with the fanfare of form as brother Eddie. Not only did the spectators howl with laughter, neither team could concentrate on playing ball for watching and laughing at Eddie going through his pre-delivery gyrations and windups. No clown could have given a better show. He would whirl that left arm around and around, then throw up his right leg as high as his head, bend his whole body backwards as if his delivery was going to be at a speed over 100 miles an hour.

Then the fun part would begin, when he let loose of the ball. It went floating in so SLOW that inevitably batters were swinging long before the ball got to the plate, and sometimes the ball couldn't make it to the plate. Dad let him pitch two or three innings, but those innings gave everyone a barrel of fun. It was evident Eddie wasn't going to be a major or minor leaguer, but in all fairness, I admit, in his own way Eddie was a darn good pitcher. With the sadness of war hanging over us, he gave us a lot of good laughs. During this period we nicknamed him Lefty Gomez.

Beer was becoming scarce, so Dad began buying as many cases of beer as possible, fearing that beer rationing was sure to come. He and brother Eddie made daily trips Monday through Friday, rotating between Pittsburgh, St. Marys and DuBois, Pennsylvania, calling on the Ft. Pitt, Iron City, St. Marys and DuBois Breweries in an effort to purchase as many cases of beer as they would sell Dad. Every evening we stacked the wooden cases, each containing 24-12 ounce bottles, from floor to ceiling in the room no longer used as a dance hall. Their trips continued until several thousand cases of beer were accumulated, which had to be sold within one year as that was the life expectancy of bottled beer. Though none of the beer spoiled, it proved to be quite a challenge for Dad as the year's end was nearing. Securing enough beer for the remainder of the war became a never-ending battle which caused Dad much anxiety. The problem of obtaining enough liquor to sell also became a problem, especially since the state of Pennsylvania controlled all the liquor.

After six months of fierce fighting, a ray of hope came June 6 with the announcement that the American Navy had turned the tide at Midway Island in the Pacific. The Americans met the Japanese armada of 200 ships, including eight carriers, eleven battleships, twenty two cruisers, sixty five destroyers and twenty one submarines with only three American carriers and 233 planes. The Japanese lost one heavy cruiser, four fleet carriers, and 330 aircraft. The Americans at last rejoiced in a well-earned victory.

A week later, the government, announced it was officially in the spy business. The United States had been the only major power without an intelligence service. President Roosevelt appointed Colonel W.J. Donovan, a World War I Congressional Medal of Honor winner, as head of the new agency called the Office of Strategic Services.

The entire country became involved in a scrap and rubber drive for the war effort. Brother Eddie, using Dad's truck, worked with the town's Boy Scout troop collecting scrap and rubber throughout the town and surrounding countryside. It was then stored behind the hotel until it could be hauled to Pittsburgh. Our nation's Boy Scouts worked diligently throughout the war and deserve a lot of credit.

On August 17, the American Army Air Force made their first major bombing raid of the war on Rouen, France, thereby joining forces in an overall strategy with Britain to gain complete air supremacy over Europe. The Americans conducted daylight raids against Germany and occupied Europe while Britain's would do the same at night.

By this time Sagamore's miners were becoming affluent working six days a week. The hotel business was flourishing as never before. Dad knew this sudden increase was as uncertain as war. He also realized that it gave him his first opportunity in 20 years to liquidate thousands of dollars in unpaid debts that he had vowed to pay years before. He began reviewing the old filing box that had stored away for years. It held the unpaid debts, yellowed with age, that worried him for so long. He devised a plan in which a certain amount of every dollar earned would go towards liquidating them. It was going to be hard because so many individual owners or corporations had gone bankrupt, or just closed their doors and walked off. Others had passed away. However, he was determined to find their heirs or learn the whereabouts of those having moved. His old ledger showed the total amount owed was $48,000, a staggering amount in the year 1942. After six years of hard work by all six members of our family, plus a full-time bartender and housemaid, he realized the fulfillment of his vow, much to the admiration and respect of those who had long ago lost any record of the bill having ever existed.

That August Dad's desperate need for a full-time bartender was resolved when Mother's sister Elizabeth and her husband John came to live in the house behind the hotel. John bartended for Dad for the next three years.

By September the war had changed everything in my life. I felt no enthusiasm about becoming a high school senior. Realizing how badly Mother and Dad needed me in the hotel business, I was torn between the desire to help them and the desire to graduate. I was determined to do both, especially since our baseball season was coming to an end. I met the challenge by assuming a schedule of all work and no play. This resulted in my missing all my high school activities, including my junior and senior prom, that in later years become the cherished memories of all juniors and seniors.

At this time other great decisions were being made in the sport of baseball. The major leagues were suffering from the loss of their best and greatest ballplayers by way of their enlisting or being drafted into the armed forces. They were facing a decision of either playing a lower quality of major league ball or disbanding for the duration of the war. Both President Roosevelt and Congress encouraged the commissioner not to disband the two leagues. They said that baseball was as American as apple pie. It was the great American pastime, and especially during wartime, it was good for the morale of the people. And so, in the fall of 1942, Philip K. Wrigley, then owner of the Chicago Cubs, met with professional baseball advisors to discuss the desperate situation. "Why not a women's professional baseball league?" they asked. Wrigley liked the idea and a plan was devised and implemented, whereby the 30 Chicago Cub scouts were sent to scout the 40,000 semi-pro teams throughout the United States and Canada. In their search for the best hurlers and sluggers, 280 girls were invited to try out at Wrigley Field in Chicago in the spring of 1943.

In November, the first year anniversary of Pearl Harbor was nearing. The daily roller coaster news reports were emotionally draining. Every American was involved in the war effort, but still they wanted to do more. News reports about the war in the Pacific, as well as numerous simultaneous battles being fought around the world, sent us scurrying for our "World Atlas" to locate geographically just where our marines, sailors, soldiers and fighter pilots were fighting. It was difficult for the poor immigrants who had no knowledge of the world geographically because of little or no education. They had never heard of Sava Island, Santa Cruz, Lunga Point, Cape Esperance, Tassafarongo, the Eastern Solomons and Guadalcanal. These were places where seven months of battles were fought in the Solomon Campaign. These islands are located northeast of Australia and scattered through the South Pacific east of Papua New Guinea. Much bloody fighting took place on these important, tiny islands between the United States and Japanese forces, in which thousands of American lives were sacrificed. Their control meant control of the Pacific. Therefore, when American forces won the battle of Guadalcanal on November 15, it was a major victory in the long, hard battle for the Solomons.

News of the Americans' victory at Guadalcanal electrified the crowd in our hotel bar. We had waited too long for good news regarding a South Pacific victory. The loud cheers rang out over and over again, along with the singing of patriotic songs and the theme songs of the Marines, Navy and Air Forces. "Praise the Lord and Pass the Ammunition," "Anchors Aweigh," "The Army Air Corps", "America The Beautiful," "The Marines Hymn," "The Caissons Go Rolling Along," "Battle Hymn of the Republic" and "God Bless America" were sung over and over again. Other favorite songs were "A Home on the Range," "You're in the Army Now," "Auld Lang Syne," I've Been Workin' on the Railroad" and, much to my surprise, "She'll be Comin' Round the Mountain." The celebrating and singing went on into the wee hours of the morning. I recall getting very little sleep that night, because in my heart, I was rejoicing with them, and many of those songs had me crying in the night.

Another cause for celebrating that November was the announcement that the Allies had stormed the beaches in North Africa at Casablanca, Morocco, and Algeria. "WE'RE GOING AFTER THEM NOW," yelled one of the men who was too old to fight. His enthusiasm left no doubt that he was a fighter in his youth.

December 7, 1942, marked the first anniversary of the sneaky Japanese attack on Pearl Harbor, Hawaii. Remembering that day reinforced America's anger. Their unified determination to win the war was strengthened beyond anything ever seen before. This determination would build the foundation for the rise of the United States from a minor power to the "GREATEST POWER IN THE WORLD."

The Japanese in the Pacific had revealed to the American people a cold-blooded, heartless, insensible enemy.

In Europe, the Germans and Italians also were proving to be equal to the Japanese in their cold-blooded, moral insensibility towards mankind.

Millions of Americans from all religious denominations, having faith in GOD, prayed for GOD'S intervention against this earthly evil spawned by the DEVIL. My confidence was intensified by the belief that "WE SHALL PREVAIL BECAUSE GOD IS ON OUR SIDE. THUS, THE DEVIL SHALL NEVER WIN."

The hotel's bar was bustling as Christmas was approaching. Soldiers, sailors and marines were coming home on leave for Christmas. Following six weeks of boot camp, they looked in superb condition, walking tall, proud and confident. The men found pleasure in games of chance such as pool, checkers, chess, Chinese checkers and card games either for sport or gain. The slot and pinball machines were never quiet. Nor was the jukebox that blared out an assortment of songs, some so sentimental even the toughest marine was seen shedding a tear or two.

"SHOOT THE JAP," a new electronic game of skill, was the rage that Christmas as uniformed men were anxious to demonstrate their shooting skills. From a distance of 40 feet, the contestant was allowed 20 shots using an electric rifle. The goal was to consecutively shoot a nine-inch-tall, continually moving Jap soldier who had a small electric target in his shoulder. Only a perfect hit on the Jap's target was counted. A contestant shooting 20 perfect shots was automatically able to continue shooting until he made his first miss, at which point the game was over.

The miners decided to have a little fun. "I'll bet Bounce's daughter can keep that Jap turning and moving more times than you," they'd say. It worked every time. "Put up or shut up," the man in uniform would say. "OK, I bet a dollar," replied the miner. The crowd hurriedly gathered around and the bets were on. Even Dad got involved in the fun. The fun sometimes went on for hours, until I defeated every serviceman in the bar. Much to my surprise, the serviceman were great sports in going along with the laughter and teasing. The miners were not interested in the betting money. They were glad to pick up the servicemen's tabs throughout the night and paid for the "SHOOT THE JAP" games. "Where did you learn to shoot like that?" the servicemen asked. "I belong to the Cowanshannock Township Rifle Club," I'd reply. Invariably, they'd smile while pointing a finger at me, saying "UNCLE SAM NEEDS YOU."

Following school, preparing our meals under Mother's supervision was one of my chores. Mother had a room next to the bar converted into a second family kitchen and dining room. This was more convenient for the family because the bar was open 20 hours daily Monday through Saturday and four hours Sunday afternoons.

Because of a never-ending seven-day work schedule, my lovely, astonishing Mother never slept but three or four hours daily. She possessed amazing stamina and an inner beauty that endeared her to everyone. Not only was she the backbone of our family, she was our role model, in essence the glue that held us together. GETTING DAD OUT OF DEBT ONCE AND FOR ALL was the families ultimate goal. My dear Mother did far more than her share. Because we understood the necessity of working together, everyone worked in every aspect having to do with the operation of the hotel. In fact, it is sad but true, in order to work full time, brother Eddie left school upon completing his sophomore year in high school.

December 31 was my 17th birthday. No one seemed to care and neither did I. My day was spent preparing meals, washing dishes and watching the merrymakers bring in the NEW, 1943.

Sagamore (left to right)
Seventh, Eighth, and Ninth Streets - workers homes - Lutheran Church building - the local theatre and ice cream parlor - Hotel Sagamore extreme right

CHAPTER XII
THE YEARS 1943 – 1944

January, 1943, the American people learned that 60,000 American soldiers had been killed since the war began, awakening those Americans of my generation to a reality of war of which our parents had already experienced in World War I, the heartbreaking sacrifices of losing loved ones much too young to have died. Nevertheless, Americans were resolved to win, little realizing that 300,000 American soldiers would lose their lives or be missing by the end of the war.

Three years and three months had passed since World War II began in Europe with the invasion of Poland September 1, 1939. No one envisioned a war of such magnitude that it would involve fighting on three continents, and three oceans, and eventually involve 57 nations.

On January 24, President Roosevelt and Prime Minister Churchill of Great Britain had agreed that the war would not end until they had achieved and "unconditional surrender."

With the absolute defeat of the Japanese at Guadalcanal, the North African campaign became our deep concern. Defeating the German General Rommel, nicknamed "THE DESERT FOX" was proving to be costly in lives and armament for the Allies. The Allies would not defeat the Axis resistance there until May.

On the homefront, a new slogan was going around: "USE IT UP, WEAR IT OUT, MAKE IT DO, OR DO WITHOUT." It seemed there was nothing that was not rationed. The sale of coal to civilians was frozen, making it difficult to obtain enough coal in which to heat our homes. The coal company did allow that any coal having fallen along the railroad tracks could be salvaged for civilian use, if anyone wanted to hand pick and carry it home. However, this was a back-breaking job. I was filled with compassion for the young girls as they struggled, often falling in their attempt to climb the steep hill behind the hotel, while carrying a sack load of coal on their backs. I could not believe their fathers would permit it. It was a difficult feat for a man, let alone a young girl. We were fortunate in that we had a pickup truck in which to haul coal that was purchased from small coal bank operations that were not controlled by the government.

During the fall and winter months I worked regularly with weights and calisthenics. "My muscles are going to be toned and ready. There will be no charley horses for me this spring training," I thought.

Following the long, hard winter, the coming of spring was beautiful. The snow turned to slush, then into water followed by the usual nasty mud. The yellow dandelion blossoms peeked out, birds chirped and March winds dried the mud.

Then spring training began, and the beginning of my third year of men's semi-pro baseball. Dad was hard at work rebuilding our team after having lost several players to the armed forces. Daylight hours were longer now, allowing more hours for practice on weekends and after school.

I had no difficulty in hitting a ball between the infielders and outfielders since my first year playing as a regular on a 90-foot regulation baseball diamond. However, opposing outfielders invariably played in on me, thereby robbing me of would-be hits. Dad and I were often exasperated by the problem. To overcome this disadvantage he devised a plan that proved to be a work of brilliance on his part. In the fall of 1942, and on into the spring of 1943, he diligently trained me hour after hour in the art of bunting. Much to his surprise I had a natural talent for it and had mastered it to perfection. I could place a bunt anywhere he signaled me to do so. He wanted no publicity about it, nor did he want me to bunt during pre-game practice, because he anticipated my bunting to be an unexpected surprise to the opposing team, and indeed it was. He called for my bunting in very close and decisive times during a game, such as bunting along the first base or third base line with the bases loaded, depending on where the weakest link of the opposing team was. I could bring a run in every time and many times it was the winning run. Performing daring feats like that brought the excited and thrilled fans to their feet, as did my stealing bases and sliding in head first. Dad's attempt at teaching me the art of sliding feet first was a disaster. It was head first with me or not at all. The aggressive desire to get there head first could not be overcome, so he finally conceded, contenting himself by calling me "BULLHEADED." But the fans loved it, and so did I. However, my bunting ability gave me confidence and faith in facing any pitcher. Fearing no pitcher, I preferred a fast pitch, the faster the better, whether it be high, low or a curve ball. They posed no problem, for I learned to bunt them all.

I was five feet, two inches tall now and weighed 117 pounds. My biceps measured 13 inches, and my strength surprised even me. I recall performing feats of strength in which I held 200 pounds on my chest while doing the backbend and 200 pounds on my shoulders as I did a forward split with arms outstretched. Years of weights, calisthenics and playing baseball made it all possible. I felt in control and I liked it. "IT'S A MAN'S WORLD FROM WHAT I SEE, AND I'M GOING TO BE A SURVIVOR," I thought. By this time I experienced some hard knocks in baseball along with aching muscles, nasty bruises, and a broken finger, and I knew there would be more to come.

World War II was correctly named, no mistake about it. Thousands were losing their lives fighting in the South Pacific on the land, air and seas of the vast Pacific Ocean, as well as the Atlantic Ocean. In the east, the European theatre, devastated by years of war, left no country untouched in one way or another, and death were in the hundreds of thousands. Fighting on the Russian front alone was beyond belief, claiming millions of lives. The battles being fought in the North African desert were like no other in history, and lives lost were in the thousands. When the Germans and Italians surrendered on May 12, 1943, nearly 250,000 troops were taken prisoner.

On July 10, the Allies invaded the southwest top of the island of Sicily, and successfully occupied the island by August 17. Then the Allies focused on a full-scale invasion against the Italian mainland. The war was moving rapidly on every front, east and west.

On the homefront, baseball history was being made in the spring of 1943 when 280 girls ages 15 to 30 from 16 states and five Canadian Provinces arrived at Wrigley Field in Chicago for tryouts for the first women's professional baseball league. One hundred were selected for spring training. Of those, 60 were contracted at $50 to $125 per week. These girls became the first four teams of the ALL AMERICAN GIRLS PROFESSIONAL BASEBALL LEAGUE.

New rules and regulations were created for this new baseball, and gradually would change throughout its 12-year existence, bringing it closer and closer to men's baseball. During that period the distance between bases would change from 60 feet to 85 feet, the pitching distance from 40 feet to 60 feet and the ball from 12 inches to 9 ¼ inches in circumference. Pitching would graduate from the fast underhand whirlwind pitch in 1943, '44 and '45, then include the sidearm pitch in 1946 and '47. By 1948, only the overhead pitch was allowed as in men's baseball.

Little did I realize at age 17 that at the age of 19 I would be the first girl from Pennsylvania to play in the league.

My graduation from Cowanshannock Township High School was nearing. Preparations were being made for the biggest event of the year, the junior-senior prom. I enjoyed working on the decorating committee, although I had no plans to attend the affair. My priorities and plans did not call for dating until I was 21, a decision having been made years before.

All was not happy for our family that spring of 1943. Brother Eddie's draft induction notification came on his 19th birthday, April 28. Ironically, he was to report for army induction 10 days prior to my graduation, which was May 27. On May 30, he was shipped to Ft. McClelland, Alabama, for boot camp training. I was devastated, never having thought much about Eddie going to the army. Now, it was real, and I could not accept it. In the quiet privacy of my room, I recalled the past memories of our lives together, of the good and bad times, hard and sad times, fun and happy times. A feeling of emptiness filled the pit of my stomach. I felt rebellious and angry as I struggled with my thoughts: "EDDIE IS GOING OFF TO WAR. IT CAN'T BE TRUE. MAYBE ME, BUT NOT EDDIE. HE ISN'T A FIGHTER. HE'S TOO GENTLE AND EASYGOING. BESIDES, HE CAN'T SHOOT A GUN. I SHOULD BE GOING, NOT HIM. I CAN SHOOT, AND I'M STRONGER THAN HE IS. THEY CAN'T DRAFT HIM, NOT EDDIE. HE FAINTS EVERY TIME HE SEES BLOOD." I wanted to do something to stop his being drafted, knowing in my heart it was not possible. Feeling helpless, I began to pray for courage to accept what was happening, praying also for Eddie and all the family, knowing Mother was heartbroken. Thereafter, all my worry and prayers for his safe return from the war was confined within my heart and private world between God and me.

Things were changing fast now that he was leaving. First, he taught me to drive the pickup truck. A week later I passed my driver's test and had replaced Eddie as Dad's driver. Dad hated driving. Besides, no one would ride with him because he was such a terrible driver.

199

Mother possessed numerous talents, but that of her beautiful sewing could not be disputed. During my 17 years, all my clothing except a half dozen items or so were sewn by her. However, graduation and Eddie's leaving for the service were two special occasions, one happy, the other sad. This called for a store-bought dress from Molly Ann's, because she insisted on a family portrait in memory of both occasions. So we drove to Rural Valley where Mr. Boyer produced our first and only family portrait. Dad was 45, Mother 40, Eddie 19, I was 17, Johnny 15, and Nicholas 12.

There was no party or fanfare about my graduation. It just came and went, like all my birthdays did. One week following graduation, my graduation ring went washing down the drain along with the washing machine water, lost forever with no possible way of retrieving it, and only adding to my disappointment.

However, no disappointment was greater than learning that I would not be attending college in the fall. It had been my dream for years. With Eddie in the army, and help difficult to find, Dad depended on me more than ever. After all, I was his bookkeeper since age 14. In addition, there was my baseball career with practice every day, and helping Mother with her tremendous responsibility of cleaning a 62 room hotel along with the cooking, baking, washing and ironing demands of such a large public building. The 40-year-old coal town of Sagamore still had its dirt and gravel sidewalks and streets presenting an ever-constant struggle to keep the hotel free and clean from dirt and mud.

Brother Johnny also felt the impact of Eddie's induction when his full work schedule was doubled. It was more than any 15-year-old boy should have to carry, but carry it he did with never a complaint. He especially worked long, hard hours in the gambling hall, besides being a regular pitcher on our team. He was the best pitcher we ever had. I can't praise him enough, With him on the mound our team's confidence was second to none. He inspired us, and we performed in backing him. His calm and confident pitching performances of great speed and control carried our team to greater popularity. This and the fact the "THE KOVALCHICKS," as we were called, had a girl on their team aroused the curiosity of teams everywhere, and before long we were scheduling games to be played in 1944.

Dad furnished all the team's equipment, including gloves for most of the players, and he special ordered black and white wool uniforms from Pittsburgh, wool being the uniform material of those days. The team's name, "KOVALCHICKS," were embroidered in black across the chest. Black knee socks, belt and cap embroidered with a white "S" for Sagamore completed the impressive-looking uniforms which Mother kept immaculate by regular laundering. However, my trademark uniform was tennis-style shorts and peasant blouse, because my allergy to wool prevented me from wearing the wool uniform.

Everyone missed Eddie. Gone were the laughs we enjoyed when watching him pitch. He had also been the team's driver and equipment caretaker. Now Joe Stanavich Sr. had become our driver, and Nicholas and Johnny looked after the equipment.

The season before Eddie had converted our pickup truck into a mini bus by installing benches along both sides of the pickup bed. These benches accommodated 12 ballplayers. The equipment and water cooler were stored in the center. As many as three sat in the cab. Fans also furnished transportation for players. To protect player from sun and bad weather, brackets were installed to support a tarpaulin that could be rolled up or let down on the sides and back.

I chose to ride in the back of the pickup with the boys as we traveled to play, as I realized our team's success depended largely on their accepting me as their equal, especially with our lineup constantly changing due to the war. I wanted them to see me as a baseball player, not as a girl. I wanted to share our wins and losses with them. We praised each other's feats when we won, and vowed to play harder and practice longer when we lost. We told stories and laughed a lot, but never a vulgar word was spoken, nor a cigarette ever smoked, or alcohol ever seen amongst them. As we got to know each other, the togetherness unified the team as I had hoped. I developed a deep respect for them, and they in turn respected me.

Because barnstorming was taking us to towns and cities further and further away from Sagamore, gas rationing was becoming a problem. However, we were fortunate that so many loyal followers came to our rescue. They shared their gas rationing stamps, and even organized car pools, enabling them to continue following the team.

It was becoming quite an embarrassment to teams we defeated. You can imagine the razzing those players took when they lost to a team with a girl ballplayer. We began noticing that teams were made up of bigger and better players with more experience, because they were being solicited from surrounding towns and cities. At times we were dwarfed by them. Still, we never backed out. Dad said, "A COMMITMENT TO PLAY IS THE SAME AS YOUR WORD OF HONOR." The fact is, the challenge accounted for a more exciting game. Our players played harder, and as tension mounted spectators cheered louder, spurring us on.

The secret of our success actually was owed to Dad, who throughout his baseball career had learned to play the game as a science, because he was only five feet, four inches tall. He overcame his disadvantage by studying the opposing players, taking advantage of their weaknesses, as well as their strengths. No man had mastered the game better than he had. When he asked a scout to look at one of his ballplayers, they responded immediately, because they had great respect for his ability to recognize a potential professional ballplayer.

Sagamore lies in the beautiful foothills of the Allegheny Mountains of west central Pennsylvania. The townspeople loved those hills, calling them by name, such as Cherry Hill, Ballground Hill, Marshall's Hill, 8th Street Hill, and Reservoir Hill, only to name a few. Those hills surrounded the town, and were covered by a variety of wild vegetation and forests of hardwood trees. There were all kinds of berry bushes, fruit and nut trees and abundant mushrooms.

I frequently climbed those hills, as they fulfilled my need for a private place away from the rest of the world.

It was on one of those private visits that the first of many spiritual experiences came into my life. There is was like out of nowhere, a beautiful lush green grass clearing in the middle of the dense woods hidden away from civilization on that high plateau on the top of Ballground Hill. Directly in the center of the clearing stood an eight-foot black charred tree trunk – the remains of a once gigantic oak, exposing a huge split in its trunk where a deadly bolt of lightning had ended its life a long time ago.

There was no evidence of anyone ever entering the clearing as it was encircled by a thicket of trees and underbrush. I was mesmerized by the serenity of it all. It was so close to nature and God in this peaceful, quiet place on earth.

I found myself thinking of how it was as a "Lost Horizon" and felt the spiritual presence of God. At that moment, I claimed it as my own "Lost Horizon" that had been touched by God's hand – a place I could come and meditate and pray, pray for the war to end and for Eddie to come back home safely. "Yes, Eddie will need a lot of prayers," I thought.

Then, I began plotting a hidden entrance through the thicket that surrounded my "Lost Horizon," making mental notes of certain trees and shrubs and even a rock or two.

The following day I returned with all the necessary items for making an altar in the huge split in the charred tree trunk. It was perfect, it even had a place for kneeling to pray, and a safe place for storing the items while I was gone.

For the remainder of the war, my "Lost Horizon" remained my special place for rejuvenation of my strength, faith and hope.

When Eddie was sent to Ft. McClelland, Alabama, for boot camp training on May 30, we knew that one day he would be coming home on leave before being sent to one of the many war fronts throughout the world, and we prayed and worried constantly about it.

In October, his 10 weeks' training in motor mechanics and seven weeks' basic training at Ft. McClelland were near an end, and he was coming home on a seven-day leave before having to report to Ft. Meade, Maryland. His basic training was cut short because of his 10 weeks in motor mechanics, which was one of the 14 specialists divisions of his company.

Everyone was excited, Eddie was coming home, and immediately plans got underway.

Our four-story hotel with its 62 rooms was cleaned and polished as if we were preparing for the arrival of some famous dignitary.

Mother and I baked his favorite Czechoslovakian nut and poppyseed rolls and his favorite foods. Dad walked around joking and laughing with everyone. It had been a long time since I had seen him in such a happy mood. And Mother engaged Mr. Boyer to make a portrait of Eddie in his uniform.

Dad met him at the bus station in Indiana, Pennsylvania. Gone was the boy I grew up with, and in his stead was the most handsome soldier I had ever seen. He was walking tall and confident, and was handsomely tanned by the hot sun of the South. I was so proud.

Mother wrapped her loving arms around him and cried. The realization of how much she loved him enveloped me. It touched my heart so, that I went into another room to wipe away the tears.

That October, our bar was filled with soldiers home on leave. Our hearts were heavy because we knew they were being shipped overseas upon leaving Sagamore for Ft. Meade. However, they seemed resigned to "WHAT WILL BE, WILL BE" as they laughed, joked and drank a lot. There was no sign of being afraid to face the unknown that lie ahead as they went off to fight a war for the sake of freedom.

Yes, they were proud soldiers – pillars of courage, strength and determination. But there were times when another side was revealed, especially when they were drinking, and the juke box was playing a heartbreaking or sentimental song, stirring within them memories of present or past loves, or thoughts of having to leave their wives and mothers and others close to them. Many times I saw their tears.

Such was the case with one soldier, who had no girlfriend or sisters, but wanted to take something overseas with him that belonged to a girl. "CAN I TAKE YOUR BEADS OVERSEAS WITH ME?" he asked. I reached and took them from around my neck, then handed them to him. "I'LL BRING THEM BACK WHEN THE WAR IS OVER," he said. True to his word, when he returned he brought them to me and said "I WANT TO THANK YOU. YOU WILL NEVER KNOW HOW MUCH YOUR BEADS MEANT TO ME AND THE GUYS IN MY SQUAD. THEY WERE PASSED AROUND TO ALL THE GUYS. THEY JUST WANTED TO HOLD THEM OR WEAR THEM AROUND THEIR NECK FOR AWHILE WHEN THEY WERE LONESOME FOR THEIR WIVES OR GIRL-FRIENDS BACK HOME." He reached for his shirt pocket, pulled out the beads, and handed them to me. Then, thanking me again, he turned and left the bar, and I never saw him again. Today those pearl beads are among my mementos from the war.

Eddie's leave was a fast and furious one. He enjoyed every minute of it, hardly stopping to sleep. He was a people person, just like Dad, and knew thousands of people for miles around. It looked like he was trying to visit every one of them personally to tell them good-bye.

Time seemed to pass too quickly. Suddenly sadness was everywhere as Eddie and many others were leaving for Ft. Meade. Gloom weighted heavy on our hearts, especially Mother's as tears flowed down her cheeks. An unsettling, intuitive feeling filled my very soul. It was one of the saddest days in my life.

At Ft. Meade, Eddie, along with thousands of other soldiers, was issued clothing, then immediately sent to the port of embarkation in Norfolk, Virginia. There, all necessary overseas shots were administered. Then, trucks transported them to their ships. Eddie's ship departed Norfolk on November 3, 1943, and arrived in Oran in Algeria, Africa, on Thanksgiving Day, 21 days later.

Back home, November brought in our first snowflakes as usual around Thanksgiving Day. Because the stressful circumstance of war weighed so heavily on our hearts, Thanksgiving Day was sad. However, we gave thanks to God that we were Americans and lived in the land of freedom. We asked God to watch over our soldiers, especially those closest to us, knowing they were facing the horror of war in the cold winter ahead. And, not knowing on which front they were fighting increased our anxiety.

On Christmas Day, Eddie's company shipped out from Camp Lion Mountain in Oran for the port of Naples, Italy, occupied by the Allies since October.

At home, Christmas and my 18th birthday on December 31 were the saddest ever. Regardless of how bad the weather, every day I visited my "Lost Horizon" on Ballground Hill to pray for Eddie, the United States and our Allies.

Since childhood, I felt a bond between Eddie and me, as though he was my responsibility. Not that I did not love Johnny and Nicholas just as equally, but, Johnny's bigger-boned physique and stature gave me a feeling of security about him. I felt that he would make it, that he would be all right. As for Nicholas, I was proud of his intelligence and confident in his ability to climb to whatever heights he set out to accomplish. But Eddie was different. He was not robust, being only 118 pounds when he went off to war, and his trusting and easygoing nature left me in doubt as to his future. I had an unexplainable intuition that he needed me and my strength.

We listened intently for news about the fighting in Italy, feeling certain that our boys were being shipped there. We learned that the Germans had retreated towards the Apennine Mountains, the central spine of Italy which ran 800 miles from the North to the Straits of Messina in the south. This "Gustav Line" was dominated by Monte Casino, a 1,703 foot high peak on which a beautiful 1,300-year-old Benedictine monastery stood at the entrance to the Liri Valley, blocking the only road north to Rome, 75 miles to the northeast, and the Allies had to capture it.

Eddie's ship arrived at Naples on New Year's Day, 1944, and immediately his company was sent to the front lines at Monte Cassino, where they desperately needed men. Conditions were atrocious. Mountain fighting in freezing cold weather was taking a heavy toll on the Allied troops. The Germans were well entrenched. The battle raged, and the death toll mounted. And, Eddie, with only seven weeks of boot camp training, was thrust into one of the worse battle fronts being fought in the war, not as a motor mechanic, but as an infantryman. The battle would eventually take a toll in lives of over 100,000 men and six months of bitter fighting.

In an effort to relieve pressure on our Allies fighting in the mountains, troops were landed behind German lines at Anzio 30 miles South of Rome on January 22.

As we listened to the news and read our newspapers regarding the fierce fighting and large death toll, we feared that Eddie was at either Monte Cassino or Anzio.

Monte Cassino was not accessible by truck or other heavy equipment, but it was accessible on foot or with mules. One day Eddie was sent out ahead to scout with his mule, and by nightfall he became lost behind enemy lines for three days. There he huddled in the cold, protected from freezing to death by his loyal mule as they both laid quietly day and night within hearing distance of the Germans. Fear enveloped him as he snuggled closer to his mule, and shared his rations with him. On the third day, he heard the voices of American soldiers. As he ventured from his hiding place they greeted him with surprise. "Only the hand of God had protected us," he said. The love he felt for his mule Jake would never leave him.

A few days later, on February 4, a bullet found its way through his helmet, sending him to the hospital.

At home, February 4 was no ordinary day for me. The moment, I awoke, I knew something had happened to Eddie. I jumped out of bed, hurriedly dressed and rushed downstairs. Then, grabbing my coat, I ran for Ballground Hill and my "Lost Horizon." Breathless, I set up my altar, knelt down and began to pray. During my deep meditation and prayer, time passed and the snow began to fall. The snow was turning into a blizzard, but my thoughts were only of Eddie and the unexplainable feeling that he needed help. Tears were falling as I begged God to please help Eddie, that He (God) was the only One with the power. The wind was blowing harder, making the temperature fall faster, and the snow was fast becoming inches deep. Still, I knelt in prayer and determination, praying that Eddie was all right.

I began to feel a dull numbness in my feet and hands, as coldness began to overtake me. It diverted my thoughts, awakening me to the realization that what at first appeared to be a normal snowfall had developed into a bad blizzard. I hastily started towards home, finding it difficult to walk in the high snow because several inches of snow was blown in by the blizzard, adding to the snow already on the ground from the day before. After plodding through the snow for sometime, freezing cold and tired, it occurred to me that our hotel should have already been in sight, yet nothing looked familiar. I was lost but not frightened or discouraged, and decided to rest for awhile, away from the cold-cutting wind before trying to acquire the right sense of direction. A nearby ravine seemed perfect, and I climbed inside. Soon a sense of comfort and warmth overtook me and I began to fall asleep, when off in the distance voices were calling my name, but only my mind could respond: "HERE I AM, OVER HERE. I'M OVER HERE." I thought over and over again, "YOU'VE GOT TO FIND ME. I'M OVER HERE." I could hear the voices coming closer and closer, and then a voice called out, "HERE SHE IS, OVER HERE, HERE SHE IS." The three men carried me home after rubbing may hands, face, feet and legs. Luckily, Mother saw me leaving that morning, and had sent them to find me.

Returning home was an experience never forgotten. Mother's dunking me in tub after tub of cold water, then following with brisk massaging, which brought warm blood flowing back into the numb parts of my body. The big, warm blanket she wrapped around me, and the hours spent in the hotel's furnace room, sleeping in the warmest bed in town to hasten my recovery.

Then one day the sad letter from the War Department arrived. It read, "WE REGRET TO INFORM YOU THAT IN THE LOYAL SERVICE OF HIS COUNTRY, YOUR SON, EDWARD J. KOVALCHICK, WAS WOUNDED IN BATTLE AT MONTE

CASSINO, ITALY, FEBRUARY 4, 1943." Only I and I alone knew something had happened to Eddie that day.

In the privacy of my bedroom, I quietly prayed, strangely feeling that somehow he was all right.

Two weeks after Eddie was wounded and still hospitalized, our armed forces at Monte Cassino and Anzio Beach were still engaged in fierce fighting and encountered horrendous losses in men. In desperation the Army called upon the wounded who could walk and carry a rifle to return to fight on the front line. Surprisingly, every man possible climbed out of bed, including Eddie, and volunteered to return to the front.

The volunteers were informed that they were being trucked to Naples, where they would board ships bound for Anzio Beach. The need there was desperate. The allies stood to lose what they had already fought so valiantly to secure.

As their ships approached Anzio Beach, landing seemed impossible while the Germans were bombarding them with everything they had. Days passed while deaths and destruction mounted. Everything and everyone was in a state of confusion as they prepared to storm the beach. In all the chaos Eddie heard an officer yell out orders as they neared the beach, "YOU'RE ON YOUR OWN, MEN. IT'S EVERY MAN FOR HIMSELF. DIG IN AND FIGHT." Eddie jumped into the water, heading for the beach with bombs bursting and shrapnel and bullets flying within inches of every part of his body. He made it to a foxhole, but many of his buddies did not make it. He claimed a Power greater than himself led him safely to that foxhole.

For the next three months life was pure HELL as our soldiers fought courageously, gaining ground and then losing ground time and time again, before breaking through the German defenses on

May 23. Eddie had met and escaped death numerous times in those three months.

At home, I decided it was time to enlist in the Army now that I was 18. Dad would not hear of it, but I persisted. After all, I was strong, unafraid and a sharp shooter. Nothing would sway my determination that is until the day Dad announced that we were going to the recruiting office in Greensburg to enlist. Little did I know at the time that Dad had made an appointment after engaging the help of the enlisting officer in a scheme to erase once and for all any desire I had for enlisting in the army. I believe that enlisting officer was the rudest man I ever met, and I was angry. "HOW DARE HE," I thought, ending my desire to join the army. Dad's plan had worked. I felt the army recruiter had caused the army to lose one of their best soldiers ever, and that he wasn't working for the good of the United State and should be reported. Dad agreed with a big suspicious-looking smile as we drove home.

Following my enlistment disappointment, my thoughts turned to spring training just as Dad had hoped.

With Dad losing ballplayers to the armed forces every year, he worked harder and harder to organize a team capable of maintaining the hard-earned reputation his team, "THE KOVALCHICKS" had gained since he organized it in 1939.

As in years past, our team in 1944 was indisputably a team hard to beat. We defeated CLYMER 2-1, SAMPLE RUN 9-1 and 7-6, FORD CITY 7-6, INDIANA 8-5, PUNXSUTAWNEY 6-3, ERNEST 4-3 and 4-1 only to name a few.

The highlight of most games was the banquet following the game, which was part of Dad's agreement to play the town's team. THE DAY WE DEFEATED AULTMAN, our highly anticipated banquet was never consummated. They were so ANGRY that they stoned us out of town - yes indeed. Following the game, I was sitting in the back of the pickup as we were driving to the banquet hall, when stones began to fly from every direction. I felt that the act of not defending ourselves was an act of cowardice, so I began to shout, "COME ON BOYS, LET'S CATCH THE STONES AND THROW THEM BACK." We grabbed our gloves and did just that as we hurriedly drove out of town, abandoning our plans to attend their promised banquet. I do not know if Aultman ever offered Dad an apology.

It was common to lose five pounds when playing nine innings or more. To sustain the grueling physical demands of the game, peanut butter and jelly sandwiches were my mainstay. I sure loved those peanut butter and jelly sandwiches and could make one fit for a king.

The news media was beginning to call us the "COLORFUL KOVALCHICKS," a nickname that prevailed for years. We always had a team of unusual players, like six-foot, three inch Zip Zentner and two fathers, Joe Stanavich Sr. and Dad. Joe's two sons played until they left for the armed forces. There were times Dad and us four children – Eddie, Johnny, Nickie, and me – played at the same time. Also, there was Bo Long, a black man, who played shortstop. Our team was always diversified with old timers and young boy, the tall and the short, and best of all were the potential ballplayers that would one day play in the minor and major leagues, like BILL HUNTER, ALEX KVASNAK, BUD SOUCHOCK, GENE POMPELIA, BROTHER JOHNNY and MIKE GOLIAT.

While our baseball team was enjoying a winning streak since the season began, the war continued to rage on all fronts.

Eddie was still at Anzio, where after four months of fierce fighting, the Allies had at last broken through on May 23 and were heading towards Rome. At the same time, Allied troops were moving up from the South to join forces with them.

An Allied victory looked more and more inevitable to the Germans. They decided to retreat in order to prepare for new defensive positions at the Gothic Line along the Arno River. To disguise the fact that the Germans were retreating, Hitler announced that they had withdrawn to prevent the destruction of Rome, the oldest culture center in the world.

Allied troops from Anzio and those from the South linked up on May 25 and entered Rome on June 6, 1944. It was a glorious time, with cheering, tears, and joy, but Eddie felt no joy upon entering Rome. Most of his buddies were dead. After three months of fierce fighting, he was numb from battle fatigue, and seeing the cruelty and starvation that had been inflicted upon the Italian people by the Germans broke his heart.

In an effort to provide for the millions of homeless and hungry Italians, the Allied Military Government of Occupation (AMGOT) was set up to feed the starving, keep the streets clean, issue money, and carry out other essential duties of government. As the Allies continued in pursuit of the Germans, Eddie again was on the front lines.

On the same day that the Allies entered Rome, the Allies' liberation of Europe, named "OPERATION OVERLORD," began the D-DAY invasion of France as 5,000 ships and 154,000 men landed at Normandy Beach, located on the Northern coast of France. The liberation of France was completed at the cost of thousands of lives on August 25, 1944.

On the Russian (Eastern) front, after three years of the most violent fighting in the history of warfare, the Germans were on the verge of defeat by July, 1944. The Russian people fought with a determination never seen before. Of all the countries that would fight in World War II (57 in all) Russia would be the only country to recruit women to fight on the front lines. Russia's Red army impressed and terrified the Germans with their bravery and savagery, which they had never experienced before.

In the South Pacific, the Japanese had underestimated the resolve of the United States. From the beginning of the war, it was devastation, death, and more devastation and more death by the thousands as the Allies fought from island to island. President Roosevelt and his commanders had at last developed strategies called "island-hopping" to deal with the Japanese resistance. "Island-hopping" was a process whereby smaller and weaker islands were captured first, then used as bases to isolate and neutralize larger Japanese concentrations in the area. In doing so, by 1944 the Allies were ready to liberate the Philippines.

Due to the war, HOTEL SAGAMORE was doing a booming business like never before. No longer did Dad have to wait for payday to roll around, as the crowded bar, pool hall, and gambling room were continuously bustling with music and excitement 20 hours a day. Dad continued allotting part of every dollar the hotel earned towards paying off old debts from the days of the coal strike and Depression.

Bad news was beginning to hit many families as letters from the government informed them of loved ones either wounded or killed in service.

Many could not cope with the death of their loved one. Such was the case of Lena, who worked for us. Her grief broke my heart. Mother, also heartbroken, tried desperately to help her. She and Joe were desperately in love and wanted to marry. However, both families were feuding and would not hear of such a union. So, Joe enlisted in the service not knowing that Lena was pregnant. Lena had the baby and prayed for Joe to return one day and marry her. Unfortunately Joe was one of the first in Sagamore killed in the war.

Life came to an end for Lena that day. She worked as always, but never laughed, smiled or talked to anyone. With all of Mother's pleading, she till refused to eat a bite of food all day. However, she always carried a small flask in her dress pocket, which she sipped from during the day. Before long, it was obvious Lena had turned to drinking and was slowly becoming an alcoholic. Her life was short, as the alcohol took its toll. Then one day she at last found peace in death, feeling in her heart that she and Joe would be together in heaven.

Since the war began, the government encouraged everyone to grow a "VICTORY GARDEN" because food was in short supply for civilians. A "VICTORY GARDEN" was a trademark of real patriotism and everyone had one. Mother's "VICTORY GARDEN" was amazing. No one in town had a more productive one. She had what we called a green thumb and could grow things that no one would even attempt to grow, such as flowers and vegetables that were known to grow only in the South. She loved her garden and spent many hours there. You might say it was her "Lost Horizon" just as I had mine. One day Dad built a greenhouse for her, because she had such a passion for flowers. She was always generous with whatever her garden produced and flowers were always free to anyone who wanted them. Every fall she canned hundreds of jars of vegetables and made the best jellies ever from our native fruits. I guess you could say Mother had a "VICTORY GARDEN" all her life.

I cannot recall why I was not at baseball practice on July 12, 1944. Instead, I was working with Dad and Uncle John in the bar. It was close to five o'clock in the afternoon when a strange premonition enveloped me, and thoughts came flashing through my mind: "Eddie's been hurt. Eddie's been hurt bad. Oh God! Oh God! No! Oh no! He needs me!" "Dad, I've got to go. I've got to go right away!" I said, and ran out the side door headed for Ballground Hill. The heat was intense. By the time I reached my "Lost Horizon" my clothes were soaked through. It is hard to explain the intensity of what was happening. A sure certainty that Eddie was wounded and wounded bad was in my being. I knew it. I could feel it like it was happening to me. I prayed and prayed, but felt just prayers were not good enough. He needed more. He needed strength. He was losing it and losing it fast. "OH GOD, he needs strength, OH GOD, he needs strength. What can I do? I've got to send him mine." I prayed. I knelt with eyes closed, holding the cross of Jesus. While deep in meditation, I tried to pull the strength from my own body in an effort to send it to Eddie by way of a spiritual power greater than I. I do not know how long I remained in this meditated trance, but I could feel my body growing weaker and weaker and weaker until I fell unconscious to the ground. When I became conscious again, I began to cry like a child, saying over and over again, "Eddie, you've got to make it. Eddie, you've got to make. You can make it, Eddie. Take my strength. Oh God, let my strength reach him."

Night was falling when I returned home, but I told no one of my premonition.

Weeks later, for a second time the government letter came saying, "We regret to inform you that in the loyal service of his country, your son Edward J. Kovalchick was wounded on July 12, 1944. Yes, I already knew. Eddie was wounded north of Rome, three miles south of Leghorn, Italy. After nine close encounters with death, Eddie's luck had ran out when an 88mm mortar shell exploded eight feet away from him, and 238 pieces of fragmentation penetrated his body. His condition was classified as critical, but he was alive, much to the surprise of the hospital doctors and nurses.

We continuously worried and prayed as July passed into August and September. We learned that he was in the 5th Army General Hospital in Rome. Occasionally a letter written by a hospital volunteer came informing us of his slow progress. The fact that they were not written by Eddie led us to believe that he was seriously wounded. We felt helpless with him overseas, thousands of miles away.

In our effort to handle the stress and anxiety, we kept busy, working harder, practicing more, and the team played ball like never before, like they too felt the tension and anxiety, for everyone loved Eddie.

In one way or another everyone was effected as the war raged through-out the entire South Pacific and Europe. Death and destruction dominated every radio broadcasting station and newspaper headline of the day. We felt that our sacrifices were small in comparison to those of our brave soldiers. Outwardly, we responded with joy as the tide slowly turned in favor of the Allies. Inwardly, we prayed continuously for our fighting soldiers, and prayed and grieved for our dead and wounded.

When at last Eddie was removed from the critical list, doctors and nurses called it a miracle. One day, his doctor told him that only his youth – he was only 20 – saved his life, and that an older soldier's body could not have withstood such a traumatic impact of an 88-mm mortar shell explosion at such a close range. And, Eddie being himself as always, responded, "No, doctor, I'm alive because I've got God on my side and He's not ready for me yet." Five months would pass before doctors felt he could be moved to the hospital in Naples for rehabilitation.

As for Dad's brothers serving in the war, when the war began with the bombing of Pearl Harbor on December 7, 1941. Dad's brothers – Nick 35, Mike 27, and 21 year old twins George and Andy – owned and managed the Kovalchick Salvage Company. During the war their company furnished the government thousands of tons of scrap metals that were recycled for the manufacturing of warfare equipment for the armed forces.

George was called to service, but was refused for health reasons. However, Andy was inducted June 16, 1944, and was awarded two bronze medals while serving under General MacArthur in the

South Pacific. Following Japan's surrender on September 2, 1945, he was one of the first American soldiers to set foot on Japanese soil.

Back during the '30s Dad had added a two-story addition to the right side of the hotel. The bottom section intended for a grocery store never materialized, and from time to time it was used for various functions. Since the war began it was empty, so in or about the summer of 1944 Dad installed a juke box along with chairs and a snack bar, turning it into a teenage dance hall. He thought it would keep the teenagers off the streets and out of trouble.

The management of the hall was turned over to me to run as if I owned it, just as Johnny was in full charge of the gambling and pool hall. My first thought was to enforce strict rules and regulations. No smoking, drinking, profanity or unruly behavior was allowed and everyone was advised of the rules.

There was no charge, except the cost of the juke box that played a record for a nickel. When the teenagers were out of money or appeared to be, I kept the music going until 11 o'clock closing time.

All was going fine until one night in September. Everyone was talking about General MacArthur's fighting in the South Pacific when a soldier on leave entered the hall with a bottle of beer. A hush fell over the crowd and everyone looked towards me. After all, I made the rules, now I was being tested. "This is a teenage dance hall and no drinks, smoking or profanity are allowed," I said. He responded by lighting up a cigarette, and offering them to several of the teenagers. Again I asked him to leave. He then responded with profanity. I could read the minds of the crowd as things were getting tense. I reached for his collar, and pushed him out the door. Then all H——— broke loose, as they say, as a real fist fight ensued. Having learned to box at the age of seven, I began to draw on the knowledge I'd learned, and was holding my own, until the soldier got in a blow to my vulnerable right eye. I decided to call on Dad, who was working in the bar. "It's your fight, not mine," he said. "You're running the place, not me." As I left the bar, there was brother Johnny taking up the fight where I left off. Someone had informed him of the fight and he came running, and surprised me with his ability to handle himself in a fight. He was great and I felt real proud of him. School started the following Monday, and the dance hall was closed.

Months later a letter of apology came from the soldier with whom the incident occurred. I appreciated it, however I had forgiven him a long time before, knowing that he was drinking and everyone during that time was tense.

That fall, at the cost of millions of lives, the Allied forces were succeeding on all fronts. At last the war picture was taking a positive direction.

In October, we cheered when General MacArthur announced, "PEOPLE OF THE PHILIPPINES, I HAVE RETURNED." As the United States Sixth Army landed on the island of Leyte.

The beaten German army had retreated from Russia, and the Russians were advancing on Germany itself.

On the Italian front the Allied troops were advancing towards northern Italy. And, now that France was in the hands of the Allies, Germany was being bombed continually. It looked like it was only a matter of time before Germany would be defeated.

Again the country rejoiced when history was made with the re-election of President Franklin D. Roosevelt for a fourth term on November 7, and Harry S. Truman was elected Vice President.

Then an unexpected surprise came in the mail – a letter from Tim Dewicked saying he was with the army fighting in Germany. Four year had passed since he left Sagamore and I had forgotten him. Now the memories of him came rushing back. I recalled his mean streak and thought about how cruel he could be. "I'D HATE TO BE AN ENEMY IN HIS PATH," I thought. His letter talked about the sure victory of the Allies and of the horrors he had witnessed. Again, I recalled his own nature. "LIKE CALLING THE POT BLACK," I thought.

Then he wrote about coming home when the war was over, and that he was planning on our getting married. Again, just as four years before, I said out loud as I read those words, "OVER MY DEAD BODY." Then, I tore the letter into pieces. Yet I knew that one day there would be a showdown between the two of us.

Our first snowflakes fell on Thanksgiving Day that year and everyone was predicting a cold winter. However, no one foresaw the influenza and pneumonia that would plague us all winter.

As Christmas was approaching, Mother worked many hours baking her traditional Czechoslovakian nut and poppyseed rolls. And, as always, much to her disapproval, Dad traded them out for Mr. Sottile's homemade Italian wine and Mr. Bryan's Syrian baklava. Then, realizing we would not have enough left for Christmas, she and I hurriedly baked another batch at one o'clock in the morning.

Mother decided for the first time ever that our Christmas tree should be in the living room on the second floor, as it seemed more appropriate there than in the kitchen. I volunteered to cut a tree from Grandma Kovalchick's tree farm just outside of town, and with Johnny's help, we cut down a beautiful Spruce, then tied it to our big sled and pulled it home.

The bar was buzzing with excitement over the holidays with all the service people home on leave. They brought excitement and laughter to the older coal miners, whose lives were dark and dreary otherwise, and they loved and admired their men in uniform. Each had their exciting war and boot camp stories to tell, besides hundreds of the funniest jokes. Best of all was when the singing broke out. The miners would stomp their feet and clap their hands to the Marines' Hymn, "From the halls of Montezuma, to the shores of

Tripoli," The Caissons Go Rolling Along, "Over hill, over dale, we have hit the dusty trail". Anchors Aweigh "Anchors Aweigh, my boy, Anchors Aweigh;" The Army Air Corps' "Off we go into the wild blue yonder," and many more were sung way into the night.

December 31 was my 19th birthday and once again there was no cake or birthday party. "OH, WELL," I thought, "NOW THAT I'M 19, IT DOESN'T MATTER."

However, shortly before Christmas, a birthday gift arrived by way of a letter from Italy. After five months in the 5th Army General Hospital in Rome, Italy, Eddie was transferred to the army hospital in Naples to undergo rehabilitation. That was the best news we had received since he was seriously wounded on July 12.

This Certificate Presented by

THE NATIONAL BASEBALL HALL OF FAME

to

DOROTHY KOVALCHICK

In recognition of her outstanding contribution to women's baseball as a member of the All-American Girls Professional Baseball League. The league was in existence for the period of 1943–1954.

Donald C. Marr, Jr.
President

November 5, 1998

CHAPTER XIII
THE YEARS 1945 – 1946

By January 1945 no family seemed untouched by influenza or pneumonia, including ours. Only days following my 19th birthday, both Mother and Dad came down with pneumonia. I felt a deep sense of dedication to carry on the daily 24-hour task of managing our 62-room hotel until their recovery. I knew I could do it with Johnny managing the gambling and pool hall after school. Also, there was Joe Reno, the barber, our bartender, the upstairs maid and Nicholas to help me.

For days the temperature hovered near zero degrees. The hotel's huge coal furnace burned day and night. Our bartender and I kept it burning during the day, and Johnny slept on a cot in the furnace room and kept it burning all night. Soon we were running out of coal and there was no one available to replenish the coal bin. Realizing that time was running out, in desperation I headed for our pickup truck and Mr. Kimmells's coal mine located just outside of town. As I climbed the steps to his porch, the bone-chilling wind whipped against my face and penetrated my clothing. The door opened and I quickly stepped inside. "Mr. Kimmell, I'm Bounce Kovalchick's daughter Dorothy, and I've come to buy a load of coal for the hotel. We're just about out," I said. "Do you have anyone with you?" he asked. "No," I replied. "Well," he said, "I can't cut and load the coal myself. I've got to have another man to help me." "There's no one available right now, and I've got to have the coal," I pleaded. "Mr. Kimmell, I can help you mine and load it up." But he was unyielding and so was I. We debated the issue back and forth with neither of us relenting. "Mr. Kimmell, I'm not going home without any coal and I mean it. I can help you. I know I can. Just give me a chance. I'm strong and I know I can do it. Just show me what to do. I've got to have the coal."

Finally, he agreed to give it a try, and we headed for the shanty, where we put carbide lamps on our heads. Then, we loaded picks, shovels and dynamite in a coal car and headed into the shaft, pushing the coal car on the track ahead. When we reached the heading, we drilled holes in the coal vein, filling them with dynamite. Then ran for cover behind the coal car as the blast went off and crumbled coal fell to the dirt floor. After the dust had settled, he yelled, "O.K., let's go." I took up my shovel and matched him shovel for shovel as we loaded the car, then pushed it out and unloaded it on the pickup bed. We continued until the bed could hold no more. Returning to the shanty, we stored our picks, shovels and carbide lamps in their usual place.

"I sure would like to see you marry my son Ralph," he said. "It would be a great pleasure to have you for a daughter-in-law." I didn't tell him that I was already very fond of his son, who was in the Army. "Well, we shall see," I replied, then thanked him and headed home with my pickup load of coal. I repeated the experience several more times that winter, and each time thanked God for Mr. Kimmell.

Managing the hotel proved to be a greater responsibility than I had imagined. After weeks of hard work and stress, my body cried out, "No more. I want sleep and rest," and I fell to the floor from exhaustion.

Dr. Debutcher, the town's doctor, administered a sedative from which I awoke after 36 hours. While recovering, I thought about our service people. When and how did they get sleep or rest while being bombarded day and night as they huddled trapped in their miserable foxholes? No matter how brave they were I knew they had to feel fear and anxiety. Luckily they had God to sustain them, I thought.

This experience gave me an understanding for coping with Eddie's erratic behavior, called shell shock, when he returned from the war.

Happily, my burden of managing the hotel came to an end by the end of February as Mother and Dad slowly recovered from their bout with pneumonia.

World War II was rightly named. Every day our newspapers and radios blared out good and bad news from every corner of the globe. Because we had no TVs, our imaginations played havoc with our emotions as we envisioned their horrific stories of death and destruction. However, there was no doubt in out hearts that soon we would be victorious. The tide had turned because man's love for freedom throughout the world was a dynamic force that could not and would not be defeated.

By March, the Allies were fighting on German soil, on both the Eastern and Western fronts. Premier Stalin of the USSR, Prime Minister Winston Churchill of England and President Franklin D. Roosevelt of the United States met at Yalta, USSR, and created a New World Order with each agreeing on how the conquered countries would be divided.

Our U.S. Marines made history when on March 16 they raised the American flag on Mount Suribachi, Iwo Jima, a small island in the South Pacific. Twenty six days of fierce fighting for this small island of only a few square miles of volcanic ash cost the Marines 20,000 casualties.

The Japanese resistance ended in Manila in the Philippines, and General MacArthur freed our prisoners, who looked like skeletons after suffering terribly in Japanese camps.

At last, we received long-awaited news. Brother Eddie, along with other soldiers who had been wounded, were returning to the states in March. However, Eddie would not be coming home until his discharge from the Army.

Also, in March a second letter came from Tim Dewicked, who was still in Germany and also due to come home soon. I knew that one day we would have a bad but decisive encounter between us, contrary to his plans to marry me, in my heart I knew with absolute certainty that I could not and would not marry our town's bully of years past. Again I destroyed the letter, and my mind turned to Eddie's coming home and baseball.

Baseball fever had set in and I hoped for an early thawing of the ice and snow. Again, like every season since the war began, Dad would reorganize our team. An exciting thought filled my mind: "Some of our old teammates will be coming home from the war and rejoining us. We're going to have a great team and a great year." This propelled me into a daily training program of calisthenics, weight lifting and 100 push-ups.

Also there was daily bunting practice. My skill at bunting was a valuable asset to the team, and I strove for perfection. Dad enjoyed the reaction of opposing teams when I bunted. When he'd say, "Nice going, Honey. You did great," I would feel like a million dollars. The thrill of placing a bunt exactly where Dad wanted it is a thrill hard to describe. There was the thrill of facing a pitcher who was the team's cream of the crop. He could be six feet tall, more or less, weighing 200 pounds or more, Walking up to the plate, I'd swing my regular Louisville slugger with the confidence of Lou Gehrig. Still swinging away, I'd step into the batter's box like I was going to hit the ball out of the ballpark. It was an act intended to throw the opposing team off guard. The opposing team would shift their positions. Outfielders came in a little, and infielders moved back a little. The pitcher stepped up to the mound, grim and determined looking. I could read his mind. It was the same with all the pitchers I ever faced. They were thinking, "Don't let this girl get a hit or they'll never let me live it down." Then the windup and the pitch, released by a powerful arm, and with the speed of lightning the baseball headed toward me. Simultaneously the grip on my bat changed to a relaxed choke hold along with my footing position which almost faced the pitcher. This dangerous-looking move always ignited the crowd with shock and excitement, fearing that the ball was going to hit me. Luckily in all my eight years of playing it never happened. I was off and running for first base the second my bat placed the ball where I wanted it. Then there was the thrill of beating the throw to first base, and if I succeeded, then other thrills followed like stealing base after base and sliding in head first if it was going to be close. I never could master the art of sliding in feet first. In my way of thinking, head first was faster, and the only way to go.

I never understood why Dad was always secretive about plans concerning me and my three brothers, or about problems that he should have shared with us. Even Mother was shut out from them. But, secrecy was an inherent part of his character that tormented him mentally in his latter years. Perhaps that characteristic was the reason that his brothers and sisters never understood him, nor realizing how relentlessly he secretly worked to open doors that paved the way for their ultimate successes in life. He also did the same for friends and a number of major and minor league ballplayers. Unbeknownst to them, Dad had paved the way for their success.

Two of Dad's secrets took me by surprise in April. The first happened the first week of April when I learned that Dad had taken Johnny to Washington, D.C., for a tryout with the Washington Senators and to meet with their owner, Clark Griffith.

The plan was that Johnny would join the Senators on a two-week pre-season exhibition tour, and upon their return he would be sent to one of their minor league teams as determined by the Senators manager.

Unfortunately, the team had left the day before their arrival. So, Clark Griffith sent Johnny to Lewisburg, Pennsylvania, where their Williamsburg, Pennsylvania, minor league team had begun spring training. Again, misfortune befell Johnny. Most of the rookie players were Cubans who were very eager and determined to sign contracts with the Senators. Their determination initiated a conspiracy against the other rookie players, and Johnny's chances for signing a contract with the Williamsburg minor league team was greatly hindered because the Cuban catchers continually told the Cuban batters what pitch Johnny was going to pitch.

Disappointed and discouraged by the Cubans' betrayal, he decided to leave Lewisburg after being hit by a wild pitch.

He hitchhiked to Olean, New York, as he heard they had an independent team in the Pony League. Olean signed him to a contract the following day.

The realization that Johnny would not be with our team for the season saddened me. I thought our team would never be the same without him. He was our best pitcher and carried us to victory after victory. "Brother Eddie is gone, and now Johnny," I thought, and in the privacy of my bedroom I cried.

On April 12 our shocked nation mourned the unexpected death of 63-year-old President Franklin D. Roosevelt, who passed away at 3:55 P.M., two hours after suffering a cerebral hemorrhage. Vice President Harry S. Truman was on Capitol Hill when the President died, and was sworn in as the 33rd President of the United States.

Then on April 18 the nation mourned the death of the nation's most loved war correspondent, Ernie Pyle, who at age 44 lost his life in the thick of action, elbow to elbow with G.I.'s on Iwo Jima in the South Pacific.

Eight thousand Allied troops were the first to break into Germany from the West when they crossed the River Rhine on March 7. However, the Soviets were the first to enter Berlin, when on April 21 the first Soviet tank entered the city. As the Red Army advanced through the ravaged streets of Berlin, thousands of German soldiers surrendered. Hitler became enraged. On April 29 he married his mistress, Eva Braun, and named Admiral Karl Dönitz as his successor. Then, Hitler shot himself and his wife took poison. Their bodies were burned in what was left of the Reichschancellery.

In the last week of April Dad and I traveled by train from Pittsburgh to Chicago. I assumed he was going on business as he frequently did, and I was going along for company. I did not suspect his real reason, even when he said, "Be sure and pack your baseball gloves." We often took them with us in case we got an opportunity to practice. Also, when I signed a contract I assumed that I was signing as a witness to a business agreement that Dad was making.

Not until the day before he returned to Pittsburgh did I learn the real purpose of our trip. I was shocked when he revealed that the contract I had signed was with a girls league called the All American Girls Professional Baseball League (AAGPBL) for $75 per week, which he thought was very good, and that after having played four seasons in men's baseball, playing in a girls league would be a piece of cake. I felt angry because I was not consulted before making such an important decision concerning my baseball career. It was beyond my understanding. Also, I was not aware that such a league existed.

Speechless, I listened as he enthusiastically talked about the girls league, which was in existence since 1943. He was confident that I had much to give and would be an asset to the league. Then, as all caring fathers do, he lectured me with fatherly advice. I was touched by his concern for my safety, like fathers do when their daughters leave home for the first time. "I'll write you when I get home." He said with tears in his eyes, and seeing his tears, all the hurt and anger disappeared. I reached up and put my arms around him and he did the same. I knew he was proud and happy for me, but deep within there was a sadness. I slept very little that night, but prayed a lot because I did not want to disappoint him.

The morning after he returned to Pittsburgh, I was driven to a beautiful park on Lake Michigan where the AAGPBL teams were already in spring training. I watched in awe at the sight of approximately 100 girls in uniforms of short pastel colored dresses, baseball spikes with knee socks and caps to match.

A feeling of intimidation came over me because I had never seen a game of softball back home in Pennsylvania, and had no knowledge that there was such a game. The ball was 11 ½ inches in circumference, and I had played only with a 9 ½-inch ball. The girls were pitching sidearm and underhand, and I had only faced overhand pitching. The diamond was smaller than those I had played on. I soon learned that the girls were the best softball players in all of the U.S. and Canada, and that some had played sandlot baseball at one time or another. The game had been modified and was neither softball as it was being played at that time, nor was it baseball as it was being played by men. However, the plan was that the game would be modified continuously and would eventually be played like men's baseball.

Directly, a man approached and asked if I might be Dottie Kovalchick, and I replied that I was. He politely welcomed me, then introduced me to a chaperone who briefed me on the rules and regulations of the league. Following her briefing, I joined the girls in practice, feeling bewildered by all that was happening so fast. After practice I was issued a pastel cranberry-colored Fort Wayne Daisies uniform.

The following day, my manager Bill Wambsganss, who we called Wamby, asked me to catch behind home plate. In all honesty I replied that I had never played any positions except first base and right field. "You're too short," he replied. "I'm very good on first base, Mr. Wamby. I wish you'd try me," I said. I thought about the newspaper write-ups back home that lauded my ability and showmanship for playing first, even though I was only 5 foot 2 inches tall and weighed 125 pounds. I felt confident and therefore determined, so again I asked for just one chance to show him how capable I could handle the position. But in an absolute voice he replied, "You will play third base and center field." I said no more, but was very disappointed.

On the third day, after hitting away a few times during batting practice, I said, "Mr. Wamby, I'm very good at bunting. Would you want me to bunt a few?" "Fans want to see home runs, not bunts," he replied. Again, I was disappointed, and thereafter said no more. However, I thought about Dad, who gave every player the opportunity to try any position they chose, because they were most productive when they realized their most adaptable position.

At the close of spring training our six-team league was divided into three sets of two teams each for the purpose of entertaining all the Army camps and hospitals in several states with two weeks of exhibition games. The Fort Wayne Daisies were paired with the Grand Rapids Chicks. It was a stroke of luck for me because while traveling together by train, I became friends with Connie Wisniewski, who was a Grand Rapids Chick pitcher. Connie was known as "Iron Women" and "Polish Rifle." She was five feet, eight inches tall and weighed 147 pounds. During her eight-year career with the league she was a five-time All-Star and in 1945 she was Player of the Year.

Following our first exhibition game she asked, "Where'd you learn to throw a ball like that?" I replied, "Back in Sagamore, Pennsylvania. I played baseball on a men's team." "I'm Connie Wisniewski," she said. "I pitch for the Chicks. You got a powerful arm. I sure wish you played for us." "Thank you," I replied. "We have a Polish family in Sagamore by the name of Wisniewski. You must be Polish. I'm Czechoslovakian. My name is Dorothy

Kovalchick. Everyone calls me Dottie. I'm a rookie." "That's O.K.," she said. "I was a rookie too." From then on we were friends.

Our tour was filled with excitement and the best hospitality ever. Following our games, we were treated to chow in the mess hall. One day someone circulated the rumor that we were served by German prisoners. Hearing the rumor provoked me to anger. I thought about brother Eddie being wounded and how terribly he suffered. My anger mounted as I thought about the horrible stories we heard about D-Day, the Battle of Normandy and the Battle of the Bulge. Then, I noticed a tall German-looking soldier standing by a trash receptacle, collecting and emptying trays. I felt certain he was a German prisoner. As I approached him carrying my tray, I angrily glared intensely with my meanest look possible. "He's got to know how angry I am," I thought as I rudely handed him my tray. After leaving the mess hall, the thought occurred to me, "Oh my gosh, maybe he wasn't a German prisoner after all." Suddenly, I felt embarrassed and ashamed because I loved and appreciated our men in uniform. Unfortunately, I never learned the truth and neither did any of the girls as we left the camp immediately following our meal.

We were treated to a dance following one of our afternoon exhibition games. After the rigorous demands of our tour, we were ready for a night of dancing. The music was the best I'd ever heard, and the girls never missed a dance – that is except me. No one asked me to dance and I was disappointed. But at last a soldier came forward and asked me to dance. I realized why I was a wallflower the moment he said, "I asked you to dance because you remind me of my sister. She wears pigtails too." I had forgotten to comb out my pigtails and was the only girl wearing them. I'm sure the soldiers thought I was just a kid, and there I was 19 years old wearing pigtails to a dance.

During our exhibition tour, I rarely played in a game, but did get a lot of practice. After having played four years as a regular in men's baseball and with teammates who went on to play in the major and minor leagues, I felt it was a waste, sitting on the bench envisioning myself in every play on the field.

However, after the season officially opened, I played third base or center field in a number of games in which I did very well and had no errors. I have since learned that some records were lost from the early years of the league before 1946. Unfortunately, my records were among them.

Many important events of May 1945 are forever recorded in history. The most significant – the surrender of Germany. On May 7 German representatives at Reims signed a document providing for unconditional surrender, and on May 8 the heads of the three German armed services signed a similar instrument in Berlin that officially proclaimed May 8 V-E Day.

There are no words adequate enough to describe the feeling that enveloped me. "Now Johnny won't have to go to war," I thought. I prayerfully thanked God, knowing that only through him winning the war was possible.

Oh, how exhilarating was the taste of victory as the Allies celebrated their hard-won victory with jubilation, whooping it up in Times Square, patriotic victory parades and tears of joy and prayers of thanks to God that at last World War II was over in Europe.

Now an all-out effort was directed towards the defeat of Japan, our one remaining war front.

But, with all the happiness and celebrations of victory, the Allies were faced with the worst horror of the war, the Buchenwald and Dachau death camps. Many of our G.I.s could not bear to look at the Nazi legacy – the fate of six million Jews, brutalized, beaten, starved, worked to death, and after being gassed in gas chambers, the lifeless bodies were stacked in ovens. Those still living were so emaciated they were hovering near death. Their eyes were so sunken that they could hardly see, and their hands were too weak to turn the page of a book. Volumes can be written on the terrible atrocities of World War II. It was as though mankind had turned into animals.

The week following the surrender of Germany, Johnny, seriously ill with influenza, returned home from playing minor league ball for Olean, New York. For weeks Mother, nursed him back to health, after which he returned to playing on Dad's team – the Kovalchicks.

Johnny was a senior when he left school in April to play minor league ball. Based on his excellent grades, he received permission to by-pass his final exams and received his high school diploma on graduation day.

I looked forward to Mother's weekly newsy letter about our baseball team and other happenings going on back home. But, none were as exciting as the day she wrote that Eddie was being discharged from the Army on June 15 and was coming home at last. I felt a peace and joy like no other, and gave thanks to God. After praying two long anxious years for Eddie's safe return from the war, he was coming home at last. Sadly, on that joyous day I could not be there.

After two months with the All-American Girls Professional Baseball League I made a decision as to what direction I wanted to go with my baseball career. This time it would be my decision, not Dad's. Even though I would miss the girls and all the friends I had made, I decided to leave the league. I wanted to return to playing baseball on a men's team, and Dad accepted my decision. I was released with the agreement that I could return to the league at any time I desired.

At the train depot, everything seemed all right. I was making the right decision, I thought. Then, a sadness came over me and tears filled my eyes. "Maybe I should stay. I'm no quitter," I thought.

This was overruled by the thoughts of what awaited me back home in Pennsylvania.

After two years I would be seeing my brother Eddie again. I had to see him. He was only 19 when he left for the army and weighed only 118 pounds. Everyone loved Eddie. He was so handsome and gentle-natured. When we were growing up, he always fainted at the sight of blood and here he was back home. Now, he was a man of 21 with two Purple Hearts and an Oak Leaf Cluster, earned in the service of his country, and I was very proud of him.

I boarded the train, and as it pulled away from the depot, the tears fell. Wiping away the tears, I promised myself that I would not look back, only forward to barnstorming on Dad's all-male baseball team, the KOVALCHICKS.

As the train slowly pulled into the Pittsburgh depot, Dad and Eddie were standing on the depot platform eagerly looking at the coach windows as they slowly went by. I pressed against my window, waving in the hopes that they would see me. I cannot describe the excitement of the moment. I noted how thin Eddie was. His face was gaunt, yet his good looks could not be denied. When the train came to a halt, they saw me, and within minutes we were embracing and I was crying. It was a moment never to be forgotten.

I soon learned that Eddie was a victim of one of the most terrible aftermaths of war, known as shell shock. In a sense, he was the same happy-go-lucky Eddie, yet he was different. He learned to drink, smoke, and chew snuff in the service, and his attitude towards life was disturbing. His philosophy was that he was going to live for each day because he may be gone the next. Which meant that he would live life recklessly and with abandon. This attitude, however, was experienced by many families when their loved ones returned from the war. It would bring Mother and Dad much mental anguish, because they felt so helpless and were so concerned, expecting him to immediately return to being the same Eddie that went off to war. Little did they realize that it would never be the same Eddie, and that for the rest of his life he would be plagued by the shrapnel pieces still embedded in his body. X-rays revealed that he had more than 100 shrapnel pieces in his body at the time of his army discharge and was given a disability classification.

Eddie would wreck two vehicles his first year home, which put him in the hospital with cuts and bruises, but no broken bones. He frequented all the drinking establishments for miles around and spent money recklessly, even burning paper money of all denominations as he jested about life.

My welcome at home was as if I, too, was a soldier returning from the war. I never saw Mother so happy. For the first time in two years the entire family was together.

I had hardly caught my breath when I rejoined Dad's team, the KOVALCHICKS and spent hours practicing on the ball field. The team was having a good year, and there was a renewed spirit in all of us.

I cannot say that we won every game, but I do attest to the fact that the opposing team had to play mighty good ball to beat us.

In reviewing some of the tough games we did lose, I recall the game we played before I left for Chicago in April. It was a battle like no other. It was a hard-fought game driven by revenge that began in the fall of 1944, when we defeated the Punxsutawney All-Stars by a score of 6 to 3. It was a crushing blow to the All-Stars, because they were defeated by a team with a girl playing at first base. They wanted revenge and engaged us to open the 1945 baseball season. Punxsutawney is renowned nationally for its annual Groundhog Day, when the groundhog named Punxsutawney Phil comes out of his winter hibernation hole and predicts the end of winter or six more weeks of winter based upon whether or not he sees his shadow.

Preparing for their revenge game, Punxsutawney solicited the best of the best, and found it in a newcomer to the mound, George Carlson, and a second pitcher named Bruno. They held us to six hits and defeated us by a score of 12 to 1. Dad brought in the only run. The loss was a crushing blow to us, because we played so hard to accomplish so little.

Another team determined to beat us at all cost was the DuBois Vulcans, reputed as being the best in the area. With their reputation at stake, they could not afford to be defeated by us. They also solicited the best of the best, and found it in pitcher Laborde. It was entirely a pitchers' duel between our pitcher, Ashman, and their pitcher, Laborde. Only five hits were given up in the entire game; DuBois got two and we garnered three.

I believe DuBois and Punxsutawney were the two hardest-fought games we ever played and lost.

Some losses were truly heartbreakers. Like the time we played Ford City. Our pitcher, Roman, struck out 21 men and we still lost the game 4 to 2.

That same day, we drove 40 miles to play Clymer and lost to them 7 to 4 after outhitting them.

Even after suffering those hard-fought losses, people called us an unbeatable team, and no one could say we did not thrill the crowd.

It is only natural everyone is determined to beat the best in any sport, and to beat us was every team's goal. Therefore, we had to play harder to sustain the reputation we worked so hard to achieve.

I always felt that my being a girl added pressure on the men. At that time in history, no team wanted the stigma of having lost to us. However, the tougher the competition, the harder we played and the more we enjoyed it.

There were overflowing crowds of spectators everywhere we played because so many boys were returning from the European theatre since the surrender of Germany and Italy. We were proud to see their uniforms throughout the crowd. They demonstrated more excitement than the civilians with their yelling and cheering. They wanted us to win, thinking we were the underdogs with a girl on the team. They were unaware it was my fifth year playing the game. Their loyalty inspired us to play even harder to give them a great game. It was our way of saying 'thank you' for fighting for our country and freedom.

I believe that our game with Adrian July 15, 1945, was the turning point in my baseball career.

I made first base on a safe hit, then stole second, third and home. This feat caused quite a stir. Reporters lauded it in the newspapers as quite a feat for a 19-year-old pigtailed girl, playing men's baseball on a 90-foot regulation ball diamond, and whose uniform was none other than a peasant blouse, tennis shorts, ball cap and spiked baseball shoes.

Newspaper articles called us the colorful KOVALCHICKS. Our lineup changed often. It could be made up of two fathers, five sons, older players, very young players, very tall and very short players, one Black man and woman. Everyone thought we were quite a novelty, and we were.

Following the Adrian news article, reporters representing the Pittsburgh Sun Telegraph and the Pittsburgh Press arrived in Sagamore to do their own news story. Within weeks pictures and write-ups were circulated throughout the United States and even the Stars and Stripes newspaper in the world.

Fan mail began to arrive from everywhere. Fans expressed the kindest and most encouraging comments about my playing baseball with men. I was flabbergasted by the number of marriage proposals that were offered from men I did not know. I concluded it was just fascination with a novelty. I kept all correspondence with fans on a friendly basis.

At age 19, I had never dated because my baseball career took precedence. I decided I would not date until I was 21, nor would I marry until age 25. I often joked about that, saying that the first man who came knocking on my door with a proposal of marriage on my 25th birthday, I would marry him. And I did exactly that.

There was one especially persistent fan, and two others who corresponded until they realized I wasn't interested. Joe Davis was one of them. I will write about him later.

The press coverage initiated many requests from cities in states other than Pennsylvania who wanted to schedule games with us. Dad decided against it, because we were already scheduled a year in advance with more and more doubleheaders scheduled to accommodate the demand.

In August, concern about the war with Japan was at an all-time high. It was only a matter of time until we would be fighting on Japanese soil, which meant that thousands more of our men would be killed. We prayed daily for some miracle to bring the war to an end. That miracle did come by way of an atomic bomb – the most powerful weapon ever created by man.

After much mental anguish and deliberation, President Harry S. Truman made the decision to release the bomb over the city of Hiroshima, Japan, in an effort to bring the war to a final end. The 20,000-ton bomb was dropped on Hiroshima August 6, 1945, by a B-29 bomber, the Enola Gay, killing 78,000 people and injuring another 78,000. However, Japan did not surrender. Another bomb was dropped three days later on the city of Nagasaki, killing 26,000 and injuring more than 40,000. Only then, on August 14, did the Japanese Emperor Hirohito address the Japanese people. He indicated that the war was not necessarily going to their advantage. It was as close as the Emperor got to admitting defeat. However, on September 2, 1945, aboard the battleship Missouri, two Japanese officials surrendered to Allied forces led by General Douglas MacArthur, thus ending the worst war the world had ever seen.

As the war came to an end, two superpowers dominated the globe – the United States and the Soviet Union. More than six million Russian soldiers were killed and 14 million were wounded. If civilian deaths were counted, the Soviet Union lost some 20 to 30 million lives. With the exception of one attack by a Japanese seaplane, no bombs fell on the continental United States. There were 16 million American service people in uniform in World War II. Of these, more than 400,000 were killed and a half million were wounded.

As a result of the war thousands of factories sprang up almost overnight. Hundreds of fortunes were made and today America has a standard of living rivaled by no one on the planet.

When the final announcement was made that Japan had surrendered and that World War II had ended, the atmosphere in our bar was a circus. The crowd of servicemen and civilians, overwhelmed with emotion, went wild. There was dancing, laughing, singing, drinking, crying, smoking and cursing, and adding to all the noise was the juke box playing as loud as the volume allowed. For several days the bar did not close because the crowd would not disburse. Each servicemen had stories to tell of his experiences in the war. The stories went on and on into the night.

Soon the servicemen were coming home more rapidly and were anxious to begin again. They talked about going to school under the G.I. bill, which paid for their education. Many had learned new skills in the service and planned to pursue jobs using those skills. Very few desired to become miners, as their fathers were. And then there were those who could not adjust. The war had done something to their outlook on life. Their adjustment would take longer, even years.

For a town so small, Sagamore was indeed a proud, patriotic town. There were 255 men and women who served in the war. Of these 10 lost their lives in the service of their country.

The rationing of shoes, tires and most foods had ended. A demand for public housing and more jobs began. President Truman ordered full resumption of consumer production, free markets and collective bargaining at last.

It was no surprise, when in late September, like a ghost from out of the past, I came face to face with Tim Dewicked in the lobby of our hotel. Years had past since I last saw him. He looked handsome dressed in his Army uniform, and he still had that same mischievous grin.

"Hello, Honey," he said. "I told you I'd be back." I resented his calling me Honey. Only Mother, Dad and my three brothers ever called me Honey. He wasted no time before turning on the charm. It was obvious he was no amateur at it. He said he had come on behalf of his mother, who wanted me to come for dinner. I refused with a polite, "Thank you, but I work nights with my Dad and I am really very busy." He persisted, following me halfway up the stairway. I realized he wasn't accepting no for an answer. I turned and looking directly at him, I said, "Tim, I am not interested in going anywhere with you. Besides with your reputation, my parents would never allow it." I saw the anger in his eyes. Without another word, he walked down the stairs, across the lobby and out the front door.

For weeks he constantly followed me, trying to convince me that he no longer was that wild kid of the past, but instead a man seriously wanting to marry me, if only I would give him a chance. Firmly, with resolve, I explained that we could never be anything more than casual friends. He was not convinced and became more determined.

Then one day after closing the bar with Dad about two a.m., I found him waiting in my bedroom suite. "What right do you have being in this room?" "How did you get in? The door was locked," I asked. He did not respond to my questions. Instead he replied, "Get some clothes together. We're going to get married." In a firm, decisive voice I said "I'm not going anywhere with you, Tim."

Suddenly, he grasped my arms with a tactic I am sure he had learned in the service, then hurriedly carried me to my bedroom. His intentions were obvious. This ignited an anger in me that generated unbelievable strength. My yelling brought Mother running. She pounded furiously on my door, causing Tim to loosen his grip, which allowed me the opportunity to run and unlock the door. With little success Tim tried hiding under the bed. Mother pulled his half-emerged body out, and began beating upon his back. When he succeeded in breaking away, he went running down the hall and out the back door.

His second attempt followed a week later. One morning about three o'clock there was a thumping sound on my second story windowsill. The steady thumping sound slowly brought me out of my deep sleep. I jumped out of bed and headed for the window to investigate the cause of the thumping. There was Tim, climbing up a two-story ladder that was anchored against my windowsill. He had carried the ladder from the other side of the hotel where it was temporarily being stored by painters who were in the process of painting our four-story hotel.

I immediately grabbed for my bathrobe and left the room, locking the door behind me. I hurried across the hall and entered room No. 8, as it was vacant. Safely inside, I locked the inside latch, then crawled into bed and went back to sleep. A long time afterwards, I could hear Tim returning the huge two-story ladder to its storage place.

The next morning, I entered my bedroom to find it in shambles from pictures to furniture. It angered him when he found my bed empty, but still warm, knowing that I had just left it. Destroying my bedroom was his way of getting his revenge. Because of the incident with Mother and him the week before, I said nothing to her.

However, the following night his anger continued when he threw huge rocks against the hotel beneath my second-story window. Observing the rocks the following morning, I could not imagine anyone strong enough to throw such huge rocks. Still feeling confident that I could handle the situation on my own, I said nothing to Mother or Dad.

Then, a week later, there was a knock on my door. Thinking it was Mother, I unlocked the door before realizing it was Tim. He had climbed the hotel fire escape that serviced the front of the hotel, then walked the full length of the hotel's flat roof to the fire escape that serviced the back of the hotel. There he entered by way of a window that he had unlocked during the day. Again, he demanded that I go with him, threatening to kill Mother and Dad if I refused. "I'll go with you," I said. "But let me get some clothes," and I opened the door. There stood Mother. Quickly Tim said "Mrs. Kovalchick, I'm going to marry your daughter. We're leaving tonight." Mother replied, "She is going nowhere with you, and I've called the police. You better leave right now." "Let her decide," he said as he tightly held on to my arm. I answered, "Tim, I'm not going with you without my parents' consent." He stood there as if in shock. Then, walking past Mother, he turned down the hall to the back stairway, and exited by unlocking the back door.

However, he still had one more trick up his sleeve. I learned of it from one of our ballplayer. Tim was spreading the lie around town that I was pregnant by him. "Well," I calmly said, "Let's just wait nine months and see this miracle virgin birth." We both laughed.

The next day, I was wrapping nickels from the nickelodeon. The owner of the machine was unable to come often enough to remove them. Therefore, when the coin box was full, we removed the coins, rolled them, recorded the amount, and divided both his and our share. I was proud of his trust, and was all the more careful not to do him out of one nickel.

While rolling the coins, I heard the shuffling of footsteps enter the lobby, and head toward my office door. I looked up as it opened, my eyes not believing what I was seeing. There stood several of our ballplayers. In their midst stood Eddie Arthur, so covered with blood he was hardly recognizable. Stunned, I rushed toward him yelling, "What happened. Oh my gosh, Eddie, what happened?" "I got him for you," he said. "Got who," I said. "What on earth happened to you, Eddie?" I could not believe the story that evolved, nor the loyalty of this friend. He had confronted Tim with a challenge. He must retract the lie and apologize to me and to those he had told. It was common knowledge that no one challenged Tim without a knock down, dragg out fight.

The results of that fight was standing before me. My heart hurt for him. It was so sad. He refused to allow me to wash the blood from his head and face and hands. His swollen lip painfully made a small smile. Again, he said, "I got him for you." I cannot describe the hurt I felt for him. He looked so terrible. I thanked him, then kissed him on his bloody cheek.

With no further conversation, they turned and left. Why I never saw him again, I do not know, except I was sure that Tim, at some time during that fight, had threatened to kill him. Perhaps Tim carried out his threat, because he himself left town. Strange that no one could tell me what had happened to Eddie Arthur after that day, nor did they know where Tim had gone.

"How ironic," I thought. "All this, and I haven't had my first date yet." Little did I realize the worst was yet to come.

By November, the KOVALCHICKS greatest baseball season had come to an end. We were ready for a rest. Many times we departed Sagamore at 10 or 11 a.m. and did not return until late in the night. But, ask any player and he would not trade it for anything. The excitement was never-ending.

The coming of Thanksgiving was exciting because the whole family was going to be together, and with the war ended, everyone had so much to thank God for. The season's first snow fell a few days before Thanksgiving, adding to the beauty of the holiday.

Our business boomed during the holidays. The bar was always filled with miners and soldiers. With hunting season ended, as always, it was time to visit the bar and brag about how they shot that big 18-pointer. They hunted just about everything in our part of the country. I concluded they got more joy from bragging about their hunting feats than they did from the actual hunting itself. Some stories were questionable. I had hunted since 1941 and found many of their stories hard to believe. Especially the ones in which they had a near-death experience. However, the soldiers' stories were very dramatically told and at times moreso than the hunters'.

I loved hunting, not for the purpose of killing animals, but for the exercise. It is great for any athlete. I thought deer were the most beautiful and graceful animals and I refused to kill them. Having seen so many dead squirrels, rabbits and pheasants while growing up enabled me to cope with shooting them. Besides, I loved the challenge. Rarely did I miss, and that was important to me.

The highlight of my hunting trip was lunch time, when I would sit on the ground to eat my peanut butter and jelly sandwich, which I made with more peanut butter and jelly than bread.

I worried about the difficult time brother Eddie was having adjusting. He could not shake the shackles of his shell-shock attacks. Mother and Dad made every effort to help him, but their efforts failed. They endured a tremendous amount of stress, worrying about him.

As the holidays were approaching, so was the cold weather. Eddie's wounds could not tolerate the cold. He suffered unbearable pain. This caused him to drink even more as he tried to cope. As a result, it initiated more frequent shell-shock attacks.

Mother and Dad could not control his behavior when he went into a shell-shock attack. However, because of some unexplainable spiritual bond between us, I could calm him and bring him back to reality.

During one such attack, he had taken off at midnight, running a mile up the highway in his bare feet in the snow, wearing nothing but his long-john underwear. When I finally caught him, it was so pitiful seeing him re-enacting the war, shouting and screaming, "ra-ta-ta, ra-ta-ta.' As he relieved his war experiences, over and over again. "It's all right Eddie. This is Sis," I yelled as I tried to hold his arms. "You're all right Eddie. The war is over. This is Sis. You're home safe. You're in Sagamore, Eddie, and you're all right. This is Sis. Come on, let's go home." Slowly my words began to calm him.

Mother had given me a pair of slippers and a robe before I took off running. I put them on him as he began to cry. Then, we slowly walked down the snow-covered road with our arms around each other as he cried and cried. And so did I.

With the war over, it never occurred to me that Johnny would be drafted for the Army. However, he was drafted on December 10, 1945, and stationed at Fort George G. Meade, Maryland. There he was assigned to Special Services with the 2101st A.S.U. Station.

So many thoughts raced through my mind. "What are we going to do without him? He can't go to the service. The war is over. Why are they drafting him?" Nothing seemed to make sense. "The boys are coming home from the war, not going to war. It's over," I thought. It was something I could not accept. But, he was gone, and there was nothing I could do about it.

Ringing out the old and bringing in the new that December 31 was one of the most celebrated I had ever seen in Sagamore and in our bar. What a joy it was to see everyone so happy after the worry and stress of the past four years.

However, no one remembered that December 31 was my 20th birthday. Oh well, after 20 years, it did not matter.

Two major world events followed the end of World War II during 1945 and 1946. First, the United States sponsored and helped organize the United Nations, in which 60 countries took part in writing the charter in April of '45. It pledged to maintain world peace and security to let residents of colonial areas to gradually develop their free political institutions.

Second were the war trials to both Germany and Japan. Allied resolve that justice must be done resulted in the creation of the most extraordinary trial of the 20th century. The Nuremberg trials, named after the city in Bavaria where they took place, began November 20, 1945. On September 30, 1946, 11 Nazi leaders were sentenced to death by hanging, three were acquitted, and eight faced long prison sentences. Four committed suicide before the trials began and one disappeared.

The Far East trials were not concluded until November 1948, when seven Japanese military and political leaders were sentenced to death and 19 others were given life imprisonment.

No words can adequately describe the terrible atrocities, suffering, death and destruction of World War II.

Meanwhile people in the United States resumed their lives. Dad began building a stronger team in preparation for the upcoming 1946 season. He knew that with all the good ballplayers returning from the war, we would be facing stronger competition.

However, my baseball career took an unexpected turn. Dad was up to his secrecy again. After I left the All-American Girls Professional Baseball League. The National Girls Softball League offered me $75 weekly to play for the Chicago Queens. Unbeknownst to me, Dad was planning for me to go. I had no intention of accepting their offer. "You don't have to stay if you don't like it," he said. To please him, I agreed to give it a try. So, there I was sitting in our pick-up truck on my way to Chicago with brother Eddie and his friend, Joe, that last week of April.

I signed a contract with the Queens the second day following practice. However, I did not feel that I belonged there, and wished I was on my way back home with Eddie.

The Queens' publicity director, Eddie McGuire, made lodging accommodations for me with the Eleanor Club for Women, located just off State Street approximately two blocks from the elevated train. All games were played at night and I was to get to and from the games by way of the elevated train. As unfamiliar as I was with city life, this disturbed me, thinking it was a dangerous situation, because I was the only ballplayer staying at the Eleanor Club and would be riding the train alone at night. I soon learned that sometimes I would be returning from a game as late as 11 p.m.

My suspicions soon proved correct. One night, I was hurriedly walking across the vacant platform of the elevated train at 11 o'clock and suddenly I was stopped by an intuition feeling that all was not right. The train had gone, so I decided to proceed with caution. I hugged my baseball mitt and spiked shoes under my arm. Then clenching my fists, I began walking and prayed, "Lord I am in Your hands. Help me get back to the Eleanor Club safely." As I approached a dark alley leading to a loading dock, a shrill scream came from the

248

pitch-black alley, and a chill went down my back. "Help! Help! Somebody help me! Help me!" Then again the cries came, "Help! Help! Somebody help me!" The pleading cries of the woman's voice triggered an instinctive urge to run down that alley to help her. Forgetting all else, I started toward the alley. Suddenly, as I approached the entrance, a voice within me said, RUN! RUN! GET OUT OF HERE, HURRY RUN!" Frightened by this sudden inner voice, I immediately began running faster that I had ever run, until I entered the Eleanor Club, dripping wet from perspiration.

The next morning. All the girls were talking about a woman who was found murdered in the alley not far from the Eleanor Club. I felt sure it had to be the woman I heard yelling for help. Maybe she was lured down that alley by screams, just like I could have been lured down that alley and murdered.

I had been at the Eleanor Club for several weeks when late one night our club chaperon came upstairs to my room. "There is a gentleman here in an Army uniform to see you. He said he is your brother. He is waiting in the living room," she said. I was delighted, expecting to find brother Johnny. Instead, there stood Tim Dewicked, who quickly reached out, putting his arms around me. "Hi, Sis," he said, and before I could say a word, the chaperon had left the room. He quickly maneuvered an arm lock behind me, and said, "We are walking out of here slowly and quietly, and if you make one mistake, I will break your arm." At that moment, I complied for safety's sake, and did exactly as instructed without conversation as we walked down the alley to the elevated train. The night was black as pitch, and not a soul was waiting for the train. The platform lights allowed very little light for a public train depot.

"We're going to get married," he said. I replied, "We have already gone over this many times, Tim. I am not going to marry you, and I am not getting on that train with you." His patience snapped as he angrily said, "You will or I will throw you off this platform!" Then, unexpectedly, he picked me up, raising me above his head as he walked toward the platform railing. "You will come with me, or I will throw you down from this platform." The platform appeared to be 100 feet or more above the concrete alley below. I could hear the elevated train off in the distance. His arms began to sway back and forth, back and forth as though he was going to throw me. This angered me more than it frightened me. For a brief second I recalled the incident from years past, when as a kid I was dared to climb the third diving board and jump in even though I could not swim. I accepted the challenge and jumped, and almost drowned. Now, I was being challenged again. "I am not going with you, Tim!" I said angrily. "Let me down!" The train was coming closer. I had to think fast. His swaying was becoming more threatening, and for a second, I felt he was going to throw me over the railing. I had only one more chance before the train would come around the curve. "This is it," I thought. "Make your decision, Dorothy!" With my anger snuffing out any thought of the consequences, I yelled out, "Go ahead, Tim, throw me down! I would sooner be dead than married to you!" It seemed an eternity as I waited, remaining as still as possible, because if I caused his grip to slip, indeed, I would fall over 100 feet o the concrete below. He stood swaying and swaying, perhaps hoping to frighten me into submission. I said nothing. Then, slowly, he lowered me to the platform and said, "If you would sooner be dead than married to me, then you need not worry, for you will never see me again."

I did not reply as he boarded the train. He did not turn or look back. When the train pulled out, I stood there, shocked by all that had happened. I knew I had won the final battle. However, I did not feel happy with my victory. Instead I was sorry for him and felt a deep compassion toward him. He made his choices in life and took the wrong path. He chose to be a bully, hurting others, and now he was a very miserable person, reaching out for something that could never be. Did he think I could bring him happiness? Or was I simply a challenge to him, someone who said "Over my dead body," when six years before, when he said he was going to marry me. To this day these remain unanswered questions. However, I learned that he did marry, and has since died. No other information is known to me, but true to his word, I never did see him again.

Still in shock, I walked back to the Eleanor Club resolved to leave Chicago. The following day, made arrangements to leave the league, and boarded the train for Pittsburgh.

I arrived home just days before Memorial Day, vowing that never again would I return to noisy Chicago. How wonderful it was to enjoy the quiet of a small town again.

A doubleheader was scheduled for Memorial Day, and I was back playing men's baseball. Dad had built an excellent team. They were older and well seasoned. I saw that he did not have to spend time training his new crop of players. With Johnny in service at Fort Meade, Dad was fortunate to have found several good pitchers who had just returned from the service. They carried us to many victories that season of 1946. I was proud of our team, especially brother Nick. He could cover second base better than any player I ever saw. He was dependable. That gave me a lot of confidence.

Playing baseball with men has given me thrilling moments and never-to-be-forgotten memories, like the time we played Dayton. Dayton's catcher was trying to get acquainted with me, or maybe he had a sister my size, or maybe he felt sorry for me. Whatever, the reason, I do not know. But, when I was at bat, he was telling me what pitch the pitcher was going to throw. This frustrated me, so I stepped out of the batter's box, and in a voice loud enough for all to hear, I said, "I can see what he's throwing. You don't have to tell me." That was mistake number one. The next pitch came straight for my head, knocking me to the ground. I laid there half conscious. Players came running and the crowd was overwhelmed with concern. Dad was yelling, "Get a runner down at first." "Oh no, he's not knocking me out of the game," I thought, and in a stupor, I said, "I don't need a runner. I'm O.K. I'll do my own running." I struggled to my feet and staggered down to first. That was mistake number two.

Still dazed when I got to first, I rounded the base, and proceeded toward second, and found myself in a dog chase. Back and forth they closed in on me. They all got into the action, the first baseman, the second baseman, the shortstop and even the center fielder and right fielder came running. I went sliding head-first into second. That was mistake number three. Everyone came crashing together, and when the dust settled, it was like the game of football. They were all on top of me. I yelled, "O.K., ya all can get up now." Their embarrassment was evident. Dad came running. As I got to my feet, he said, "Well, are you satisfied now?" He then pulled me out of the game. That just wasn't my day. I'm still carrying scars from my slide into second. Scars made by players' spiked shoes when they came crashing down.

One of the most miraculous plays I made happened when we played Indiana, Pennsylvania. Indiana's team was determined to win, and so were we. It was an especially hard-fought game. An Indiana sportswriter was there with his camera, kept stationing himself where he felt the action would be, making certain that he caught a decisive play in action.

Indiana was at bat, and in the batter's box was their reputed best hitter. He was big and muscular, so we all stepped back a few steps. He acted like he was about to put one out of the ballpark. I yelled at the pitcher, "Come on, let's go. Throw it in there, Pitch. He'll never see it. This is not his day. One, two, three, he's out." The pitcher wound up and delivered and the batter connected with all his power, sending the ball at lightning speed down the third base line. It looked like it was a clean hit, and the crowd cheered. I rushed for first base because our third baseman had made a spectacular play by stopping the ball. He scooped it up and fired toward first. The throw was much too high, and the crowd screamed louder than I had ever heard. Never before did I experience what happened next. I leaped for the ball, my gloved hand reaching high into the air. The screams from the crowd were deafening. All of a sudden, I felt that it wasn't me jumping that high. It was as if I was being lifted by an unknown force. I heard the ball hit my glove and my body fell back to the ground, but the player was safe. However, we did retire the side without a run.

When I came to the dugout, I learned the real reason for the screaming that had overtaken the crowd. The reporting photographer had stationed himself near first base, hoping to get a good picture of me in action. When the batter hit the ball and it looked like a sure hit, the reporter watched no further, and turned his attention toward the crowd. No one expected that I would catch the third baseman's high throw. It looked like a wild pitch, and it was headed straight for the photographer's head. He was unaware of the danger he was in. I was told that had I missed that ball, the photographer could have been killed. They called the catch miraculous. "It wasn't me," I said. "It was some force greater than me." I never forgot that catch because I could never forget the feeling of that unknown force I felt in that brief moment.

Billy Hunter, who played six years in the major leagues from 1953 to 1958, and then managed Baltimore in 1977-78 played for Indiana. Dad solicited him for games when we were scheduled to play some really tough teams. The first game he played with us I knew he was destined to play professional ball. It was evident he had it all. Just as I knew Bud Souchock, Mike Goliat and Alex Kvasnak would make the majors too. There's something about a ballplayer that' got it, and brother Johnny had it, too. If it were not for "Uncertain Destiny" he would have made the majors. Also, many players that we played against went on to play in the minor leagues.

When we played a doubleheader with McIntyre, Dad solicited Billy Hunter to play with us. In the first game, Billy was playing shortstop and brother Nick was at second when a line drive was hit between them. Both made an effort to recover the ball and collided with an impact that fractured Nick's left wrist and forced him from the game. Another time, Billy threw a ball to first with such powerful speed that it almost tore off my mitt.

We won the first game and McIntyre was sure getting angry. In the second game, it was evident they were committed to win, and not necessarily by being fair and square. We were at bat. Billy was safe on second with a double. Our next batter hit a line drive deep into center field. Billy took off running, tagged third and headed for home. He bumped McIntyre's approximately 240-pound catcher in his effort to go around him, as he was blocking his way. In a split second, the catcher hit Billy with a vicious blow, knocking him unconscious. As he recovered, Dad summoned the team. We loaded our equipment and quickly made our departure, vowing never to play McIntrye again.

When I returned from the All-American Girls Professional Baseball League, Mother copied the design of their uniform, and sewed one for me to match the KOVALCHICKS uniform, which were black and white. However, I still preferred my peasant blouse and tennis shorts, just a habit, I guess.

Our season was going great when another unexpected surprise came. The day after Labor Day, brother Nick, who was a junior in high school, was leaving the team to attend high school in Indiana, 20 miles away, and would be living there with Aunt Julia. Mother believed he would acquire a better education foundation there in preparation for college.

I was disappointed because we were a great team together. For the balance of the season, Dad replaced Nick, who played second base, with Andy Gulish or JoJo Stanavich. Both were excellent ballplayers. We immediately made a good team like Nick and I did.

We played baseball late into the fall, fulfilling our commitments. The season was long and hard fought. The team was ready for a rest.

A year had passed since World War II ended, but the United States struggled with adjusting to peace. Strikes prevailed, as 4.5 million workers went on strike, crippling the coal, auto, electric and steel industries and interrupting rail and maritime transportation. Prices skyrocketed as people resorted to purchases done under the counter. It was a difficult time for America as man-days lost to strikes went to 113 million. However, strikes were for the most part calm, unlike strikes of the past, and labor profited by raises in their wages.

The United Mine Workers of America (UMWA) had walked out on strike twice. Workers had gained health, welfare and safety benefits in their first walk-out in April. Then they lost their second walk-out because they had violated a no-strike pledge and were fines $3.5 million. Sagamore was deeply affected by both walk-outs.

Our first indication of the coming of winter was Thanksgiving Day, when the first snow flakes of the season fell. It brought a feeling of holiday excitement that stayed until the middle of January, because we Greek Catholics celebrated Christmas and New Year's by the old Russian calendar, which had Christmas falling on January 7 and New Year's on January 14. However, we also celebrated on December 25. When we were kids, we thought it was great, having two Christmases.

Adding to the excitement of the holiday season was Johnny's discharge from the army on December 11. Many of the servicemen were being released after one year of service, because the United States was no longer at war.

Sometime during my early years, I had resolved never to date until I was 21 and never marry until I was 25. That December I was 21, I was not especially excited about it, nor had I anyone in mind to date. I was confident that I would cross that bridge when I came to it. I wondered if anyone would remember my birthday. You are right, no one remembered. However, in our bar, there was a grand celebration as January 1, 1947, was ushered in.

CHAPTER XIV
THE YEAR OF 1947

In January, Dad and Johnny attended the Joe Strip Baseball School for three months in Orlando, Florida, and the New York Giants' tryout camp in Palatka, Florida, for one week. As a result, both the Boston Braves and New York Giants offered Johnny a contract after he returned home.

A contract arrived by mail from the New York Giants on a Friday. Dad being overly anxious, insisted that Johnny sign with them, and immediately mailed the signed contract back against Mother's advice to wait. The following day, Johnny received a telephone call from the Boston Braves offering him a contract with a $10,000 bonus. Much to Dad's regret, that was one time he should have taken Mother's advice.

Johnny seemed to be plagued with misfortune. Just days before he was to leave for Peekskill, New York, for spring training with the Giants minor leagues, he attended a roller skating party and perspired with intensity while skating, With his body still wet from perspiration, he left for home in the cold weather, and soon developed a serious case of influenza. It was obvious he was unable to play ball in his condition. However, Dad insisted that he go on to spring training. The Giants had no choice but to release him, and he returned home. Once again, Mother nursed him back to health.

March winds had quickly dried the mud. By April, Eddie was able to drag the diamond and our team was at practice.

Baseball history was made that April of 1947, when Jackie Robinson became the first Negro to play major league baseball in modern times. Robinson played first base for the Brooklyn Dodgers in the season opener on April 15.

Also, in the national news, four million veterans of the war were taking advantage of the housing, business and educational opportunities offered under the G.I. Bill. Though the bill helped ease the adjustment to civilian life, returning from war was still difficult for servicemen and women. In 1946 more divorces were recorded that ever before in American history as returning young men and waiting young women found themselves strangers. Some had not known each other well before they wed, but rushed to form a bond before death might prevent it. Other couples knew each other well before, but war had changed them. Women had been holding down jobs and balancing checkbooks. All of a sudden the husband was taking charge.

President Truman signed the National Security Act, uniting the armed forces under the Department of Defense, and a National Security Council would advise the president on military policy. The Central Intelligence was established, and the Army Air Force became independent as the U.S. Air Force.

The Cabinet Committee on World Food Programs reported that the United States had sent a record of 18,443,000 tons of grain and other foodstuff to Europe. The record-breaking volume did not meet the world's urgent postwar needs, as there were still millions of desperately hungry people.

After having worn the baseball uniform copied after the All-American Girls Professional Baseball League during 1946, I decided on a new black and white satin one that I thought would stand out and be showy. So Mother sewed a white satin blouse trimmed in black pipping with KOVALCHICKS in black letter across the chest. The shorts were black satin bloomers with white stripes on the sides. The outfit also featured black kneesocks, white baseball shoes with metal spikes and a black cap with a white initial "S" for Sagamore.

Our baseball season was under way my May 1. Nick returned to the team when Indiana High School ended it's second semester, and Johnny returned following his recovery from influenza.

One of Dad's secrets surfaced again when I read the Kittanning Leader-Times. The article reported that the KOVALCHICKS had joined the Eastern Section of the Kittanning Independent League, and that the Eastern Section would be livened with a girl first sacker playing for the KOVALCHICKS. A schedule of the games were listed beginning May 18, with the final game being June 19. The teams of the Eastern Section were Dayton, Elderton, Kovalchicks, NuMine, Rural Valley and Yatesboro. Each team would be playing three games every week.

Our team did not win the championship, but we played some great games, and again Johnny did some great pitching. Each game was hard fought, close in score and thrilling all the way.

Following the final game on June 19, a total of 22 All-Stars were chosen from the Eastern, Western, Southern, and Kittanning Sections. Johnny and I were two of the six players chosen from our Eastern Section.

On June 29, the Armstrong County Amateur Federation sponsored a game between the 22 All-Stars of the Kittanning Independent League and one of the best amateur teams of the Pittsburgh area, known as Pie Traynor and his Cockran Stars. The team was managed by Harold (Pie) Traynor, baseball immortal and one-time manager of the Pittsburgh Pirates, and sponsored by Ottie Cockran, who was president of the Pittsburgh Amateur Baseball Federation. The All-Stars lost to the Cockran Stars by a score of 11 to 5.

The newspaper reported that the attendance was well over 3,000 people, which was one of their largest crowds of the year. They also reported that I had laid down a sacrifice and played an errorless game at first.

I am sure that because of that game, the Pittsburgh Sun-Tele-graph contacted me, requesting my personal written life story. I worked diligently at writing one as brief as possible, feeling very inadequate about doing the story for such a large newspaper. However, it was published exactly as I had written it, along with a picture of me in my black and white satin uniform.

After leaving the ball diamond, the photographer stopped at the hotel, because he wanted a picture of my bedroom. After seeing my ruffled curtains and flowered bedspread with no baseball pictures on the wall, he changed his mind. Mother and I knew it was because it was contrary to his expectations of finding my walls covered with baseball pictures, as well as other sports pictures.

That June, Shorty Katchur asked to take me to a spaghetti supper being sponsored by the Roman Catholic Church at the miner's (UMWA) union hall. It was my first date. Mother agreed to cover for me should Dad come looking for me, as he often did.

We walked to the union hall along Sagamore's main highway, Route 210. The night was beautiful. We talked about the war and about his service in the war. My expectation was that he would bring up the subject of baseball, but he did not, so neither did I. I wondered if he even knew about my baseball career. We enjoyed talking to those we knew during supper, which was delicious, but we did not linger long, as it appeared that seating was limited.

We arrived home about 10 p.m. At the back door, he held my hand and said, "Ya tebby lubim," which is Slovak, but I did not know what it meant. So I said, "Thank you, good night." Mother was waiting in the kitchen. "What does 'Ya tebby lubim' mean?" I asked. She replied, "It means I love you. Why?" "Oh! How stupid!" I said. Then, I told her what had happened. I was so embarrassed about not knowing, especially since we were Czechoslovakian, and I had responded by saying, "Thank you, good night." I decided that I must apologize, and explain that I never learned the language. But I never saw him, nor heard from him again. To this day, it remains a mystery. It was a very sad way to conclude my first date, because I really did like him. That was the first time I regretted not having learned Slovak, especially because Mother wanted to teach it to me.

Following the All-Star game with the Cockran Stars of Pittsburgh, Johnny played two days a week for Ward 1 in the Indiana Baseball League. At the same time, he played for us, as dad had scheduled barnstorming games all season. Sundays and holidays were generally doubleheaders, which were sometimes played in two different towns or cities.

On July 15 or 16, Dad drove me to Johnstown, Pennsylvania, where I attended the Pittsburgh Pirates' three-day baseball school and tryouts at Cricket Field. I was the first girl ever to report to any baseball school in the area, which drew much attention. I played first base during the workouts, and was pleased to read an article in the Altoona Mirror, that commented on my performance. It said that veteran scout Joe Brehany, who conducted the tryout drills with his assistant, George Chacko, marveled at my ability, and said that from the 74 baseball hopefuls attending the school, they almost placed me on their All-Star team.

The day after Dad and I arrived home, I received a letter from Pittsburgh Pirates scout Charlie Johnson, which was followed by a visit from him. He offered to contract me with Olean, New York, an independent team in the Pony League, with the contingency that Mother would also sign as my chaperone for the remainder of the season. Mother said she absolutely would not even think about it, because it was an absolute no. She said that she had only one daughter, and did not want to see me killed on a ball diamond. Thus, my opportunity to make history was ended.

Our huge dining room on the second floor of our hotel was no longer thriving as it had in the past. Since the war ended, the prosperous times had almost come to a halt, as miners were working only one or two days a week.

However, Mother was prepared to serve customers at any time. Therefore, it was no surprise to see a stranger walk into our dining room at lunch time requesting room and board on a hot sweltering day in August. But one particular customer was unlike any other that we had ever seen around our part of the country. He was definitely different in every way. We could see that he was no miner, nor a business individual of any kind, and he did not look like a farmer from our part of the country. He did not look Amish, either. When I walked up to his table, he asked if I was Dorothy Kovalchick, and I said that I was. I was unprepared for what happened next. He identified himself as Joe Davis, a baseball fan, and said that he had come all the way from Springfield, Missouri, to take me back to Springfield as his bride. I looked at this man in bib overalls and thought that surely this is a dream. He must be kidding. I was at a loss for words, but my mind was racing 90 miles an hour when 21-year-old Frank Gandy, who did odd jobs for Dad, walked into the dining room. A light went off in my mind. "That's my fiance," I said. "We're getting married. I'm sorry, but I could not possibly marry you." He looked at my hands and said, "You are not wearing an engagement ring." Quickly, I answered, "We're going to get our rings tomorrow." Mother saved the day when she walked up to take his order, and I left to find Frank.

"Frank, you have got to help me!" I said, and related what had just happened. Quickly, he headed for home to borrow his sister's engagement ring. When Mr. Davis asked for me at breakfast, Mother said I had gone with Frank to pick out an engagement ring. At lunch, I walked up to his table wearing the engagement ring belonging to

Frank's sister, Jenny and happily showed it to him. "When's the wedding?" he asked. "Not until spring," I said. "Give the ring back," he said. "I have a big house on a 280 acre farm, and I can give you a lot more than this boy can." It took a week to convince him that I was not going with him to Springfield, Missouri, before he would leave Sagamore. However, the problem was not resolved because Frank liked the engagement idea, and wanted it to be real. Then again, I was searching for an excuse as to why it was impossible. All I could think of was that I was not 25 yet. "What does that have to do with it?" he wanted to know. After several weeks, he realized I would not marry him. Shortly thereafter, he too left town for Connecticut, and I never saw him again.

After a one and one-half year listing to sell our hotel, our real estate agent in Cleveland, Ohio found an interested buyer for the hotel, and negotiations between them and Mother and Dad began. However, it would be several months before it would be consummated.

Even though school had started, we played until it was too cold to play. Nick had returned to Indiana High School to finish his senior year, and Dad replaced him with an excellent second baseman. No one could spot baseball talent as well as Dad. For that reason, scouts wasted no time in looking over a ballplayer that he had recommended.

I was often asked by women or young girls if I wore any protection, and if I had ever been hurt playing ball. Those questions always seemed to be of most interest to them. I explained that I wore no protection whatsoever, and that none was available for women. I had many injuries. Some I have mentioned previously. In addition, at one time or another I suffered a broken finger, a dislocated knee, a dislocated hip and a front tooth knocked loose. My worst injury came when we played our last game of 1947 with the town of Heilwood.

The game was close. We had men on base, and I was next to bat, when Heilwood's coach pulled his pitcher and sent in a replacement – a tall husky left-hander. I thought he was the biggest ball player I ever saw. Dad had been watching him warm up in the bullpen, and saw that he couldn't throw the ball anywhere near the catcher, who was warming him up. He walked over to me and said, "Honey, I'm taking you out of the game. I've been watching that pitcher warm up, and he is wild, I mean wild. He can't throw a straight ball. He's going to kill someone." The thought came to my mind that the crowd would think that I always got pulled out of a game when the going got tough. "Dad," I said, "It won't look good for our team if you pull me out. I'm not afraid of him. I'll try to bunt him, if it's O.K. Let me try it?" It was against his better judgment, but he said, "O.K. Honey, be careful," and walked back to coaching along the third base line. Again, I should have taken his advice.

The pitcher who weighed at least 240 pounds, stepped onto the mound. He positioned himself, then drew back his left arm, threw up his right leg and let go of the ball with the speed of lightning. It headed straight for my legs. I jumped, but the ball caught me in the right ankle just above the ankle bone. The players carried me off the diamond, and the Heilwood coach pulled the pitcher out of the game following that one pitch.

In looking back, I guess my greatest thrill was trying out at the Pittsburgh Pirates' baseball school in Johnstown.

I will never forget our first game ever played under lights against East Brady. The score was tied in the sixth inning when it began to rain. Neither the fans nor the players wanted the game called. Everyone wanted a winner, so we continued playing in the rain. The seventh, eight and ninth innings came and went with no runs scored. Our uniforms were dripping wet. Our balls, gloves and bats were wet and slippery, and the ball field looked like a mud field. Still, the fans yelled to keep playing. They wanted a winner.

The managers and the umpires called for a meeting and decided that the first team to score a run would be the winner. The 10th inning came and went with no runs. Then in the 11th inning, the potential winning run was on third and it was my turn to bat. On the way to the batter's box, I picked up my Dad's signal. He wanted the ball bunted just inside the first base line at a speed just fast enough that I could follow the ball to first base. I did exactly that, and in all the confusion our man made it safe at home and I was safe on first. We had won.

The crowd went wild with excitement, rushing to get out of the rain as everyone was soaked through and through. I went rushing to the high school's dressing room, anxious to get into some dry clothes. In the dressing room, I came face to face with a full length mirror and could not believe my eyes. My black and white satin uniform was soaked through and clinging to me like a tight glove. It almost looked like I had no clothes on. A deep embarrassment enveloped me. No wonder they wanted to keep playing, I thought. They were getting a free show. I hurriedly changed clothes and rushed to find Dad, as I was angry. "Why didn't you tell me you could see through my uniform." I yelled, feeling overwhelmed with embarrassment. "I was too busy playing the game," he said. "I wasn't paying attention to your uniform or anybody else's." What else could I say? It was done and there was no undoing it, that was certain. But I did appreciate the fact that not one of our players or anyone else made mention of it. However, never again did I wear that uniform. I did not want to bring back memories to myself or anyone else.

Five years later, I returned to East Brady with Dad on business. I sat on a wooden bench on the front porch of an old general store waiting for Dad. Soon an elderly gentleman walked up and sat down beside me. He had a chew of tobacco in his lower lip, which he rolled around a few times, then spit out over the edge of the porch. "Where ya all from?" he asked. I replied, "Sagamore." He pondered awhile as he rolled that tobacco around in his lower lip, and once again spit out over the edge of the porch. "Sagamore, Sagamore," he said, "I remember. They had a baseball team, and they come up and played us, and they had a girl on their team, and everyone was bettin' on that girl. They was bettin' she couldn't hit the ball. She wouldn't git on first base. She'd make an error or couldn't ketch the ball. I won $50 on that girl that night, and after the game was over, I tried to find her. I wanted to give her half the money, but I couldn't find her. You wouldn't happen to know that girl, would ya?" I looked up at him, nodded and smiled as I pointed to myself. "That was me," I said. He hesitated awhile, just looking at me. Then, he rolled that tobacco around his lower lip again, an spit out over the edge of the porch, once, then twice. "Well, I'll be doggoned" he said, looking at me. "If I'd a knowed I was gonna see you again, I wouldna spent that money."

By the end of 1947 season, the KOVALCHICKS had played in 64 towns and cities in western Pennsylvania. A list of towns and cities are herewith listed for those who may be interested.

Our prospective buyer for the hotel and Mother and Dad were still trying to have a closure on a sale. However, due to the uncertainty of Sagamore's future, no bank would risk carrying a mortgage on the hotel, leaving Mother and Dad no choice but to owner finance the sale. The final closure came on November 24, 1947, just one month short of 25 years, since Dad's brother Joe had agreed to purchase the HOTEL SAGAMORE with a handshake when he was intoxicated. With the sale finally closed, Thanksgiving Day was a very happy one for the whole family. And Christmas was celebrated like never before.

Yes, you guessed it. I was 22 on December 31, and again no birthday party.

KOVALCHICKS BASEBALL TEAM 1941 - 1947
TOWNS AND CITIES PLAYED IN WESTERN PENNSYLVANIA

1	ALTOONA	25	FORD CLIFF	49	SMICKSBURG
2	ADRIAN	26	FREEPORT	50	SHELOCTA
3	APOLLO	27	FULTON RUN	51	SAGAMORE
4	ARMAGH	28	GAS TOWN	52	SLATELICK
5	ATWOOD	29	HEILWOOD	53	SPACES CORNERS
6	ARCADIA	30	HOMER CITY	54	TRADE CITY
7	AULTMAN	31	INDIANA	55	VALIER
8	BEYER	32	JOHNSTOWN	56	VANDERGRIFT
9	BUTLER	33	LUZERNEMINES	57	TEMPLETON
10	BLAIRSVILLE	34	LEECHBURG	58	WATERMAN
11	CLYMER	35	MARGARET	59	WEST KITTANNING
12	GOHEENVILLE	36	MARION CENTER	60	WORTHINGTON
13	CRAMER	37	MCINTYRE	61	YATESBORO
14	CREEKSIDE	38	NUMINE	62	TROUT RUN
15	COAL RUN	39	PUNXSUTAWNEY	63	SEMINOLE
16	BIG RUN	40	PLUMVILLE	64	CADOGAN
17	DUBOIS	41	PENN RUN		
18	DAYTON	42	NEW BETHLEHEM		
19	DIXONVILLE	43	RURAL VALLEY		
20	ELDERON	44	RIMERSBURG		
21	EAST KITTANNING	45	ROSSITER		
22	EAST BRADY	46	SALTSBURG		
23	ERNEST	47	STARFORD		
24	FORD CITY	48	SYKESVILLE		

OTHER CITIES AND STATES PLAYED IN BY DOROTHY & JOHNNY KOVALCHICK

1. BARSTOW, FL   2. COLUMBIA, SC   3. FAYETTEVILLE, NC

**Dorothy 1947 Bartow Florida
Baseball School**

CHAPTER XV
THE YEAR OF 1948

Dad felt that his world was coming apart following the sale of the hotel. Nick was graduating from high school in May, and had enrolled at Penn State University. He would attend Clarion State Teachers College in September, because all Penn State freshmen going into Civil Engineering were required to spend their first year at Clarion.

Johnny left for Bartow, Florida, in January to attend a four-month baseball school. In February, Dad and I drove to Bartow in our new Frazier car to visit him for two weeks. While there, I had the opportunity to enjoy a little warm-up practice with some of the Dodger ballplayers, who were having their spring training there. I was thrilled, and must say they were absolutely great. I think they were amused watching me playing in my peasant blouse and tennis shorts.

Our second week there, Mother called. She was crying hysterically. The third floor of the Hotel Sagamore was on fire. Dad and I grabbed our belongings and headed for Pennsylvania at 80 to 90 miles an hour all the way, non-stop, except for gas and food, which we ate in the car. The police stopped me in South Carolina, North Carolina and Virginia. We explained about the hotel fire, and each officer warned me to slow up for our safety, as well as for others', and sent us on our way without giving us a ticket. I have always felt a deep appreciation for policemen ever since that day.

Arriving home, we found that the fire had been contained. The damages were estimated to be between $3,500 and $5,000. With Dad having owner-financed the sale of the hotel, I understood why he was so worried and stressed all the way home from Florida. Luckily, I was driving, or we would not have made it.

269

When Johnny's baseball school ended on April 14, he signed a contract to play for the Greenville, North Carolina, Greenies' of the independent South Atlantic League, known for its high-quality ballplayers. Many players from the league eventually went to the major leagues.

Because Eddie was unable to tolerate the cold weather, he was in Orlando, Florida, attending a mechanic school under the G.I. bill, along with several of his army buddies.

Then Dad's biggest blow came. I announced that, after dedicating eight years to baseball, I was giving up the game. He argued that at 22, I was at my peak and could not quit. "Dad, that's how I want people to remember me, at my peak, not when I am on my way down," I said. Again, he spoke in anger, "If you quit, I will disown you, and you can leave home."

Determined to hold to my decision, I went to live with Mother's sister, Mary, in Warren, Ohio. Uppermost in my mind was the desire to own my own business. I had a talent for arts and crafts, and felt that an arts and crafts business would be successful in the town of Indiana. I approached the owner of such a store in Warren and offered to work without pay, because I wanted to learn the business. I told her about my plan, and she agreed to give me a chance. We soon developed a very compatible relationship, and I was learning more than I had ever hoped, especially when she put me in contact with suppliers, who were eager to help me get started. But apparently that was not my destiny, because after three months, Dad came to Warren and, with tears in his eyes, asked me to come back home. "You do not have to play ball anymore, if you don't want to." he said. It was so heartbreaking seeing him that way, so I agreed to return with him. I, too, was crying inside, because I knew my plans were perhaps lost forever.

When I returned home, I learned that Dad had purchased a Dad's Old Fashioned Root Beer franchise. He also purchased a truck and hired a couple young boys to help him. I thought that being a root beer distributor at the age of 50 was not for him, but said nothing. However, I quickly opened up a simple set of books that he himself could handle.

Dad was worried about Eddie being all alone in Florida with no family there. He talked about Eddie coming home for the Fourth of July, and thought it would be a good idea, if I went back with him and kind of looked after him. I could read his mind. He was worried about his drinking. Also if Eddie got another of those shell-shock attacks and no one from the family was there with him? Something could happen to him and we would not know anything about it. Then suddenly I realized why he wanted me home. He knew I could handle Eddie, and he knew Eddie was coming home for the Fourth and he wanted me to return to Florida with him, to take care of him. I knew the second he mentioned it that I would go, because I loved my brother Eddie, and he needed me.

Eddie arrived home on July 1 with plans to return to Florida on July 5. I hurriedly washed and was ironing clothes and making other preparations when cousin Betty stopped by to visit. "How would you like to go to Florida with Eddie and me?" I said in a whimsical voice. "When?" she asked. "Tomorrow," I answered. "O.K. I better hurry home and get packed," she said. We agreed on a time and place to meet, and the following day the three of us were headed South.

Our first destination was Greenville, North Carolina, for a couple days' visit with Johnny, who was playing for the Greenies. Then, on to Orlando and into a life I only read about in books. The next 10 days were filled with fun, fun, and more fun. The crowds amazed me as everyone was so scantily dressed. Even the elderly were scantily dressed and did not act a bit embarrassed about it. "So this is Florida," I said. "Well, there' no modesty here, that is for sure."

After two weeks, cousin Betty boarded a bus and returned to Pennsylvania, and I stayed to look after Eddie. We rented two rooms and a bath from a private home owner. A small two-burner stove was available for cooking and we shared the bath. Eddie returned to mechanic school, and I attended a vocational school from 8 a.m. to 3 p.m. five days a week.

Soon our funds were running low, Dad did not mention sending money to us, so I assumed we were on our own. Desiring to continue vocational school, I decided that waitressing at the Red Rooster after school would be the solution. The Red Rooster was known as the best place to eat in Orlando. The fact that I was raised in Hotel Sagamore got me the job immediately, but not for long. Meals at Hotel Sagamore were served the old-fashioned way, called "boarding-house reach." I was not familiar with the modern professionalism that was required at the Red Rooster. In spite of my inexperience, I was not fired until a couple weeks later.

My unemployment lasted but two days, when I found a quaint restaurant resembling a railroad car. Mr. Cloyde, who reminded me of Dad, was the owner and cook. With him, my job was secure as I was exactly what he was looking for.

In August, Dad had cousin Joe Jr. deliver a 27-foot house trailer to Eddie and me, so we moved into a trailer park. It was great help financially. The cost of parking was six dollars weekly opposed to $50 weekly that we were paying for two rooms.

I realized Eddie and his Army buddies were drinking heavily and living pretty wild into the wee hours of the morning. It was evident that no amount of talking was going to change the situation.

One day he brought a very pretty girl to meet me at the trailer as he claimed to be in love with her. Within minutes, I knew the relationship would spell disaster for him, and hoped it would soon end as a passing fling.

At school, everyone ate lunch at a luncheonette located in the building. One day, two police officers who were attending the school offered to share their table as no vacancies were available, and we became friends. This proved to be Eddie's salvation. The officers, Joe and Larry, who went to class during the day and worked nights for the Orange County Police Department, were discussing the arrest and imprisonment of a rowdy trouble-making group of guys, whose ringleader, Ed Kovalchick, had a Jeep station wagon. The next time he was arrested, they were going to see that he got sent up the river.

I interrupted their conversation. "What name did you say?" I asked. "Ed Kovalchick," Joe answered. "That's my brother," I said. "My name is Kovalchick. We're from Pennsylvania. He has a Jeep station wagon. He's going to mechanic school here under the G.I. bill because he was wounded in service and has two Purple Hearts and an oak-leaf cluster. He can't stay in cold weather, because he still has so much shrapnel in him. That's why I'm here. My Dad sent me down to take care of him because he drinks a lot and could go into another shell-shock attack, and I can handle him when he does. He's a good boy. He's not mean and he doesn't mean anybody any harm. He's only 17 months older than me. You can't put him in jail. It would kill him. He doesn't mean to get in trouble. I know my brother Eddie, and he has never been in trouble ever."

There was a long silence while Joe and Larry looked at each other in disbelief at what I was saying. Then Larry spoke in a slow but very sincere tone of voice. "Your brother has already been arrested several times on various complaints or disturbances and I am sure he will be again, as he is traveling with a bad bunch of boys. He needs to get away from them. Now listen carefully. Give us your telephone number, and if we pick him up again, we will call you immediately. You get down to the police station as quick as you can and we will release him to you. Otherwise we will have to book him. Then we will not be able to help you." I thanked them and agreed to work with them as planned.

Trailer park living was interesting and different as everyone was from other parts of the country and freely shared their life stories. One of the residents, Nancy, who was 21 became my friend. I felt sorry for her. She was a beautiful girl with delicate features and long blonde hair. There was a sad and timid way about her that gave her an air of mystery.

One day Nancy suggested that we attend a local Halloween party. She had been confined for some time due to complications caused from two suicide attempts. She did not volunteer any details, nor did I ask her. However, I agreed to take her. I went about creating costumes for the both of us, which brought smiles and enthusiasm from her for the first times since I met her.

The hall was filled with loud and happy Halloweeners. I preferred watching the revelry and kept a constant watch on Nancy as she danced quite often. Suddenly, I became concerned. Nancy was not on the dance floor. Then I noticed the two men who were with her last dance partner. The men had separated, as one of them crossed the other side of the hall. Then they began exchanging nods and gestures.

It was obvious something was amiss. Then they began walking slowly toward the foyer entrance, which was vacant because all the revelry was in the dance hall. Momentarily, they were lost in the crowd, but they reappeared as they entered the foyer. Within seconds, the third man, who had been dancing with Nancy, entered the foyer with her and was coercing her toward the exit door. As quick as lightning the picture was clear to me.

I took off running through the crowd, colliding with those block-ing my way. The men had already gone out the door. I thrust it open, ran across the entrance-way and jumped over the flight of stairs, crash-ing into the two men. With determination and courage that could only come from having played baseball, I grabbed the man pulling Nancy, and shouted in a voice that conveyed anger than I can de-scribe, "Take your hands off her, or you're a dead man!" I clenched my fists, ready for a fight. The men apparently thought I was a po-licewoman in disguise or a judo expert, and they were off and run-ning as fast as their legs could carry them.

Nancy, screaming hysterically, threw her arms around me. "Nancy," I said, "Don't you ever, and I mean ever, let anyone take advantage of you, do you hear me?" With tear streaming down her cheeks she answered, "Yes, I hear you." We walked to the car, arm in arm, and slowly drove to the trailer park. We remained friends long after I left Florida. One day she wrote that she had married a wonderful man and was very happy, and I was happy for her.

Just days following Halloween, the dreaded phone call came at 3 a.m. Joe and Larry had picked Eddie up with some of his buddies. They were caught taking a boat from a boat dock. I rushed to the police station, praying for God to please help me and Eddie. Joe and Larry released him to me, with a warning that he should leave town and remove himself from the bad influence of his buddies. For the fist time Eddie realized the seriousness of the situation he was in.

The following day he brought his girlfriend to our trailer, who I had hoped was already a passing fling, and announced that we were leaving Orlando for Pennsylvania, and that he and Debbie were get-ting married along the way. Between the two of us we had about $100. Neither of us had a checking account or a credit card. "We can't make it on that," I said. "We'll try," he answered, "We can sleep in the trailer and eat what we have with us." Reluctantly I agreed.

Eddie and Debbie were married in North Carolina. But plans did not go as expected because Debbie, who thought Eddie was rich, being that his family once owned a hotel, had to eat in restaurants all the way. While she ate expensive meals every day, Eddie ordered coffee and I ordered Coke. She would not believe that we were running out of money.

When we got to Virginia, it was evident we might not make it. Not only were we running out of money, the trailer was too much for the little Jeep station wagon to pull up the hills and mountains we were facing. Eddie's solution was to cut off the motor once we got to the top of a hill, then let the Jeep and trailer roll down the hill at full speed. The force would propel us as far as possible up the next hill before we would throw it into second gear, in the hope we could make it to the top. It was working successfully until we got 70 miles from home.

The gas tank was on empty when the Jeep and trailer started to roll backwards on a hill. Even the brakes could not stop it. Eddie yelled for me to jump out of the Jeep and throw rocks, stones or anything I could find under the wheels. I was doing as he asked when a truck pulled up behind us. The driver leaped out and threw blocks under the wheels, which he carried with him for emergencies just like ours, saving the trailer. When we got everything under control, we told him we were out of gas and money. Again, the man resolved our dilemma, by pulling us up over the hill and to the first gas station. He paid for filling our tank and gave Eddie $10 on which to get home. I have never forgotten the kindness and generosity of that wonderful man.

Thanksgiving was only days away when we arrived home, and that was a Thanksgiving that we had much to be thankful for.

I had mixed emotions about the world events of 1948. The news that Israel was recognized as a new nation was certain to cause war the Arab states, who opposed the partitioning of Palestine.

I did not agree that it was wise for President Truman to sign the Marshall Plan that allocated $6 billion for overseas economic and military aid. I could not fathom that amount of money. I felt it would never be appreciated by the generations that would benefit by it. Time seems to make everyone forget, and I am referring to those countries that profited by the plan.

When the high courts ruled to prohibit prayer in schools, I felt a real sense of sorrow, especially for the children, as they would lose that feeling of hope and faith that a prayer in school brought them every morning.

When I read about the Soviet Union's blockade of Berlin, I instinctively knew it would fail, and it did.

I was glad that President Truman signed the Selective Service Act, requiring men 18 to 25 to register for military duty. Eligible 19-year-olds would be called for 21 months' duty. I realized that our country needed to be ready at all times to defend itself. And when the President issued an executive order to integrate the armed forces, I thought that also it would be good for our country's unity.

I felt a sadness reading about death of famous baseball slugger Babe Ruth, who died of cancer, for everyone loved him.

I thought it was a great advancement when Dr. William Schuckley invented the tiny transistor that would revolutionize electronics.

As for television rapidly becoming a permanent part of American life, I felt very skeptical.

We had a beautiful, white Christmas. Nick was home from Clarion College. Johnny was home from Greenville, North Carolina. Eddie and I were back from Florida. And Mother cooked and

277

baked enough for all of Sagamore. As for Dad, he seemed to be melancholy. I think he was discouraged over his Dad's Old Fashioned Root Beer Distributorship. It was more work than he had anticipated. I sensed that he wanted to give it up but did not want to look like a quitter.

There is nothing to report about my 23rd birthday, which was December 31. There was no birthday party, and I did not expect one. The new year's Eve celebrations were all I needed.

CHAPTER XVI
THE YEAR OF 1949

Our three-story house behind the hotel had 15 rooms and a cellar. With all that space, Mother and Dad gave Eddie and Debbie a four-room apartment on the first floor, having it own private entrance, It was the warmest place in the house, and with winter upon us, it was perfect for Eddie.

Nick returned to Clarion College after Christmas, and Johnny helped Dad until he returned to North Carolina, where he played for Pine Top part of the season and Farmville part of the season. Both teams were in the Bright Belt Independent League.

As for me, as usual, Dad had plans. I was leaving for Sykesville, Pennsylvania, to work for the KOVALCHICK SALVAGE COMPANY AND REAL ESTATE DIVISION, WHICH WAS OPERATED BY Dad's brother, Michael, whom we called Uncle Mike. He was the seventh of Grandma's 10 children.

Their second office was located in Indiana, Pennsylvania, and was operated by Dad's brother, Nicholas, whom we called Uncle Nick. He was the third of Grandma's 10 children.

Dad's sister Veronica, whom we called Aunt Ronnie, was office manager for Uncle Mike in Sykesville. She was the eighth of Grandma's 10 children.

Dad's twin brothers, George and Andy, also worked for Uncle Mike. They were the ninth and 10th of Grandma's 10 children. I hope I haven't confused anyone.

In 1948, Uncle Nick and Uncle Mike had purchased 12 coal-mining towns, having 1,800 house, from the Buffalo and Susquehanna (B&S) Coal and Coke Company. The B&S had closed the mines in those towns and had no further use for the houses. I would be working for both the salvage and the real estate division under Aunt Ronnie.

For the first month, I lived with Aunt Ronnie. Then it was decided that I would stay at Uncle Mike's beautiful camphouse on his own small, private lake, located behind the iron and steel scrap yard of the Kovalchick Salvage Company. It was not beautiful structurally, as you might imagine, but it had a charm all its own as it was built to suit no one but Uncle Mike, who was 35 years old and never married.

The dictionary describes eccentric as an odd individual differing conspicuously in behavior, appearance or opinion, and that describes Uncle Mike. The family hoped that I would bring a little homelife into his lonely life by preparing home-cooked meals or just being there for him to talk to.

One day he gave me $100 to cover the cost of preparing a gourmet supper with all the trimmings. After hours of planning and preparing, as I wanted it to be perfect, I announced that supper was ready. He walked up to the table and looked down at the beautiful setting. A white tablecloth covered the table and there were flowers and burning candles in the center. Our food was already served on white china dinner plates, and there were individual white cloth napkins. He just stood there, admiring it all like a child fascinated with a favorite toy. "That sure is nice. Yes, indeed, that sure is nice," he repeated over and over again, as though mesmerized by it all. "Sit down and eat, Uncle Mike. It's getting cold," I said. "You go ahead and eat," he replied. His next words absolutely shocked me. "Feed mine to the dog," he said and walked out of the room. After recovering from his shocking statement, I did exactly as he said. I fed his supper to Pingo, his mongrel dog.

Uncle Mike purchased a new Cadillac every year. That was all he would drive. Every day he drove me home from work. One day he drove up in his new Cadillac with Pingo sitting on that beautiful velour-covered seat. "You can sit in the back," he said, forgetting that he had already removed the back seat, which he did with all his Cadillacs. So that he could haul scrap iron in the back if necessary. "Move over Pingo. She'll have to sit up front," he said. Pingo had the seat dirty with mud and grease, and I refused to sit on it. "Get in or walk," said Uncle Mike. So I sat on that dirty seat and washed my skirt when I got home.

The story is told that he once drove to Chicago to meet several important businessmen. He offered to drive them to their destination. When they opened the back door, only then did Uncle Mike realize that he had forgotten to put the back seat in. The men returned to their office to get their own car.

Just before Easter, there was a heavy, steady rain that set in for the night. The pitter patter of the rain had lulled me to sleep. At one o'clock in the morning, I heard a pounding on my door, It was Uncle Mike, standing there drenching wet. "Get dressed and get your umbrella," he said. In minutes I was dressed. "Come on," he said, and started walking up the hill. I followed, asking no questions, but I wondered where we were going and why would we be climbing this hill in the dead of night in the rain. I struggled over rocks and shrubs and branches, trying to keep my footing. I closed the umbrella. It was of little use and was getting torn by the tree branches. We kept walking up the hill, drenching wet and cold. At last we reached the top of the hill. We could see the lights of the town in the distance below. Uncle Mike sat on a dead log. I joined him and raised the umbrella. We sat there quietly, watching the town's lights. Then, he began to speak. "Look, look at the town below," he said. "I own everything as far as the eye can see, but what good is it, to own everything, to have everything that money can buy, to have all the material things of life, when you cannot have the one you love to share it with?" Then he cried softly as he told me the story of Eva.

He had fallen in love with Eva when he was 14. She was the town's beauty, a vision of loveliness with golden, curly hair, porcelain skin and emerald green eyes. At that young age he decided that he would marry her. He was so captivated that he wanted to lay the world at her feet. Nothing would be good enough for her. He had to be worthy of her, so he had a plan.

Uncle Mike quit school upon finishing the eighth grade. He had to set about making his mark in the world. Eva never knew of his plan, but the plan drove him relentlessly. Day and night, night and day, no rest, no sleep, no proper food or proper clothing. The iron and steel industry was where he chose to make his fortune. For eight long year he labored, never losing sight of his dream. At the age of 22, he was a success. He had attained riches. He could give Eva all the worldly things her heart would desire. He was ready to go to her and ask her hand in marriage.

He decided the day would be Christmas Eve, which was also his 22nd birthday. Carefully he planned. A new suit and new shoes. A visit to a fine jeweler, where he purchased a beautiful pearl necklace. The pearls were wrapped in silver paper. He placed the box in his pocket, walked down the snow-covered street and climbed up the steps to the front porch. He knocked on the door once, then twice. Eva's mother opened it. "I've come to call on Eva," he said. She then told him the shocking news. Eva was upstairs getting dressed for her wedding. She was being married that very evening. He watched her descend the staircase in her beautiful wedding gown. He turned and ran from the house with tear-filled eyes, not believing what had just happened. As his world tumbled down before him, he thought about his mother and what she had said a long time ago. She told him that pearls brought tears.

And that was why he never married. And why his work was his life, and his dog his constant and only companion.

At last I understood why Uncle Mike was the way he was. The tears rolled down my cheeks. I was filled with such compassion for him that I felt that my heart would burst. Yet I knew he was not going to try to change his lot in life. He was going to continue the way he was.

The following Friday about 10 p.m., Uncle Mike asked if I had gone to church that day, because it was Good Friday. "No, I did not," I answered. "Then why didn't you?" he asked. "Because we worked all day," I replied. "Get your coat, we're going to church. It's not right. Everyone should go to church on Good Friday," he said. I knew there was no use arguing. So I got my coat and we drove the 15 miles to the Greek Catholic Church in Punxsutawney. "I never heard of anyone going to church at 11 o'clock at night," I said. "God doesn't care what time you go to church on Good Friday, just as long as you go,: he answered.

The sanctuary was filled with beautiful flowers. I reached up and cut one carnation off its long stem for remembrance. "You put that back. You're not taking flowers from the church," he said. "It's only one carnation, Uncle Mike. There's hundreds of flowers. This is only one," I replied. However, nothing I said would appease him. I had to put the flower back knowing it would shortly die because the stem was too short to reach the water in the vase.

Uncle Mike put a $100 bill in the basket in front of the sanctuary. "Uncle Mike," I said, someone might be tempted to take that much money out of the basket. You shouldn't leave that much money. Why don't you send it to the church?" I asked. "Well," he replied, if they take it, it will be their sin, not mine." The we left the church and arrived back home past midnight.

I hated to leave Uncle Mike. I felt so sorry for him and wanted to help him. But Dad called on May 1 and wanted me to return home.

I do not recall having said good-bye to Uncle Mike. I barely caught the bus for Indiana after hurriedly packing and telling Aunt Ronnie good-bye.

Dad met me at the bus terminal in Indiana. During our 20-mile drive to Sagamore he brought me up to date on happenings at home.

Eddie and Debbie had moved from our house and were renting a house from the Kovalchick Salvage Company – Real Estate Division. Sagamore was one of the 12 towns that they had purchased from the Buffalo and Susquehanna Coal and Coke Company in 1948.

Dad had given up his Dad's Old Fashioned Root Beer Distributor Franchise and was making preparations for going into the wholesale meat business. A huge walk-in refrigeration room was being installed in the two-story building behind our house, which had been built years before. He was purchasing a five-ton refrigeration truck and part of the two-story building would be used for preparing customers' orders for delivery. He had hired a young boy by the name of Pete Catanese, who was hard working and a tremendous help to him.

As for me, I was to set up his books for the wholesale meat business. Also, I was to open a small grocery store on the first floor of our house as it was now vacant since Eddie and Debbie had moved. I knew that the bookkeeping would be no problem, but I did not know one thing about a grocery store. Well, I soon learned the hard way. I can see now how the wholesaler tried to steer me in the right direction when I placed my first order. I was so naïve. I just ordered things that I liked, which was far from what actually would sell in a small grocery store in a small town. So the family ended up having to eat most of what I had purchased. Mother placed the orders for the store from then on, and I knew why.

When Nick finished his freshman year at Clarion College on June 8, he immediately left to do his required route surveying field work for four weeks. Having completed it, he helped Dad until he left to attend Penn State University in September as a sophomore.

During the summer, Johnny was dating his first girlfriend, while playing ball in Greenville, North Carolina, and was madly in love. Freda would be the best thing that ever happened to him. He is always quick to tell anyone that he and his ballplayers buddies were eating at an ice cream parlor when Freda and her girlfriends walked in. The second he saw her he told his buddies that he was going to marry her. Then he walked over to her table and told her straight out that he was going to marry her, right in front of her girlfriends. True to his word, they married November 23, 1949. He was 22 and she was 19.

Business was slow in our little store. Even selling gasoline did not improve the business. Since the mines closed in 1948 the Kovalchick Salvage Company was dismantling the mines and the Real Estate Division was offering the houses for rent or sale. Those beyond repair were torn down. As a result, people either rented or purchased a house or moved out of town. Those who remained commuted to work and did their shopping near their work.

In August, Dad announced that Mother would operate the store with the assist of a girl who could handle the bookkeeping and assist with the housework. I was going to work in Indiana for an architect named Don Winslow. I rented a room and kitchen combination with a bath, and walked to and from work as it was only four blocks away.

I did not realize how hungry I was for knowledge until I began working for Mr. Winslow. I fell in love with everything having to do with architecture. I could not imagine anything more intriguing, and I learned more and more every day.

As Halloween was approaching, Mother wanted me to attend the upcoming Halloween party, being held at our local roller skating rink. It touched my heart when she handed me her Avon money to buy material for a costume. I refused, because she worked so hard selling Avon products, always climbing those Sagamore hills, making deliveries after a hard day's work. But she insisted as she wanted me to go, so I agreed.

It was difficult choosing a fabric as they were all so beautiful. I finally chose two different fabrics, a red moire and a black and red satin print. The moment Mother saw them she aid, "These will be perfect for a Gypsy dress." And went about creating the most beautiful dress I ever saw. The blouse was red with a round neck and big puffed sleeves, trimmed with black and silver lace. The skirt was gathered extra full, and had an eight-inch red flounce around the bottom. It had a pettycoat made from yards and yards of old sheets and colorful scrap material. I was so proud of that dress.

The attendance at the party was true to expectations. Every adult in the surrounding area was there, dressed in every conceivable costume imaginable. At the peak of all the dancing and merry-making, the master of ceremonies called the crowd to attention so that the judging could begin. Everyone was asked to line up six abreast along the outside perimeter of the huge hall. We were to march around and around the hall before the stage, where the 12 judges were sitting at a table. With such a large crowd, we were crammed close together. The music began and whistle blew signaling the marching to begin.

I was lost between costumed Halloweeners much taller and larger than I was, and I immediately realized that the judges would never see me, and would not even be aware that I was there. Then, I thought about my Mother. She had worked so hard sewing the Gypsy dress, and she had given me her hard-earned money for it. I thought about how disappointed she would be if I did not win at least one of the prizes. Then I thought about the huge crowd. There were so many to choose from. They would never choose me, because they could not see me. My heart sank. Then, my thoughts were drawn from my disappointment by the music. They were playing the Pennsylvania Polka. Mother had the song on a 33 rpm record, and many times I had danced to it in our living room. The polka had always brought rhythm to my feet. "THIS IS FOR YOU, MOM," I thought, and I broke out of line and began dancing and dancing and dancing, taking over the huge vacant space in the center of the hall. The music spurred me on and on as I kicked and twirled around and around with my skirt flying. It made me feel good all over. I felt energy like never before, and all I could think of was the fact that I was dancing for my Mother, as again and again I thought, "THIS IS FOR YOU, MOM."

At last the whistle blew and the music stopped. The master of ceremonies walked to the microphone to announce the winners. First there were two $5 winners, then two $10 winners, then two $15 winners, then one $20 winner. All were justified, I thought. "Now for our Grand Prize winner of $25," said the master of ceremonies as his voice boomed over the microphone. The crowd began to stir with excitement. "AND OUR WINNER IS, OUR GYPSY DANCER," he yelled out, and the crowd roared. Someone tugged at my arm, shouting, "THAT'S YOU, THAT'S YOU." Feeling stunned, I walked to the stage, thinking, "THIS IS FOR YOU, MOM, THIS IS FOR YOU."

When I arrived home, Mother was waiting. I proudly handed her the $25, telling her that I had won the Grand Prize. I never saw her look happier, and with a big warm smile, she said, "No, you won it. It's yours." I can not describe the moments of that night and the love I felt for my Mother. To this day, I have the Gypsy dress.

The week following Halloween Abe Cline asked me out to dinner. He was a very worldly man about five years my senior. He introduced me to shrimp on our first date. I could not believe anything could taste as good as those shrimp did.

Also, he was responsible for one of the most embarrassing moments of my life. "Would you like to go to the Indiana Country Club's Christmas Dance?" he asked, and I accepted. He said it was formal and quite an extravaganza, and that only who's who would be there. I had never heard of the country club, nor did I know exactly what who's who meant. However, I did know that formal meant an evening gown. I didn't have a gown, or the money to buy one. The dance was several weeks away, so I took my two weeks' pay, after a lot of sacrificing, and went to Molly Ann's, where I purchased a beautiful red evening gown that fit me like a glove. That means it was a little sexy, but not overly. To complement the dress, I wore rhinestone jewelry, black shoes, black cap, and elbow length black leather gloves. I thought it all looked very beautiful together.

Just before entering the country club, Abe informed me that leather gloves are not worn with formal wear. That was my first lesson learned. Then we entered the country club and learned that it was the wrong night. No formal dance was scheduled for that evening. Instead, a small casually dressed group were gathered and a few were dancing on he floor. I was embarrassed beyond words. However, Abe did not apologize. We danced a couple of dances and left. To think that I had spent my two weeks' pay for nothing, only to be embarrassed. That was my second lesson learned. Be sure you have the correct time and place when going anywhere.

However, there was one last and final date with Abe. He wanted me to meet his parents one Sunday afternoon. They lived about 75 miles away. I loved his parents right off. They were the kind of people I was accustomed to being with, and we got along very well, especially his father and me. When we returned to Sagamore, it was late. Dad was sitting at the kitchen table. He and Abe began to talk, so I excused myself to go to the restroom. When I returned Abe was gone. Dad gave no explanation when I asked why he left without saying goodnight. The answer came from Mother later. Abe thought that because my name was Kovalchick I was rich. He made the mistake of asking Dad, in the event he married me, how much money was I worth. I never heard from Abe again. "Good riddance," I thought. There is one consolation, however. Some years later I met a friend of his. Abe had told her that the biggest mistake he ever made was letting me go. I did not tell his friend that he did not let me go, that Dad had ordered him to go. Good for Dad.

On November 14, Mother and Dad received a phone call from DuBois, Pennsylvania, hospital. Debbie had given birth to a baby boy, and she and Eddie were naming him Edward John Kovalchick Jr. after his father.

As for world highlights of 1949, there were many. Here are a few:

1. Harry S. Truman began his first full term as President on January 20.
2. The 321-day Soviet blockade of Berlin came to an end in May. During the blockade 2.5 million tons of supplies were flown into Berlin by American and British planes at a cost estimated to exceed $200 million.
3. The cornerstone for the United Nations building was laid on October 24.
4. Some 500 million people had come under the rule of a Communist Government in China.
5. San Diego, California, received its first snowfall in 99 years.
6. Joe Louis, 35, retired from boxing after reigning as Heavy weight Champion for 11 years.

On December 31, I was 24. Again, there was no birthday party. "This is getting old." I thought. When will I ever get that birthday party?"

Dorothy

CHAPTER XVII
THE YEAR OF 1950 to FEBRUARY 1951

On January 2, I learned that Mr. Winslow was seriously ill. There was talk that he might be forced to close his office. His draftsman, Carl, continued working on pending plans, and I continued typing specifications and helping Carl in every way possible in order to keep our clients serviced.

It seemed that suntans were the rage at that time. Everyone wanted to be first in showing off their beautiful suntans, thereby making sunlamps very popular. I was no different than others my age, I purchased a sunlamp. Not until I suffered severe burns due to overexposure did I realize that I should have followed the directions. A doctor's visit confirmed that I had third-degree burns and sun poisoning. For weeks I nursed my burns. The miserable burns behind my knees made it difficult to walk up or down the stairs.

During this time of my healing, we were anxiously waiting for word concerning Mr. Winslow's condition. Then in early February, we were notified that the office was closing. It was very sad saying good-bye to all my friends. They were leaving my life, maybe forever.

I packed my clothes and tearfully said good-bye to my wonderful landlady. Within days after returning home, The Dritz Company of New York and several other arts and crafts suppliers contacted me, inquiring as to what I had done towards opening my arts and crafts business, because they were anxious to do business with me. I explained what had happened since meeting their representative in Warren, Ohio, the year before. They were interested in helping me by extending credit with no interest or monthly fees. They offered to install stock on consignment, and to send their personnel for a period of time to help me get started. Their encouragement gave me the incentive to give it a try. I found an excellent location in Indiana on Main Street. The owner was willing to reduce his rent and assist in the cost of necessary renovations.

With hope and enthusiasm, I went to Dad for financial help. I could not believe that he refused to help me. He would absolutely not give me one cent towards getting started. He said that he needed me to drive the five-ton refrigerator truck, as no one else was available.

Nick was attending Penn State University and Johnny was married and living in Greenville, North Carolina. He would again be playing baseball for the Greenies. Eddie was chief mechanic for the Kovalchick Salvage Company in Sykesville. Mother and Helen were managing the store and doing the housework and cooking. Pete was helping Dad prepare orders for delivery.

Dad never did learn to double-clutch. Driving his five-ton truck required a lot of double-clutching in order to successfully climb the steep hills around our part of the country. He was right, there was no one else available.

It was beyond my comprehension as to why he wanted to go into the wholesale meat business in the first place. What was he trying to prove? What was he thinking about? What could it accomplish? All of these questions raced through my mind. I concluded that he had to because of his nine brothers and sisters, who had left him during his time of desperate need. He wanted to show them that, in the end he had made it, and without them. He was harboring a deep hurt and resentment over the fact that, after having given up his own dreams in order to care for them after his father died when he was only 22, not one of them had ever asked him if he needed help. Not did they volunteer to come forth during those Depression years when he fought so hard for survival.

I felt sorry for him. He was a victim of circumstances, and now I felt that I, too, was a victim of circumstances at that moment. Therefore, I agreed to abandon my plans and help him.

I contacted my suppliers and prospective landlord and explained the situation to them. They understood and wished me well, but they left all channels open for the future, should things change for me.

One day, I was asked to dinner by a young gentleman, who said that he was the nephew of a friend of mine. During dinner, we talked about many interesting subjects. I found him to be very intelligent and well mannered. It was obvious that he had a good upbringing.

After dinner, we drove throughout the countryside sightseeing and talking. The subject eventually turned to us personally. Much to my surprise, he said he would like to marry me. He talked about owning our own business, and that money was no object. "You don't really know me," I said. "And I don't really know you. I would never marry anyone I did not love, and because I've known you for only a few short hours, I cannot say I love you. Marrying you at this time is definitely out of the question." He was of a different nationality and religion, and I felt certain we came from two different worlds. I could not fathom why he would want to marry me.

When we returned from our drive, he said he understood, and that he would be returning to Michigan the following day and would not be seeing me again. The entire matter seemed weird. "Michigan," I thought. "Did he mean we would be living in Michigan?" It did not make sense at all. However, I learned from his aunt that all he told me was true. And, true to his word, he never saw me again.

Now that Indiana and all my plans for going into business were behind me, I began helping Dad. I was thankful that Eddie taught me to double-clutch. Neither of us foresaw how valuable it would be, as I faced the challenge of driving Dad's five-ton refrigerator truck up steep hills over poorly constructed country blacktop roads that were narrow and rugged and had numerous dangerous curves. There were places so hilly that more driving was done in second gear than in drive.

For four months I faced the danger, praying for God to keep His protective hand on us. Passing a vehicle was impossible. Driving off the road so that an oncoming vehicle could pass was common.

Facing these dangers every day did not frustrate or fill me with fear. I found the challenge an exciting adventure. Not only because the driving was challenging, but because the unique and awesome places we serviced were something to see, and I would not trade it for anything. Store owners were glad to see us. We were one of the few wholesalers that serviced those that were located in small and difficult places to reach.

I came to realize that not only was the Dad's Old Fashioned Root Beer Distributorship not for Dad, neither was the wholesale meat business. After working hard all his life, at age 52, I felt he should be doing something easier.

I noticed he was changing and was growing more tired. In looking back, I realize that he was going in and out of manic depression. In those days, the medical profession knew little or nothing about it. The more I tried to pull him out of it, the more rebellious he became towards my efforts. As it developed more frequently, he would lose control of his reasoning, and on four different occasions he ordered me to leave the truck, saying that he would drive the truck home himself. On those occasions, I found myself miles away from home without a cent in my pocket. I would begin walking. Invariably someone would stop to ask if I needed help, which resulted in their driving me to Sagamore. On one occasion, a car stopped, and the man yelled out, "Are you Bounce Kovalchick's daughter?" "Yes. I am," I said. I was surprised he knew me, as I was at least 45 miles from home. "Get in, he said, "I'll drive you home." When we got home, he visited awhile, and Mother served him coffee and donuts.

Later, I heard Dad driving in, and ran upstairs. "Did Dorothy get home O.K.?" he asked Mother. "Yes, she's upstairs," Mother answered.

The following day, he was back to his old self again, acting as though nothing had happened.

In the third week of June, Nick returned home from Penn State University, after having completed his sophomore year and two weeks of required field training. He immediately took over the driving of Dad's refrigerator truck. I was glad, as it enabled me to help Mother, since her helper was no longer with her.

Johnny was again playing baseball in North Carolina in the Bright Belt League. His playing was divided between Pine Top and Farmville, just as it had been the previous year or 1949.

He enrolled in East Carolina University in Business Administration as he was determined to get a college degree. And, with the help of his loving wife Freda, his goal was realized in 1952. Determination was one of Johnny's outstanding qualities. His pitching was a lesson in concentration and control. He possessed more concentration and control in pitching than any pitcher I had ever seen.

In October, the Armstrong County Amateur Baseball Federation was sponsoring a charity game in Kittanning on behalf of cancer research. The all-stars of the Federation League would be playing against the major and minor league players from our surrounding area, who had returned home after ending their season.

Dad was to co-manage the major and minor league team, and was to contact major and minor league players to seek their participation. He asked me to help, so I called some of the players. One was Ralph Erwin, a pitcher from Tunnelton who had returned from playing Class A ball in the South Atlantic League for Columbia, South Carolina which was owned by the Cincinnati Reds. I explained that the players' only remuneration was a banquet following the ball game. Ralph said he would agree to play, if I would agree to sit next to him at the banquet. I said, "O.K. since this is for charity."

The morning of the game, and with no prior notice, Dad told me he wanted me to put on my baseball uniform and play one inning in the game. After not playing for three years, I refused. "Dad, I'm not prepared. You should have told me, so I could have gotten in some practice," I said. I was stubborn in my decision and so was he. Time was running out. He had to be at the game early. In anger he said he was not taking me to the game and drove off. I too was angry because he did not try to understand how I felt about the matter.

Then, an idea flashed through my mind. "I'm going to the game, but not as a ballplayer this time," I thought. I hastily went through my clothes closet, and chose a beautiful long-sleeved, V-necked, close fitting green velveteen dress. It was ideal for a dinner date with someone that I might want to impress. I had never worn it before, and I thought, "Why not now? This will really make Dad furious." Maybe it was revenge, maybe it was anger, maybe it was my trying to make a point. "Maybe now Dad will consult me in the future," I thought. To complete the outfit, I chose rhinestone earrings, a (rhinestone) necklace, silk stockings and high heels. I combed my hair in a provocative upsweep with a cluster of curls on the top. And, last but not least, I carried a green parasol.

I have to admit that not many people watched that game, because I sat on the very top row of the bleachers with my green parasol in the sun. No one could miss me, even if they tried. I knew that all eyes in the ballpark were on me, and I knew they were wondering who in the world I was.

When I walked to the concession stand, the whistling filled the air like music. I was having a great time, laughing and waving at the spectators as they waved back. And I was right, Dad was furious. At the banquet, he would not speak to me. "Oh, Oh," I thought. "Has Dad disowned me again?"

As for Ralph Erwin, he felt like top dog at the banquet, because he was sitting next to me. He asked for a date, which I accepted. Since it would mean driving 60 miles to Sagamore, I suggested meeting him at Meadow Brook which would be 13 miles less for him to drive. Meadow Brook was the nicest dance hall in our area.

Ralph was six feet tall and weighed 190 pounds. I felt sure he had many girlfriends. He was easy to talk to and had a cheerful, outgoing personality. He loved hunting and talked about his good luck at getting a deer every year. He had been in the Army, and played on the Army's baseball team. We both were 24 years old.

We danced very little, as there seemed to be so much to talk about. Then, the Tennessee Waltz was being played, and he asked to dance. As we danced, unexpectedly he asked, "What do you think about marriage?" Being caught off guard at the moment, I said, "I guess any fool would get married." Then he asked, "What would you think about marrying me?" "Not until I'm 25. The first man that comes to my door and asks me to marry him when I'm 25, that is who I'm going to marry," I answered. He wanted to know when I would be 25. I told him December 31. "Well then, I'll see you on December 31," he said. "It's just five weeks away." "You'd better get there early," I said. "There's two ahead of you." That did not deter him, as we dated every Saturday and Sunday through December.

The news of 1950 was filled with talk of Communism in the United State, as Senator Joe McCarthy announced that he had a list of 205 names known to the Secretary of State as being members of the Communist Party, shocking the nation. Accusations were made against dozens of people. Many innocent people were hurt or literally destroyed politically by the self-promoting anti-Communist Senator from Wisconsin.

North Korea and South Korea were developed as a result of occupations after World War II and governments of each claimed authority over the entire peninsula. On June 25, North Korean forces moved south over the dividing line. And in September 1950, the conflict between North and South Korea began. President Harry Truman appointed General Douglas McArthur as commander of the Army, Navy and Air forces. One month later the United Nations gave General McArthur command of all its forces. During the conflict the United States would provide about half of the United Nations' troop strength. Hostilities would not end until July 27, 1953.

A cloud of deep concern hovered over us as we listened to the news reports about the Korean hostilities. We could not conceive that another war was on our doorstep. "When will wars ever end?" we asked. Little did we realize that the Vietnam War was yet to come.

Christmas was a sad one as our family was again personally affected. Nick was leaving for the Navy on December 29. He was the youngest of my three brothers and four years and eight months younger than me.

He had decided that rather than return to Penn State University in September as a junior, he would put his education on hold and join the Navy for four years. He successfully passed the Navy's electronics test and went into the Navy as a Seaman Electronics Technician. After one year of boot camp training and electronics school, he was upgraded to Petty Officer Third Class.

Following his training he was assigned to the Destroyer USS Picking DD685 in Newport, Rhode Island, where the destroyer was assigned to Anti-Submarine Warfare. He would remain on the ship for the entire time of his service. The destroyer would eventually serve in the Korean waters in the Korean conflict, and would make a complete trip around the world. At the time of his discharge from the Navy, he had been upgraded to Petty Officer First Class.

With all the excitement and sadness about Nick leaving for the Navy on the 29th, I completely forgot about my 25th birthday. Dad had gone to Kittanning that morning of the 31st, and Mother was out making an Avon delivery.

That day that I had been talking about for so long had at last arrived, and by noon three suitors had asked for my hand in marriage: Ralph Erwin, Donald Allen and U.S. Marine Sergeant Gene Shaffer of Camp LeJeune, North Carolina. After four years of proclaiming that I was going to marry the first man that asked me when I turned 25, my words were being put to the test. I did exactly as I proclaimed when I accepted Ralph's proposal, as he was first. I had accepted a marriage proposal, but there was again no birthday party. That was O.K. though, because now I was in love.

We were married by a justice of the peace in Chesterfield, North Carolina, on February 12, 1951, and honeymooned in Columbia, South Carolina, where he had played Class A ball for Cincinnati the season before. I had always dreamed of a church wedding with all the trimmings, with my family, relatives and friends there to wish me well. But it couldn't be because time was essential. Ralph had to report for spring training in Florida the last week of February.

Ralph left for spring training two weeks after we were married, and I made preparations to meet him in Tulsa, Oklahoma, where he would be playing for the Reds team in the Class AA Texas League.

As I prepared for the new life before me, a deep sadness filled my heart, for after 25 years of calling Sagamore my home, I was leaving. All the past memories filled my mind. I wanted to be alone, away from the world. I thought about the peace and quiet of my "Lost Horizon." I wanted to visit it one last time and pray for Nick, who was now in the Navy, as I prayed for Eddie during World War II when he was in the Army.

I dressed in warm clothes and my fur-lined boots, as the air was cold, and headed for ballground hill and my "Lost Horizon." When I reached the clearing and saw that tall, stately. charred tree trunk that had been my altar during the war, tears filled my eyes, and I felt that I could not stay. "I may never be back again," I thought, and wanted to remove my religious items from their hiding place in the charred split of the dead tree trunk, once a magnificent oak that had been struck by lightning. I reached in and found my altar items still there. I burst into tears and fell to my knees on the wet ground.

"What lies ahead?" I thought. "What trials and tribulations will I have to face? I will miss Mother and Dad. I will miss Sagamore. What will my new life be like? Will the road be harder or will it be easier? Will my dream of living in the South ever come true? Will Mother and Dad be all right when I am gone? With Eddie, Johnny, Nick and me gone, they are going to be alone." Oh, how I am going to miss them all."

Then I prayed for God to be at my side all the way, every day, because I knew that I could not do it alone.

- - - - - - THE END - - - - - -

About the Author

The Author was born in Sagamore, Pennsylvania, December 31, 1925. She attended the Sagamore elementary school and graduated from Cowanshannock Township High School in 1943.

For eight years (1940-1947) she enjoyed a career in baseball, playing on her Father's all male barnstorming baseball team and also played in the All American Girls Professional Baseball League, the first women's professional baseball team in history. Her name is etched on the All American Girls Professional Baseball League's plaque in the National Baseball Hall of Fame Museum at Cooperstown, New York. In 1977, she was inducted into the Armstrong County Sports Hall of Fame at Vandergrift, Pennsylvania.

Following graduation, she worked for her parents John "Bounce" and Anna Kovalchick, who owned the Hotel Sagamore until 1948.

From 1948 through 1950, she worked in real estate, the iron and steel business, was secretary and bookkeeper for an Architect, and worked for her father in the grocery and wholesale meat business.

She married Ralph Erwin on February 12, 1951 and moved to West Monroe, Louisiana in 1952 where she resides today. She worked 20 years as an accountant for four different firms, and 22 years in real estate, having owned her own Century 21 real estate firm. She has one daughter Denise, who is married to Thomas Evans, and one granddaughter Brooke.

Following her retirement in 1994, she created a heirloom quilt for her daughter which won second place at the International Quilt Show in Houston, Texas.

She has been active in story telling and numerous civic organizations.

Following the death of her second husband, Earl Roark, May 24, 2004, she has fulfilled her father's dying wish by writing this book, *Uncertain Destiny*.

Epilogue

Much of the greatness of American is found upon the dreams, courage and determination of nineteenth century immigrant people drawn to these vaunted shores for many different reasons. No streets of gold were discovered by those who were able to come. With little or no means, what they did find and endure was harsh physical conditions and back-breaking labor. Some of these resilient people were drawn to the coal fields of Pennsylvania where there was work available.

It is about these people that I write. It is a personal account of my family among these many people for whom coal

mining became a way of life in twenty eight states across America. The setting is a town in West central Pennsylvania, located in the rich bituminous coal region about 45 miles Northeast of Pittsburgh.

This is a true story, recounting my father's struggle and his wish to have his life's story told. As his daughter, I grew up in these coal towns of Pennsylvania. It is our story of 51 years (1899-1951) chronologically written, and set in an unforgettable time in our country's history of Wars, the Roaring 20's and Prohibition, the Great Depression of the 1930's and the story of my eight years barnstorming throughout Western Pennsylvania as the only girl on my father's otherwise all male baseball team, this ultimately lead to my playing in the All American Girls Professional Baseball League, women's first professional baseball league in history. It is a tale of love, compassion, humor and many surprises. I hope you will enjoy it.